TOWARDS JIHAD?

ERIC MORIER-GENOUD

Towards Jihad?

Muslims and Politics in Postcolonial Mozambique

OXFORD
UNIVERSITY PRESS

Oxford University Press is a department of the
University of Oxford. It furthers the University's objective
of excellence in research, scholarship, and education
by publishing worldwide.

Oxford New York

Auckland   Cape Town   Dar es Salaam   Hong Kong   Karachi
Kuala Lumpur   Madrid   Melbourne   Mexico City   Nairobi
New Delhi   Shanghai   Taipei   Toronto

With offices in

Argentina   Austria   Brazil   Chile   Czech Republic   France   Greece
Guatemala   Hungary   Italy   Japan   Poland   Portugal   Singapore
South Korea   Switzerland   Thailand   Turkey   Ukraine   Vietnam

Oxford is a registered trade mark of Oxford University Press
in the UK and certain other countries.

Published in the United States of America by
Oxford University Press
198 Madison Avenue, New York, NY 10016

Copyright © Eric Morier-Genoud, 2023

All rights reserved. No part of this publication may be reproduced,
stored in a retrieval system, or transmitted, in any form or by any means,
without the prior permission in writing of Oxford University Press,
or as expressly permitted by law, by license, or under terms agreed with
the appropriate reproduction rights organization. Inquiries concerning
reproduction outside the scope of the above should be sent to the
Rights Department, Oxford University Press, at the address above.

You must not circulate this work in any other form
and you must impose this same condition on any acquirer.
Library of Congress Cataloging-in-Publication Data is available

ISBN: 9780197769348

Printed in the United Kingdom
by Bell & Bain Ltd, Glasgow

CONTENTS

List of Figures, Tables, and Maps	vii
Acknowledgements	ix
Credits	xi
Glossary	xiii
Abbreviations	xv
Introduction	1
1. The 'Rise' of Islam after Independence, 1974–94	19
2. The 1996 'Muslim Holidays' Affair	47
3. A Prospect of Secularization? Muslims and Political Power, 1994–2004	69
4. Growth and Radicalization? Islam and Politics after 2004	93
5. 2017: The Birth of a Jihadi Insurgency	117
Conclusion	141
Appendices	
I. Foundation of the Islamic Council of Mozambique (CISLAMO), 1981	151

CONTENTS

II.   Letter from the Muslim World League to President   155
Samora Machel, 1983

III.   Law Project for Two Muslim National Holidays, 1996   157

IV.   Final Communiqué of the First National Islamic   161
Conference, 2003

V.   Transcript of Jihadi Insurgents' Video Messages,   165
2018, 2020, and 2022

Notes	171
Bibliography	215
Index	233

vi

LIST OF FIGURES, TABLES, AND MAPS

Figure 1. Types of Muslim veils   104

Table 1.	Approximate percentage of population by religion, 1975 and 1997	53
Table 2.	Approximate percentage of population by religion, 1960 and 1975	58
Table 3.	Religious self-identification on a national basis, 1997, 2007, and 2017	97
Table 4.	Religious self-identification by province, 1997, 2007, 2017	99
Table 5.	Key dates for ISIS in Mozambique	136

Map 1.	Map of contemporary Mozambique	17
Map 2.	Muslims in Mozambique, 1997	46
Map 3.	Presence of the al-Shabaab sect in Mozambique before 2017	129

vii

ACKNOWLEDGEMENTS

This book was researched and written over many years—since 1999, on and off—and I have accrued numerous debts over that time. In terms of research, I thank the Mozambican National Archives and its director, Joel das Neves Tembe; the archive of the National Directorate of Religious Affairs, of the Ministry of Justice, and its director at the time of my visit, the late Job Chambal; the Library of the Mozambican Parliament; and the Portuguese National Archives in Lisbon, Portugal, whose personnel were most pleasant and helpful. I also thank all those who generously granted me interviews and supported my research in direct and indirect ways (see the list of interviews in the bibliography). A special thanks goes to all those who helped me but need to remain anonymous.

I received financial and other support from several academic institutions: the universities of Basel, Lausanne, and Oxford, and Queen's University Belfast. In Mozambique, I have been an associate researcher at the Centro de Estudos Africanos and the Centro de Estudos da População of Eduardo Mondlane University, the Instituto de Estudos Sociais e Económicos in Maputo, and the Centro de Investigação e Estudos Económicos e Sociais de Cabo Delgado in Pemba. I have benefitted from being a senior advisor on Raufu Mustapha's project 'Muslim Leaders in Northern Nigeria', which brought me to Nigeria twice, and from taking part in the project led by Benjamin Soares and René Otayek entitled 'Islam, désengagement de l'état et globalisation en Afrique'. I also received

ix

ACKNOWLEDGEMENTS

financial support from Irish Aid for my last stint of fieldwork in 2019.

I express a warm thank you to my colleagues and friends in Mozambique for their support and encouragement: Yussuf Adam, Sergio Chichava, João Feijó, Salvador Forquilha, Feliciano Mata, David M. Matsinhe, Vali Momade, Borges Nhamire, Estácio Valoi, and Teodoro Waty. I thank my colleagues outside of Mozambique for their advice, friendship, and engagement: Michel Cahen, William Gervase Clarence-Smith, Vincent Foucher, Caroline Jeannerat, Antoine Kernen, Lorenzo Macagno, Martin J. Murray, Didier Péclard, Anne Pitcher, and Alex Vines. In Cabo Delgado, I benefitted from the professional help of Justo Nauva and Abudo Gafuro and many others who have chosen to remain anonymous. My apologies to those I have forgotten or erroneously made anonymous. All mistakes and misunderstandings are my responsibility. Finally, I wish to thank my wife and my son for their understanding, patience, and support while writing the book.

CREDITS

The book contains three chapters that were previously published in English. One chapter is a translation of an article in French. Chapter 4, the introduction, the conclusion, and the appendices are original.

All of the chapters have been edited to avoid repetition and to make minor corrections, and the references and the bibliography have been updated. A section was rewritten in Chapter 5 (about international links and ISIS) and maps were added and updated.

'L'islam au Mozambique après l'indépendance: Histoire d'une montée en puissance', in *L'Afrique Politique 2002*, Paris: Karthala, 2002, pp. 123–46 (as Chapter 1). Copyright: Karthala, 22/23 boulevard Argo, 75013 Paris, France.

'The 1996 'Muslim Holiday' Affair: Religious Competition and State Mediation in Contemporary Mozambique', *Journal of Southern African Studies*, 26(3), September 2000, pp. 409–27 (as Chapter 2). Copyright © The Editorial Board of the Journal of Southern African Studies. Reprinted by permission of Taylor & Francis Ltd, http://www.tandfonline.com on behalf of The Editorial Board of the Journal of Southern African Studies.

'A Prospect of Secularization? Muslims and Political Power in Mozambique Today', *Journal for Islamic Studies*, Cape Town: University of Cape Town, 27, 2007, pp. 233–66 (as Chapter 3).

xi

CREDITS

'The Jihadi Insurgency in Mozambique: Origins, Nature and Beginning', *Journal of Eastern African Studies*, 14(3), 2020, pp. 396–412 (as Chapter 5).

I thank the publishers for their permission to republish the material in the present form.

GLOSSARY

alim	Muslim man who is learned in religious matters
bid'ah	innovation in religious matter (Islam, usually negative)
burqa	veil, of the most concealing type
caliphate	polity ruled by a religious leader (a calif) under Islamic rule (sharia)
cofió	cap worn by Muslim men
dawah	invitation to convert people to Islam (proselytism)
Eid Ul Fitr	religious holiday celebrating the end of Ramadan
Eid Ul Adha	religious holiday celebrating Ibrahim/Abraham's willingness to sacrifice his son in obedience to Allah's command
hafiz	a Muslim man who has completely memorized the Quran, is frequently consulted, and is often made an imam
halal	permissible by Islamic law
haram	forbidden by Islamic law
imam	male leader in prayer at a mosque
Islamism	political ideology that aims to establish sharia rule
jamaat	Shia mosque
jihadism	Islamist ideology promoting the use of violence to achieve its objective of establishing sharia rule

GLOSSARY

madrasa	Muslim school, often part of a mosque
mawlana	title preceding the name of respected Muslim religious leaders, in particular, graduates of religious institutions; man in charge of the mosque (from the Arabic *mawlâ*, 'master')
Mawlid	celebration of the birthday of the prophet Muhammad
Ramadan	Muslim month of fasting
sharia	Islamic law
sheik	honorific title, in Arabic, meaning 'elder'
tariqa/turuq	brotherhood/s
ulama	community of the learned
umma	Muslim community
wilayat	province
zakat	form of almsgiving—a key obligation in Islam

ABBREVIATIONS

AMA	Africa Muslims Agency (Kuwait)
CCM	Christian Council of Mozambique (Protestant)
CFI	Centre of Islamic Training
CIMO	Islamic Community of Mozambique
CISLAMO	Islamic Council of Mozambique
DAR	Department for Religious Affairs, Ministry of Justice, Mozambique, replaced in the 1990s by DNAR
DNAR	National Directorate for Religious Affairs
Frelimo	Mozambique Liberation Front
ISCAP	ISIS Central Africa Province
ISIS	Islamic State of Iraq and Syria
LNG	liquefied natural gas
NGO	non-governmental organization
OIC	Organisation of the Islamic Conference. Since 2011 Organisation of Islamic Cooperation
PIMO	Independent Party of Mozambique, commonly known as Islamic Party of Mozambique
Rabitat	Muslim World League
Renamo	Mozambican National Resistance
SAAR	Service of Associative and Religious Affairs, replaced in 1982 by DAR

INTRODUCTION

In 2017, a jihadi insurgency began in the north of Mozambique. It started modestly, with an attack on three police stations in the town of Mocímboa da Praia on 5 October. A handful of men began the attack very early in the morning with knives, machetes, and a few guns. As they progressed, they told residents that they should stay home and that they were only targeting state officials. Crying out 'Allahu Akbar', the jihadists killed two policemen and wounded five; they stole several AK-47 guns and proceeded to battle police reinforcements as they came in—for thirty-six hours, before ultimately retreating. In subsequent months, a growing number of attacks took place in the region, first in the countryside, then in small villages, and, finally, in towns. The insurgency grew steadily, taking root and gaining in confidence, so that by the end of 2022 it affected most of Cabo Delgado province as well as the north of the province of Nampula, the east of the province of Niassa, and the areas bordering southern Tanzania. In the first five years of the conflict, the insurgents killed over 4,000 people, according to the Armed Conflict Location and Event Data Project (a number that is doubtless a serious underestimate), and displaced over a million. This is the first jihadi insurrection in Southern Africa.

The armed conflict developed in an area of the country, the far northern province of Cabo Delgado, that is one of the poorest and furthest removed from the capital. Yet it is the province where giant natural gas fields and promising graphite and precious mineral stones were discovered in the 2000s—not long before the insurgency began. Since then, international companies have moved into the area to develop mines and start work on a mega-project for the production of liquefied natural gas (LNG). This LNG project, which is currently the biggest private investment in Africa, includes an airport, a port, a workers' camp, and resettlement villages. The insurgency was of concern to investors right from the start, but, reassured by the Mozambican government that it was a minor affair, they continued with their work in the hope that it would not affect them. In March 2021, however, the insurgency scuppered the LNG project when jihadists spectacularly overran the town of Palma, next to the LNG construction site. The attack was methodically planned and affected many expatriates, some of whom were killed. Within weeks, the French company TotalEnergies declared a case of force majeure and suspended all its work. The American company ExxonMobil followed suit and announced it would delay making a final decision on investing in the same area. A much smaller LNG project led by the Italian ENI company has continued, but only because it is located offshore—48.2 km (30 miles) from the coast of Cabo Delgado.

The combination of the jihadi insurgency—which formally linked up to the Islamic State in 2019—mass poverty, major gas reserves and mineral deposits, and Africa's biggest private investment project has attracted much attention from journalists and academics the world over. The economic, political, and military stakes are high, yet, paradoxically, the insurgency remains poorly understood. This is partly due to the suboptimal conditions for conducting research and practising independent journalism in northern Mozambique; it also has to do with the related fact that scholars and journalists have proposed many, often contradictory explanations for the insurgency, some purely speculative, ranging from poverty, personal grievances, foreign interests, and geopolitics to religious extremism, transnational contagion, local or international conspiracies, and ecology. History is the poor relation of the list, with only two texts applying a historical lens to the question and only a handful of researchers spending any time trying to find out something about the insurgency's origins and history. We still know little about the insurgents' background, the historical context from which they

INTRODUCTION

emerged, the political economy of the area they come from, and the history of the state and various other local actors in the area, let alone that of the other actors in the unfolding conflict.

This book is a historical investigation of the relations between Muslims and politics in Mozambique from independence in 1975 to 2022, five years after the jihadi insurgency began. The book discusses the relationship between mosque and state, or the state's religious policy towards Muslims and how it has developed over time; the dynamics within the Muslim community and its organizations; and the demands that Mozambican Muslims have made of the state and society. While each chapter focuses on a particular period, the overall objective is to understand the relationship between mosque and state, and between Muslims and politics, from Mozambique's independence up to the present day. The book can be read 'forward' as an analysis of Muslims and politics in Mozambique progressing over time, but it can also be read 'backward' to understand where the present situation came from and what it builds on. It allows for a deeper appreciation of the contemporary situation by putting it into perspective while hopefully also providing some idea of where things might be going in the near future.

Five themes dominate the coming pages. The first is the state's policy towards religion. In Mozambique, the same party has been in power since independence: the Mozambique Liberation Front (Frente de Libertação de Moçambique [Frelimo]), though it has changed significantly over the years, from an originally Marxist–Leninist liberation movement to a patrimonial neo-liberal party at the time of writing. Frelimo's religious policy has changed significantly over the same period too, and this raises several questions: What was Frelimo's original policy towards religion, how did it deploy it, and with what effect? How did it change over time, when were the turning points, and why was change implemented? Conversely, what are the continuities in Frelimo's views and policies towards religion, and what effect have they had? The coming pages unpack government policy, its making and remaking, its actors, and the causes of change. The discussion focuses on Islam, but where useful it also considers and discusses other faiths. The analysis thus explores how the Mozambican state has been built since independence, how it has evolved over nearly half a century, what Frelimo is and wants, and how it has adjusted its objectives over time.

Secularism is the book's second major theme. The coming pages analyse Frelimo's policy of secularism and trace how it has changed from a strong (or assertive) secularism at independence to a softer (or more passive) one in later years.[1] It also looks at how Muslims have understood and responded to this secularism. Chapter 4 deals with the topic by looking at the integration of Muslims into the political bloc holding hegemonic power. Subsequent chapters return to the issue, if less centrally, to analyse how the Muslim population perceives state policy towards religion and to discuss the changes that took place in the 2000s and 2010s. Considering the extensive discussions by scholars and historical actors over the compatibility of Islam and secularism, particularly in relation to the Muslim concern that laws be made in line with God's revelation, Mozambique provides an interesting case where Muslims, including Islamists, have engaged actively with secular institutions and have happily compromised with secular politics. Islamists have embraced the state at all levels and worked ceaselessly in the hope of Islamizing institutions and society 'from above'. As the discussion reveals, their success has been modest: using Christian Coulon's expression, there has been more of an institutionalization of Islam than an Islamization of state institutions.[2]

The competition and conflicts between Sufi and anti-Sufi Muslims form the book's third focus. This topic has been extensively investigated on the African continent but only emerged as a topic of interest regarding Mozambique at the turn of the twenty-first century. Like elsewhere, distinctions in theological doctrine have always existed in Mozambique, but of note is a Wahhabi wave that reached the eastern shores of south-east Africa in the 1960s and initiated a new period within Islam in the territory. Wahhabism settled in Mozambique among a new generation of scholars who had been trained abroad and returned with new ideas; two decades later, a number of Saudi, Kuwaiti, and Sudanese non-governmental organizations (NGOs) made their way to the country and buttressed the power of these scholars with funds, new mosques, and humanitarian and development aid. This wave of Wahhabism

INTRODUCTION

articulated into several social, economic, and generational strands of Islam, to become a major source of tension and conflict among Muslims in subsequent decades. The book analyses how this happened and when, as well as its impact on the internal organization and dynamics of the Muslim community and its associations and political stance. While this subject was a major theme of the scholarship on Islam in Mozambique up to 2017, with significant agreement among authors, it has since been replaced by jihadism as the main subject of concern.

The fourth major theme is the rise of a new Muslim elite and counter-elites. This formation only became possible after the end of colonial rule and its pro-Catholic and anti-Muslim colonial administration. The post-independence regime was initially strongly secularist, even taking an anticlerical position early in its rule. Frelimo had few Muslims among its leadership, and for many years it remained biased against Islam. But in the 1980s and 1990s, new economic, intellectual, and religious elites emerged—both among Sufi and Wahhabi believers—that increasingly engaged the state. This resulted in moments of tension and crisis around the involvement of 'Islam in politics', as some journalists put it. Chapter 2 carefully examines one such moment, including allegations of conspiracy. More generally, the book explores the rise of these new elites, be they economic, social, or religious, and Sufi or anti-Sufi, and how they were positioned socially and politically. It also pays attention to minority Muslim groups, not least the revival of old Swahili elites that can trace their status back to precolonial sultanates and sheikdoms.

The book's last major theme is religious competition and conflict. At one level, it is a discussion about state policy and how this fosters competition between religious institutions and individuals. Academic adepts of rational choice see this in a positive light, arguing that religious competition leads to more religious work, evangelization, and faith. But the deregulation of religious control can also lead to ideological and physical conflict. This is what happened in Mozambique in the 1990s, an example examined in detail in Chapter 2. At another level, the theme of religious competition and conflict is also a discussion about inter-religious and intra-religious relations. Mozambique has been marked by good interfaith relations since independence, even if tensions grew with the rise of religious competition in the 1990s and 2000s. But the 2000s and 2010s have seen the appearance of exclusivist strands of faith, both Christian and Muslim, with some groups trying to withdraw from society and distance themselves from the state to operate under purely religious rules. This is best exemplified by the rise of the al-Shabaab sect in northern Mozambique in the 2000s. In the mid-2010s, the sect turned to violence to achieve its politico-religious aims in an attempt to change society as a whole. Chapter 5 traces this history.

The title of the book asks whether it is possible to identify a historical path 'towards jihad' in the relationship between Muslims and politics in Mozambique. On one level, the question is rhetorical, asking about the connections between postcolonial Muslim politics and the insurgency unfolding in northern Mozambique. The book answers this in the negative to argue that there are no direct connections between the two. Indeed, the insurgency comes not so much from a continuation of Muslim politics in the country as a rupture with it. The jihadi insurgents reject the state, society, and all existing relations that have developed between Muslims and the state since independence. While the answer is negative, the question remains important to think about the historical trajectory of Muslim politics in Mozambique across the period and to explore what connects the past with the present. Indeed, we need to identify the trajectory of Muslims and politics to understand the context within which the armed jihadi insurrection began and unfolded, and to understand what the present situation builds on, breaks with, and argues against.

At a second level, the question in the book's title is something of a parody, to critique what has become a common methodological problem in understanding the history of Islam in Mozambique. Many contemporary analysts and journalists read history backwards, to find in the past elements that explain the situation unfolding in Cabo Delgado as they write. But reading history backwards limits the view to what one thinks is relevant for the present: it misses the roads not taken and ignores elements that are not clearly and directly related to the present. It also leads to what scientists call 'teleology', a linear understanding of history where explanations are designed in terms of the purpose they serve—in this case, to understand the jihadi

INTRODUCTION

insurrection—rather than in terms of the causes from which they arose at the time. A good example of this relates to the link many analysts see between Islamism and jihadism when they assume that Islamism is the step that permitted the development of jihadism in Mozambique even though field research indicates that Islamists and jihadists constitute different social groups with similar ideologies but different social and political projects, drawing from divergent inspirations and networks.

The first three chapters of this volume were written and published before the insurgency began in 2017. They sought to understand the relationship between religion and politics and had nothing to do with a jihadi insurgency, which could not be foreseen. The chapters have not been altered in their focus, analysis, and argument, thus pre-empting any risk of teleology in the analysis offered. The last two chapters, which deal specifically with Muslim 'radicalization' and the jihadi insurgency, were obviously penned subsequently. By bringing these older and newer chapters together, this book offers a non-teleological reflection on Muslims and politics in Mozambique since independence as well as a historical consideration of the jihadi insurgency, not only of its origins and history but also its deeper history in Islamic politics in Mozambique. This enables a careful and detailed examination of the complexity of the Mozambican Muslim community, its dynamics, and the ideas that drive it, and an informed archaeological analysis of the situation that saw the emergence of a jihadi insurgency in 2017.

The longue durée

Before discussing the postcolonial history of Muslims and politics in Mozambique, it is important to look at the deeper history of Islam in South East Africa—both in its *longue durée* (long term) and its *conjuncture* (medium term), as Fernand Braudel called them.[3] This section offers a history of Islam from its arrival on the coast of East Africa up to the end of the colonial period. It explains the structural dynamics that were at play and the impact they had in the period after independence in 1975. Specifically, it sketches the roots of the grievances and tensions that existed after independence, some

7

TOWARDS JIHAD?

remaining right up to the 2020s, such as the idea that Muslims have been and remain marginalized in the national polity. This long history is presented in broad strokes, primarily in relation to politics, and focuses on issues that are relevant to the postcolonial period.

Islam arrived in East Africa in the eighth century, with Arab and Persian travellers and traders migrating to the Benadir Coast of what is today southern Somalia. As August Nimtz has noted, 'though they were probably not the first Arabs to settle on the East African coast ... these were the first immigrants who came to Africa as adherents of Islam'.[4] According to the Kilwa Chronicle, two centuries later seven sons of the sultan of Shiraz (in Persia) established themselves in the same area and, after marrying locally, established Afro-Shirazi polities. From these developed a Swahili culture, with its own language (Swahili) and faith (Islam). In the twelfth century, the Afro-Shirazi began to expand southwards along the African coast all the way to the area that would become Mozambique. They established various settlements and polities, the most important and influential being Mombasa, in today's Kenya, and the Sultanate of Kilwa, in contemporary southern Tanzania. Smaller sultanates and sheikdoms were established on the coast of the present-day Mozambican provinces of Nampula and Cabo Delgado, namely in Tunge, Quissanga, Pemba, Memba, Angoche, Sangage, and Quitanhonga.[5]

The arrival of the Portuguese in the sixteenth century along the East African coast, and their establishment on the island of Mozambique and along the Zambezi River, limited the economic opportunities of the Afro-Shirazi Swahili settlements. The expansion of African empires, such as the Zimba and Maravi, challenged these Muslim polities further, leading to a decline of Afro-Shirazi societies in the seventeenth century and to their limitation to the coast.[6] A revival took place from the mid-seventeenth century thanks to the arrival of Omani and Hadhrami Arabs from the southern Arabian Peninsula. The Omani defeated the Portuguese in Mombasa in 1698 and went on to control the region. Their influence grew significantly, not least economically, with the trade in ivory and slaves and the involvement of Indian merchants, until Sayyid Saïd bin Sultan al-Busaidi moved his capital from Oman to Zanzibar in the early nineteenth century.[7] Religiously, Omani rule saw Hadramaut

8

INTRODUCTION

Arabs disseminate orthodox Sunni Islam into the interior of what is currently Tanzania and Mozambique (being from the Kharijite sect, the Omani largely abstained from proselytization). Success was such among theYao people, near Lake Nyasa (contemporary Lake Malawi), that several chiefdoms that are part of contemporary Mozambique became sultanates, such as Mataka, Metarica, Makanjila, Mponda, Macemba, Mawinha, Jalasi, and Matipweiri.[8]

In the mid-nineteenth century, the Portuguese were still limited to the coastal areas of northern Mozambique, where they traded in ivory and slaves. The 1884–5 Berlin Conference changed that dynamic: Portugal was forced to occupy the colonies it had successfully claimed as its own at the conference. For northern Mozambique, this required Portugal to agree on a final border, first with German East Africa to the north and, second, with the Sultanate of Zanzibar, which had a presence in the territories Portugal claimed. A Luso-German treaty resolved relations with Germany in December 1886. As to Zanzibar, in February 1897 Portugal issued an ultimatum and, when this was not respected, waged a war against it. Three battles ensured a Portuguese victory and its full control of the territory up to Rovuma River, including the originally contested Quionga triangle at the mouth of the river.[9] While this ended formal Zanzibari influence over the area, trade and religious links continued. After Lisbon outsourced the northern parts of its colony to the private Nyassa Chartered Company,[10] things changed in matters of policy and trade but not in relation to faith. As Eduardo da Conceição Medeiros notes: 'The Chartered company does not seem to have been preoccupied by the Muslim question.'[11]

When the Nyassa Chartered Company came to an end in 1929, the Portuguese administration took direct control of northern Mozambique. It reorganized the territory and worked at incorporating chiefs into the state administration. Chiefly, responsibilities were expanded from taxation to justice, labour recruitment, and forced cultivation, for which they received salaries and uniforms.[12] One substantial difference between the Portuguese and the administration of the chartered company beforehand was the stance they took towards religion. From the 1920s, the Portuguese state began to work ever more closely with the Roman Catholic Church. After

9

signing a concordat and a missionary accord with the Vatican in 1940, the Portuguese state outsourced the education and health of Africans to the church, to which it also granted land, salaries, and other benefits for its work.[13] The Portuguese state also opposed, if not repressed, Islam and other non-Catholic Christian denominations.[14] This opposition did not, however, prevent the expansion of the Islamic faith. Benefitting from colonial stability and the development of new infrastructure, a network of Sufi evangelists expanded its reach under the colonial state's radar.[15] African involvement was key to the success of Sufism as well as the involvement of a former local Muslim aristocracy that reinvented itself, as Liazzat Bonate explains, by transposing its 'precolonial political networks of kinship and territory on to the *tariqa* [brotherhood] networks'.[16]

The Portuguese attitude to Islam began to change in the late 1950s when Portugal became concerned by the rise of African nationalism and the possibility of a liberation war. The administration loosened its relations with the Catholic Church and began to co-opt non-Catholic leaders in the hope of preventing them from siding with the cause of national independence. Several important sheiks were approached and given support, including some leaders of Sufi *turuq*. The state also gave financial support for Muslims to undergo the *hajj* pilgrimage to Mecca and even for the construction and renovation of mosques. But the colonial state also used force during the liberation war by arresting many Muslim leaders, not least in Cabo Delgado, where dozens of sheiks and *mwalimu* (Muslim school teachers) were imprisoned and tortured, some deported to São Tomé, and others killed.[17] This stick-and-carrot strategy might have been successful in neutralizing nationalist support from the Muslim population as a whole, but it did not make Muslims change their view that the colonial state was pro-Catholic and that Muslims were being discriminated against—a view that predominated at the time of independence.

Approaching postcolonial Islam, Islamism, and jihadism

The historiography on Islam in postcolonial Mozambique is very young. Until the 1990s, hardly any scholars researched and wrote about Islam in the country, and none focused on postcolonial Islam. Since then, a handful of authors have focused on two aspects in particular: the relationship between Islam and the state, and the conflict between Wahhabi and Sufi Muslims. Regarding the former, the issue is mostly about the repression of religion that the newly independent Marxist–Leninist regime implemented after 1975 and the subsequent decision to move away from this policy in the early 1980s towards a new regime of division and control.[18] As to the latter aspect, researchers have focused on the rise of Wahhabism since the 1960s, its competition and struggle with Sufism, and the consequent changes in Muslim religious leadership.[19] Some of the coming chapters were early contributions to this historiography.

The literature on the insurgency that emerged in 2017 is even younger. Most authors have been concerned with identifying the insurgency's causes and look in particular at poverty, marginalization, governance, and radicalization. Others debate the importance of Islam and jihadi ideals, with some arguing that these are but a 'veil' to hide material interests.[20] Among the authors who have carried out original research, the dominant view is that there are several causes of the conflict, one of which is religion, specifically Islam.[21] While many have explored issues of poverty, governance, and radicalization, hardly anyone has looked at the history of the insurgents. Only one article has done so aside from Chapter 5 in the present book, which is a revised version of an article published in 2020.[22] Much more work is needed to answer questions about the insurgency's leaders, their origins, and their motivations. What also still needs to be studied is the insurgents' ideology and discourse and the history of the Muslim community in the Cabo Delgado province (since this is where the insurgency began). Chapter 5 contributes to the history of the jihadi insurgency; Chapter 4 makes a new contribution to the issue of radicalization, which is often presumed to have taken place before the insurgency (if not as a cause of it), although no one has studied the phenomenon.

Most studies on Islam in Mozambique have focused on institutional Islam, that is, its organizations and officials. Only recently have some started to look at mosques and individuals that are independent of the main national institutions recognized by the state.[23] This institutional bias has led all authors—including the present one—to miss some important social, religious, and political developments, most notably the birth and rise of the Islamist sect at the origin of the jihadi insurgency in Cabo Delgado. As I note in Chapter 5, there is a need in the historiography not only to study Muslims outside of the associations recognized by the state, but also to do research specifically on Islamic *sects* (understood in the sociological sense of communities separate from institutional Islam and distant from society and the state). Such investigations are challenging, as it means relying less on archives (which tend to contain material on recognized faiths, leaders, and institutions) and engaging in oral and life histories, something that might now be more difficult than ever, given the state's anxiety about such research in view of the jihadi insurgency.

The approach deployed in this book is historical and sociological: it aims to identify changes and continuities in the history of the relations between Muslims and politics. I am an adept of what some call an 'opportunity structure' perspective, namely a historical approach that neither sees people as making their own history as free agents, guided purely by their free choice, nor as people acting mechanically under the constraints of predetermined (super)structures.[24] Rather, the 'opportunity structure' perspective maintains that people act within structures that shape and constrain their actions and thinking, but that, at the same time, these structures are not free-floating elements but are made and constantly remade by the actions (or non-actions) of actors of different weight and power. Key to this approach is an examination of choices made *within* constraining structures, an analysis of the evolution of these structures under the impact of individual and collective action, and a study of the resulting historical trajectory.

My approach also builds on the rich tradition of the sociology of religion. This sub-discipline is important not just to add to and complement history, to give a subject some 'thickness' as Clifford Geertz would say, or to provide additional conceptual tools. It is key also for methods that teach how to deconstruct and critically assess faith and religious institutions, away from theology. One of the dangers for researchers and authors is to reproduce the discourse

INTRODUCTION

of the agent-actors and to misunderstand it. A good example is the term 'sect', which is used among Muslims, theologians, and believers alike to describe the two main currents of Islam: Sunni and Shia (and sometimes the different legal schools). In sociology, however, the term refers to a specific form of religious group that is located within a 'church–sect' typology. The typology defines models (or ideal types) on a spectrum of institutionalization and degree of closeness to society and the state. A sect stands at one end of the spectrum, with a low degree of institutionalization, a high degree of protest, and maximum distance from state and society. A church, in turn, stands at the other end of the spectrum, highly institutionalized and close to the state and society.[25] This book draws on this sociological understanding, particularly in Chapter 5, in preference to theological categories.

If researchers need to deconstruct the discourse of actors, they should also situate themselves. I am not religious and do not have an Islamic background. I do not speak Arabic or Swahili—as far as I know, only one such scholar exists in the study of Islam and Muslims in Mozambique. But I have been doing research in Mozambique since 1994, and I have worked on Islam since 1998. In 2007, I decided to stop doing research on Muslims because I felt that I would need to learn Arabic and Swahili and invest more in the study of Islam and the Quran if I wanted to continue. I thus shifted to other issues and topics, including politics and armed conflict. But I came back to the subject of Islam and Muslims in Mozambique in 2017 when the jihadi insurgency began. For one, I became interested in the subject; for another, I saw so much basic misunderstanding and ignorance of Islam and its history in Mozambique (on the part of commentators, journalists, politicians, and citizens) that I felt I should use my knowledge to make a contribution.[26] Looking at the insurgency, I felt that there was not just a lack of historical knowledge but also a lack of clarity about what questions needed to be asked to find out who the insurgents were and what they wanted. I thus came back to the subject with the same limitations as before but also with the advantage of a decade of prior research.

Shifting to a more general point, it is worth discussing the methodological question of whether Muslims constitute an actor in

13

Mozambican history. Indeed, do Muslims think collectively, and can they be said to act as a united entity? Can one say, for example, that Muslims as a whole voted in favour of one party or another, in one or another election? In the abstract, the answer is variable and changing, depending on the level under consideration (local, regional, or national). Sometimes Muslims act as if they were a single man/woman, but at others (more often than not?) they do not—and in certain places, they tend to do so more often than in others. The issue is one of identity. Drawing on Marxism, we can distinguish between 'Muslims in themselves' and 'Muslims for themselves'. The former exist objectively, but members of the community do not act as a collective. They lack consciousness, and, as Marx noted about class, 'the similitude of their interests creates no community, no national connection, and no political organisation'.[27] In contrast, a group of individuals 'for themselves' are self-conscious of their identity and interests, and they act as a united group. The best examples of such groups can be found in communal societies where identities have crystallized and hardened and act as the main driver and mobilizer for most if not all actions—think of societies such as those in Northern Ireland, Iraq, or northern Nigeria. In Mozambique, Muslims do not form a group for themselves at the national level; there is more than one Muslim identity and community, and the communities that exist are fluid, activated in some instances but superseded by other identities (class, region, gender, etc.) in others. For this reason (as well as the fact that even in communal groups there are particular subgroups driving processes), I do not talk of Muslims 'doing X' or 'thinking Y'. Rather, I think of institutions and groups with their leaders, and of individuals in terms of their name and position, whenever possible referring to contrary positions and actors to highlight internal dynamics and the complexity of processes.

Another issue to consider is the definition of terms relating to Islam and Muslims. There is a neo-orientalist tradition in academia that describes Islam in exotic and essentialist terms, presenting Islam in need of reform or enlightenment or as a threat; conversely, there are scholars who adopt Islamic concepts and terms without any scientific distancing. Here, I avoid using terms such as 'extremist' (which is loaded and refers to a continuum between two extremes

INTRODUCTION

that are rarely explicated) or 'fundamentalist' (which originates from Protestantism). I use the terms 'Islam' for the faith that developed on the basis of the Quran, and 'Muslims' for believers of that faith (whichever version they believe in and to whichever degree). I use the concept 'reformist' to refer to people who try to change, update, or modernize religious teachings—similar to Roman Loimeier, who refers to 'reformists' as Muslims with an 'implicit or explicit program (*manhaj*) of change'.[28] I use the terms 'Islamist' and 'jihadist' to refer to Muslims who want sharia rule. While Islamists want to Islamize the existing state by peaceful means, jihadists reject the existing state and seek to overthrow it by force. Both Islamists and jihadists are not religious currents but religious political ideologies—French scholarship speaks tellingly of 'political Islam'.[29] All of these terms are general and often need qualification and nuance, as there are many subcurrents and trends: for example, Deobandism and Wahhabism are two distinct forms of Islamism.

Actors, and even some academics, may not welcome the highlighting of nuances and differences. Apart from the argument that only Muslim scholars should study Muslim societies and issues, there is an article of faith in Islam drawing from the Quran and the hadiths about the unicity of God (*tawhîd*) and the unity of the Muslim community (*umma*). The hadiths make clear that not only should the *umma* be a central objective of any Muslim but also that divisions within the community constitute a 'supreme disorder' (*fitna*).[30] This leads some individuals to reject the idea that there are divisions among Muslims, hence contesting the idea that there are differences, competition, and conflict within the community. This sometimes leads them to take issue with the very enterprise of research and to challenge sociological and historical works and findings about class, gender, racial, and other differences. The present research was not conducted in any negative spirit to reveal or stir divisions within Islam. On the contrary, the objective was, and remains, to improve our understanding of the complexity of the Muslim community and its history (in Mozambique specifically), to avoid misunderstandings, undermine simplistic ideas that feed prejudice, Islamophobia, and bad policies, and to reinforce bridges if not create unity between communities.

To conclude, let me refer to the primary sources used for the book. First, I have used archival documents, particularly those of the Portuguese and Mozambican states. I have worked at the National Archives of Mozambique, the National Archives of Portugal, and the Archives of the Mozambican National Institute of Religious Affairs (within the Ministry of Justice) and its Nampula provincial branch. Critically, I have relied on oral history and life histories to complement and triangulate written sources. I conducted dozens of interviews and life histories (see list in the bibliography). In northern Mozambique, I also contracted researchers who conducted additional interviews about the sect behind the insurgency—the names of most of these researchers and interviewees are anonymized in view of the sensitivity of the subject. Finally, I practised some participant observation—when possible, when useful, and when invited to do so—which allowed me to enrich my understanding and gain an empathic connection to the subject at hand. Overall, the book is the result of twenty years of research that has accumulated and reinforces itself, following a cumulative trajectory of questioning and investigating, hopefully ending in a coherent and helpful whole.

Map 1. Map of contemporary Mozambique

Source: Maura Pringle (Queen's University Belfast). In 2018, Swaziland became Eswatini.

1

THE 'RISE' OF ISLAM AFTER INDEPENDENCE, 1974–94

Islam in Mozambique became publicly visible and politically important in the 1990s. New mosques were built in cities, towns, and villages, and the country's president, a Catholic, started wearing Muslim garb to visit Muslim-majority areas of the country, even for his own birthday celebrations. Political parties began courting believers of the Islamic faith, and, in turn, Muslims became important actors in national affairs. This was a pronounced change. Although numerically significant, Muslims had been marginalized and their faith opposed by the Portuguese colonial state before being censured and even repressed by the new 'Marxist' government after independence. The 1980s and 1990s thus mark a dramatic shift in the position of Islam in Mozambican society, and this raises a number of questions: What is the exact nature of this shift? How did it unfold? What are its causes—internal factors, external factors, or possibly both? Is it linked to changes in Islam or the reorganization of political power, or both? What is the politico-religious situation in the country after this turnaround?

When this chapter was first published two decades ago, there were few academic texts about Islam in Mozambique and none about Islam after independence. This was partly due to the prevailing Christian intellectual hegemony that was rooted in the pro-Catholic Portuguese regime that ruled Mozambique until 1975; and partly due to the anti-religious policy of the first government after independence and the materialist approach that dominated Mozambican studies until the mid-1980s. To this, one can add the difficulty of mastering Arabic and Swahili, a barrier that almost no researcher has overcome. Be this as it may, the fact is that there was a certain vacuum in the historiography of Islam in Mozambique. It was necessary to improve our understanding of the history of contemporary Mozambique and of Islam in Africa, particularly in East Africa. Indeed, if there were few studies on Islam in Mozambique, it followed that there were hardly any comparisons between Islam in Mozambique and in its neighbouring countries (something that still holds true in 2023). Yet it is important to evaluate the differences and similarities of attitude and religious policies of the British and Portuguese colonial powers of the region, the nationalist and Marxist postcolonial regimes, and the liberal, if not neo-liberal, orientation of present governments. It is also necessary to compare the development of different currents of Islam (Sufism, Deobandism, Wahhabism, etc.) in the various countries and to evaluate the respective penetration of new Muslim organizations such as the Africa Muslims Agency (AMA), the World Muslim League, and Islamic Appeal.

This chapter is based on research in the archive and in the field, following a method that combines ethnography and history, as mentioned in the introduction. For this specific chapter, I interviewed Sufi and Wahhabi religious leaders and state officials in the provinces of Maputo, Manica, Sofala, and Nampula in 2000 and 2001. The interviews were both formal and informal, unstructured, and followed a snowball selection methodology. The chapter is organized into four sections. It first presents an overview of Islam in Mozambique before independence, including the number of believers and the divisions that existed within the faith community. It then explains state policy towards religion after independence, when the government officially adopted a Marxist orientation. The third section traces the transformation that took place within the Muslim faith community around 1981. The fourth looks at Islam's politicization in Mozambique after 1989. The chapter closes with a

Colonial Islam

The introduction briefly set out Islam's long history in Mozambique and something of the colonial Portuguese state's religious policy. In this section, I look at the divisions within Islam, how Portugal's religious policy played out in relation to different groups, and how these groups created new dynamics within the community, some of which would be important after 1975.

At the time of independence, Mozambique had over a million Muslims, representing about 15 per cent of the overall population.[1] The community was divided in ways that were determined by their time of arrival or conversion, by race and colour, by religious current and legal school, and by social class. To begin, one can distinguish between an Islam with roots in Arabia and the Swahili world and an Islam with roots in Asia. The former, following the Shafi'i school of law, was dominated by Sufi *turuq* (brotherhoods, sing. *tariqa*), such as the *tariqa* Qadiriyya, *tariqa* Shadhiliyya, or *tariqa* Rifa'iyya. It was present mostly in the north of the country, particularly among the Yao and Makua people and the old Swahili elite who converted to Shafi'i Islam in the late nineteenth century.[2] It was present in smaller numbers in the centre of the country, in particular at the important Sufi sanctuary Nova Sofala, also called Muenhe Mukuro, and in the south among communities that had migrated there from the north.[3] Islam with roots in Asia, in turn, was either of the Hanafi school of law or was Shia (of the Twelver and Ismaili branches), and it was geographically present in cities and towns along the coast, with a concentration in Mozambique's south, particularly the cities of Lourenço Marques and Inhambane. African Muslims, almost all followers of the Shafi'i school of law, dominated numerically, with more than a million in 1960, but they were much poorer than Muslims of Asian origin (about 20,000 in 1960).[4] Many Asian Muslims worked in trade and commerce; *mestiços* (mestizos) often worked as employees or artisans, linked to the Asian communities. African Muslims were predominant in agriculture, artisanship, 'informal' trading, and farming. On the northern coast, some communities were still related to the Swahili sultanates that existed before Portuguese colonial occupation (Angoche, Sangage, Quissanga, etc.).[5]

By the late 1950s, new Islamic currents had appeared in Mozambique. The first missionaries of the Ahmadiyya brotherhood (of the Idrisi orders) arrived from Tanzania and made inroads but have remained marginal since.[6] Deobandism and Wahhabism, both revivalist and scripturalist movements, also began to appear in those years, developing within the Asian Muslim community, particularly among *mestiços*; after independence, this latter current was to grow significantly, as we will see below.

These divisions within the Mozambican Muslim community led to the founding of a flurry of religious organizations but also to tensions between them. In most towns, Indians gathered into Muslim organizations. Among African Muslims, there were nine brotherhoods from two major groups by 1968—the Shadhiliyya (Liaxuri, Madhania, and Itifaque) and the Qadiriyya (Sadat, Bagdad, Jailane, Saliquina, and Macherepa)—plus a more informal brotherhood called Rifa'iyya.[7] Less organized but no less powerful were the remaining structures of the northern sultanates, such as Angoche, whose importance and influence was informal and unofficial but important nonetheless.[8] In the south, the main Asian Islamic organizations were the Comunidade Mahometana Indiana (Indian Muslim Community, founded in 1935 and renamed Comunidade Mahometana Paquistanese [Pakistani Muslim Community] after the 1961 invasion of Goa),[9] the Associação Anuaril Isslamo (a *mestiço* association under the financial control of the Comunidade Mahometana), and a brotherhood called Bezme Tabligh Isslamo Cadrya Sunni, linked to the Anuaril Isslamo mosque.[10] Still in the south, there was also the Associação Afro-Mahometana (created by Shafi'i *mestiços* from Inhambane province), the Associação Comoriana (launched by the Comorian diaspora in Lourenço Marques), and small delegations of brotherhoods from the north of Mozambique.[11]

Predictably, this diversity led to tensions and conflicts. Competition and occasionally fights emerged within Sufi brotherhoods, leading to the creation of new 'lodges' (from two *turuq* in 1905 to eight

THE 'RISE' OF ISLAM AFTER INDEPENDENCE, 1974–94

in 1968), and between different brotherhoods and organizations, usually over issues of rites, ethnicity, race, and funding. The biggest conflict was, and until the end of the twentieth century remained, between Sufi Islam and a reformist or revivalist Islam that developed within the Asian and Asian *mestiços* Muslim community (Deobandism and Wahhabism), a conflict that superimposed itself on to issues of race and Muslim law (a full discussion follows below).

Historically, the Portuguese colonial state was hostile to Islam, as we saw earlier. This was the result of the co-identification between Portuguese nationalism and Catholicism, something that was formalized in 1940 with the signing of a concordat and the missionary accord by the Vatican and Portugal. These two agreements established a formal strategic alliance between Lisbon and the Catholic Church by which the Portuguese state helped the church in the colonies and outsourced to it the provision of education and health services for Africans, giving the church a quasi-monopoly. It led the colonial government to marginalize other faith organizations. From 1940, the colonial state deployed a systematic policy of 'hassling' Islam (and other non-Catholic faiths), to borrow Michel Cahen's expression.[12] Colonial administrators closed Quranic schools on the flimsiest of pretexts, seized Islamic religious books, and forced children to attend Roman Catholic missionary schools. This policy was not without practical challenges and met with significant resistance from Muslims and even some (anticlerical) administrators.[13] The colonial state's opposition to Islam only changed when African nationalism began to gain popular traction. At this point, the Portuguese administration tried to co-opt Islamic leaders and became less repressive to prevent Muslims from joining the 'enemy'. In the 1960s, the state started to provide funding for Muslims to go on pilgrimage to Mecca and repair mosques, and the governor-general began to make official visits to leading Muslim organizations and centres. For the most part, the strategy was successful, with the colonial state co-opting, or at least politically neutralizing, most Mozambican Muslims until the end of the colonial era.[14] The only exceptions were a few young Muslims who joined the nationalist movements and a handful of religious leaders in Cabo Delgado province who sided with African nationalists and the liberation struggle and were promptly arrested,

23

deported, or executed by the colonial state. For reasons that are still unclear, Frelimo, the main liberation movement, made little effort to gain Islamic support for its liberation struggle.[15]

Marx and Muhammad

Frelimo's policy towards religion after independence was marked by a militant laicism and, soon after, by an open attack on religious organizations. Frelimo aimed to build a socialist and secular state, an effort that, seeing how the colonial state had instrumentalized religion, was not without its problems. At the time it came to power in 1975, Frelimo did not have an explicit anti-religious position towards religion or Islam in particular. It acted against some churches and arrested some religious leaders, but these actions were limited to institutions and individuals who had collaborated with the colonial political police or were perceived as imperialists.[16] Indeed, the liberation movement was still looking at restraining the power of religious organizations (not religion as such) and, in turn, ascertaining the power of the new state. In July 1975, Frelimo nationalized the property of all faith organizations including that used for social, educational, and health purposes, the overwhelming proportion of which was in the hands of the Catholic Church. Soon after, it banned several associations, some of which were Islamic.[17] Finally, Frelimo set up a policy of controlling people's movements and tried to restrict religious activities to churches and mosques, removing them from schools and public spaces. It was critical of faith organizations, but the main aim of the new government at this point was to reduce the social and political power of faith institutions rather than attacking faith itself. Tellingly, Frelimo spoke about confining religion to the private and individual domain.[18]

There were divergent reactions within the Muslim community to independence and Frelimo assuming power. Ismaili Muslims, a community of a few thousand members, left the country in 1975 following the order of their leader, the Aga Khan, after uprisings in central Mozambique took an anti-Asian turn.[19] Other Asian Muslims adopted different positions: some hedged their bets by moving elsewhere while leaving behind one or a few family members to look after their companies, properties, and goods; others stayed, adapted to the situation, and even took advantage of it, given that the independence process had led to the mass departure of their main competitors, the Portuguese settlers (the overwhelming majority of settlers left during the transition period or soon after independence).[20] As for African Muslims, and particularly Muslims belonging to brotherhoods, it is difficult to determine unambiguously how they reacted to independence. Several brotherhood leaders had benefitted from the Portuguese policy of co-optation, making it likely that they felt uncertain about the future. During an interview in 2000, a *tariqa* leader declared that he had had no choice but to go with the tide once Frelimo assumed power.[21] At the same time, most African Muslims, regardless of who their leaders were, are sure to have welcomed liberation from colonialism as it implied an end to racial, economic, and political discrimination.

At its Third Congress in 1977 (its first since independence), Frelimo decided to move away from its initial policy of merely restraining religious organizations. It transformed itself into a one-party state and adopted 'Marxism–Leninism' as its official ideology, with the aim of creating a full and effective socialist society. To that end, it posited itself as a vanguard party, opted for a planned and centralized economy, and developed an explicitly anti-religious stance. The new religious policy aimed to replace other belief systems with Marxism, materialism, and atheism. Drawing on Achille Mbembe,[22] we can say that the Mozambican one-party state embraced a 'theological pretention' by not only wanting political power but also wanting to control how people thought. Consequently, from the second half of 1977, Frelimo began what François Constantin and Christian Coulon call a 'secular holy war',[23] a policy coordinated by all elements of the party-state in charge of religious affairs, that is, the Information Department, the Ministry of the Interior, and the Ministry of Security (including the secret services, the infamous Serviço Nacional de Segurança Popular).[24] These entities used national radio to spread atheist propaganda and organized campaigns in the countryside to 'diminish the influence of religion in all sectors of society'.[25] The party-state banned the teaching of the Quran to children, prohibited Muslim men from wearing the *cofió* (Muslim cap) in cities, towns, and all party-state institutions, and put an end to the pilgrimage to Mecca (which had seen 180 participants in 1977).[26] It closed several mosques and madrasas (schools) in provinces such as Inhambane and Niassa—the official position being that it only closed religious buildings that were close to social and educational centres or that were located within the 'liberated areas' (the areas freed by Frelimo during the liberation war) to prevent 'contamination'.[27] In some cases, the police or state administrators took advantage of these operations to seize and burn religious literature found at the religious sites.[28]

Two aspects must be noted regarding Frelimo's anti-religious policy. First, it was not applied uniformly. The policy was official and coordinated from Maputo by radio messages (some of which are archived in the National Directorate for Religious Affairs [Direcção Nacional dos Assuntos Religiosos (DNAR)]). But because of human variation or tactical choice, there were regional nuances (for example, mosques were not closed in all provinces), and there were some inconsistencies or tactical concessions, such as when permission was granted in early 1980 for an Islamic congress in Tete city, attended by Mozambican delegates and 140 foreign guests.[29] Second, even if the official policy addressed all faiths equally, the Christian education of a majority of Frelimo leaders, including those in charge of dealing with religion, determined that it was applied more harshly towards Muslims than towards Christians. For example, when the country's president visited the central mosque of Ilha de Moçambique, he did not take off his shoes, shocking the assembled believers, an episode well remembered by Muslims in Mozambique to this day.[30] Some political leaders, including the president, refused to accommodate the Muslim taboo of eating pork, so that Muslim soldiers were coerced into eating pork, and pigsties were built in Muslim neighbourhoods and areas across the country.[31] Similarly, when Maputo's governor tried to prevent the closure of commercial businesses during the Eid Ul Adha celebration in 1982 and Muslim leaders came to protest, he suggested that businesses should 'just' move their celebration to a Sunday, Mozambique's official day of rest.[32] Last, the Service of Associative and Religious Affairs (Serviços de Actividades Associativas e Religiosas [SAAR]),

THE 'RISE' OF ISLAM AFTER INDEPENDENCE, 1974–94

which was responsible for the state's relationship with religious institutions, was tellingly located in the Ministry of Interior, and no one working there had any knowledge of Islam. It was not until 1989 that a Muslim was put in charge of dealing with Muslim affairs in SAAR's successor institution, the Department for Religious Affairs (Departamento de Assuntos Religiosos [DAR]; later succeeded by DNAR).

Unsurprisingly, Frelimo's anticlerical policy had disastrous consequences. In the northern Cabo Delgado province, revolts took place in several places, such as in Mocímboa da Praia in 1980 when the teaching of the Quran was banned and in Pemba in the same year when Muslim Sufi dancing was prohibited.[33] The policy alienated Muslims from the government and created the potential for latent and even open opposition against the regime. In 1979, the Resistência Nacional de Moçambique (Renamo), an armed movement established in Rhodesia in 1976, denounced the destruction of mosques, the prohibition on practising one's religion, and the demand made for Muslims to eat 'monkey meat', as Issufo Moamed, then head of Renamo's religious affairs, put it at the time.[34] Similarly, in 1980 Mozambican students at the University of Dar-es-Salaam denounced the repression of Islam in Mozambique.[35] More significantly yet, the Renamo guerrillas and their Rhodesian supporters took advantage of the anti-religious policy and how it was applied against Islam to reach out to Muslim countries. In 1978, they sent an envoy to the Gulf monarchies to mobilize financial and diplomatic support.[36] It is not known how much Muslim support Renamo managed to gain in this way, both within Mozambique and internationally. But there are indications that Renamo's military progress was facilitated in areas dominated by Muslims,[37] and several authors suggest that it received financial support from Oman, Saudi Arabia, and the Comoros as well as from elements in the Muslim community in Lisbon.[38]

Frelimo put an end to its anti-religious and anti-Muslim policy in 1981. Before discussing this shift, however, we need to analyse the development of Islam in Mozambique after independence, particularly the development of reformist Islam. This is necessary to understand how the shift away from repression took place, the

27

impact it had on the community, and how the relationship between Muslims and politics unfolded subsequently.

The rise of Wahhabism

The first signs of Islamic reform, revivalism, or scripturalism among Muslims in Mozambique go back to the late nineteenth century.[39] Debates took place about funerary rituals, the reformists arguing that sacred texts prescribed silence during the proceedings, while Sufi Muslims in the country sang, beat drums, and marched with flags in line with Islamic tradition. On more than one occasion, these differences led to controversies, if not outright conflict. In 1949, the British government had to intervene in Malawi (with the Muslim Yao community straddling the joint border), and in 1972 the Portuguese government asked an influential sheik to issue a fatwa (a ruling on a point of Islamic law) to resolve a conflict around the same issue.[40]

In the 1950s, reformism in Mozambique saw a new development with the emergence of a new *ulama* (or community of the learned) made up of Afro-Asian sheiks educated abroad. These scholars were fully trained in *ilm* (Islamic knowledge) and had developed contacts with influential international centres of Islamic religious knowledge, giving them symbolic and religious power. The first Afro-Asian sheik from this new generation was Cassamo Tayob, a *mestiço* from the capital city of Lourenço Marques (present-day Maputo) in the country's extreme south. He had studied for sixteen years in India, including at the famed Darul Uloom Islamic seminary in Deoband, a world centre for Hanafi reformist Islam.[41] On his return to Mozambique in 1951, Tayob worked as a teacher at the Anuaril Isslamo mosque in Lourenço Marques. His teaching was new, and conflict soon emerged around his personality and approach. In 1957, Nuro Amade Dulá, the son of the founder of Anuaril Isslamo and the head of the Sufi brotherhood Bezme Tabligh Isslamo Cadrya Sunni, accused Tayob of trying to use old conflicts to 'infiltrate the Deobandi sect which is subversive'.[42] Despite this resistance, Tayob gained prominence over the years and was able to exert a significant amount of influence, pushing for the primacy of the *ulama* over the particularism of mosques and what he called 'syncretism'. In 1966,

THE 'RISE' OF ISLAM AFTER INDEPENDENCE, 1974–94

many imams and mawlana of southern Mozambique considered him the top authority in religious matters.[43]

In the late 1960s, another sheik emerged who would be equally, if not more, important. Sheik Abubacar Hagy Mussá Ismael, commonly known as mawlana or Sheik Mágira, studied with Tayob before going to Pakistan for religious training and finally attending the Islamic University of Medina in Saudi Arabia, where he trained in Islamic law.[44] On his return to Mozambique, he worked at a small mosque in the periphery of Lourenço Marques, where he rapidly took leadership of the Mozambican reformist (Deobandi/ Wahhabi) movement. Helped spiritually and financially by reformists in South Africa, among whom was the Miya family in the Transvaal province,[45] he quickly came to clash with Sufi and pro-Sufi Muslims in Mozambique. The situation came to a head in late 1971. At a meeting at the Anuaril Isslamo attended by more than 800 Muslim delegates from the whole of Mozambique, including a number of brotherhood leaders from the north, mawlana Mágira attacked the dominant practice of Mawlid, the celebration of the birth of the Prophet, drawing on the Wahhabi belief that it is a *bid'ah* (innovation), because it is not referred to in the Quran or the Sunnah. He also denounced the popular Sufi sanctuary Nova Sofala in central Mozambique. His address was badly received, and several Sufi leaders wrote to the governor-general to complain about him. They accused him and his partners of destabilizing the country's Muslim community by bringing 'confusion and contradictions never seen before in the community' with 'tendentious insinuations and innovations about principles … established centuries ago'.[46] But this did not stop Sheik Mágira's campaign. When he sent a petition to the Portuguese governor-general in 1973 asking for permission to build and open a college and an Islamic school, he claimed that there were few Islamic schools in Lourenço Marques and that most of them were under the direction of associations and brotherhoods whose leaders 'were not capable to take just and correct decisions in what concerns the Islamic faith'.[47]

Despite significant opposition, the reformist movement gained supporters across southern Mozambique, mostly from people with Asian *mestiço* backgrounds. African Sufis did not accept this religious current that attacked their traditions. Some Indian Muslim associations with a Sufi orientation also opposed the reformists, with additional concern for possible racism (from *mestiço* sheiks) and caste differences.[48] Thus, until 1975, the reformist current remained in the minority and was regionally limited to the south of Mozambique. Its leaders' level of training and prestige brought them to the attention of the colonial authorities, who, in the late 1960s and early 1970s, tried to co-opt them. As we saw earlier, the colonial state had also deployed this policy of co-optation towards Muslim brotherhoods in the north, particularly in Nampula province. As a result, there were followers of reformism who supported African nationalism, but most anti-Sufi Muslims either remained politically neutral and quiescent or were co-opted by the Portuguese government—just like the majority of *turuq* leaders, who made no effort to turn the masses against the colonial power.[49] Even after independence, Wahhabism did not manage to make significant inroads in Mozambique. After 1977, Frelimo banned proselytization and even repressed religious practice. Yet the conflict between Sufism and anti-Sufism continued, if in a latent form, in a reformulated language, and on new battlegrounds. For example, the reformists fought for control over the Anuaril Isslamo mosque by creating a Revolutionary Committee of Anuaril in 1979, in whose name they then wrote to the government to ask for a change of direction of the organization and the mosque. Their letter argued that this step was necessary because some of the Anuaril leaders had been compromised by cooperating with the colonial power and the anti-independence movement during the political transition to independence in 1974–5.[50]

By 1980, Frelimo came to realize that its anti-religious policy not only caused problems but was counterproductive in that it played into the hands of the 'reactionary' cause of the nascent Renamo guerrilla movement. By the end of the year, it decided to abandon this policy and substitute it with a policy to control faith organizations. Among other things, this implied setting up umbrella bodies that would bring together all religious organizations of a particular denomination and faith, thus one for Protestant churches, one for all 'independent' churches, and one for all Islamic groupings; only the Catholic Church was to remain as it was. The umbrella bodies were placed under the authority of the DAR, which the government set up at that point and placed within the Ministry of Justice in replacement of SAAR. The umbrella bodies were created to ease their management by the state, but they were also given the mission of liaising with international and world religious organizations in order to improve the country's image. In terms of Islam, government representatives met a group of sheiks in Maputo in late January 1981 and asked them to form a national organization. The government representatives offered as headquarters for the body the Anuaril Isslamo building that had been nationalized in 1975.[51] Six months before this meeting, several high government officials and a delegation of the World Muslim League and the Saudi Arabian government had discussed the idea and agreed upon such a Muslim body. At the January 1981 meeting, without any consultation with Muslim leaders across the country, government representatives met with sheiks from Maputo, most of whom were reformist. The Muslim representatives agreed to set up a founding committee for an Islamic Council of Mozambique (Conselho Islâmico de Moçambique [CISLAMO]) within twenty days and agreed to nominate as coordinator of the new organization the contentious Saudi-connected Sheik Mágira. Soon after, the founding committee launched an information newsletter, which, in its first issue (see Appendix I), announced the creation of CISLAMO and set a particular tone for the organization by aggressively attacking the 'puppet brotherhoods', which, it stated, had been created to divide Muslims and were 'infested' with colonial political police spies who had waged 'campaigns of terror' against those who did not belong to their organizations.[52]

Unsurprisingly, several sheiks, imams, and Muslim believers in Maputo who were members of the new *ulama* but favourable to Sufism considered this new body to be controlled by Wahhabis and decided to create an alternative national organization, the Islamic Congress of Mozambique (Sunni). The latter was formally established in January 1983, after a 'historic meeting' in December 1982 between the government and all faith organizations in the country in which the government officially and publicly brought an end to its policy of anticlericalism.[53] At the launch of the Islamic Congress, its promoters explained that they were responding to the government's request for a single national Muslim organization. In a short history of its foundation a year later, they explained that all previous attempts at creating such a body had failed because 'a minority had tried by all means possible to impose foreign interest onto the majority'.[54] Like CISLAMO, the Islamic Congress was dominated from the outset by Muslims from the south of the country. However, its pro-Sufi orientation ensured that it expanded quickly throughout the whole country. Many communities, mosques, and brotherhoods in southern, central, and northern Mozambique became affiliated with it and took positions of leadership. The body met with meteoric success, and the government found itself not only with two organizations at hand but a situation where the body it launched, CISLAMO, was eclipsed by the infinitely more representative Islamic Congress.[55] Frelimo could not but abandon its plan to have a single national body for Islam, as a result of which it was unable to act against the Comunidade Mahometana (which had dropped the term 'Indiana' from its name after independence) and, ultimately, had to recognize and deal with three Islamic organizations.

The rest of the 1980s was marked by relentless competition between CISLAMO and the Islamic Congress. The government preferred CISLAMO,[56] but the Islamic Congress had incomparable popular support. A year after its foundation, it counted 239 affiliated mosques, associations, and brotherhoods, while CISLAMO, a year older, had only three affiliated mosques and associations from outside of Maputo.[57] Thereafter, competition focused on international relations with foreign governments and international organizations. Here CISLAMO had an advantage because it had started earlier, had the support of the Mozambican government, and was founded by men who had studied abroad and had created their organization in coordination with Saudi Arabia. In 1983, CISLAMO already had good contacts with the Saudi-based Muslim World League (Rabitat) (see Appendix II) and had signed a cooperation agreement with the Libyan organization Jamaat Daawa al Islamiya (World Islamic Call Society).[58] For its part, the Islamic Congress quickly affiliated itself with the World Federation of Islamic Missions and the World Muslim Congress, both based in Pakistan, and also formalized an application to become an affiliate of Rabitat. Competition was such that when the

Kuwaiti AMA visited Mozambique in 1984, CISLAMO demanded they deal exclusively with it and tried to conceal the existence of the Islamic Congress.[59] The AMA did not appreciate the council's game and, like Rabitat, refused to be partial in its relations with Mozambican Muslim organizations.[60] What followed was a difficult balancing act by AMA and Rabitat in how they distributed humanitarian aid during Mozambique's civil war, allocated scholarships to study abroad and granted subsidies to go on pilgrimage to Mecca (which the state now permitted once again). These conflicts seriously affected the interests of these international organizations: in 1988, the AMA submitted a formal complaint to the Mozambican government about being faced with 'strong opposition' throughout the country because it wished to work independently, with all Muslim organizations.[61]

As already mentioned, the Mozambican government was not neutral in this competition between the Muslim bodies, even if it accepted the existence of the Islamic Congress. All religious organizations were tied to the state via the DAR, which issued permissions for travel and for opening bank accounts and occasionally helped organizations get extra food, which was rationed due to the war. Yet, if the DAR had the official task of liaising and working with all religious organizations, it also followed the political aim of encouraging religious organizations 'so that these presented the correct image of the People's Republic of Mozambique to the exterior and obtained, by diplomatic means, support from their foreign partners'.[62] Regarding Muslim organizations, the aim was even more specific, namely to 'penetrate the reactionary monarchies of the Middle East' (as the DAR put it) that continued to hold a negative view of the country and were suspected of supporting Renamo's guerrilla war efforts in one way or another.[63] The government originally thought that the creation of CISLAMO would be enough to achieve this goal, but the launch of the Islamic Congress complicated matters. The government had to deal with two main organizations (in addition to the Comunidade Mahometana), and, at times, it played one off against the other. Despite much intervention and entryism in both CISLAMO and the Islamic Congress, in the end the government's approach showed little success. Mozambique's image in Muslim countries did not improve during the 1980s, and the humanitarian help received from these countries remained extremely modest, even though the war had expanded significantly.[64] In 1989, DAR's director referred to Frelimo's Muslim policy as a 'fiasco': the government had given back much social and political influence to Muslims but had gained little in return.[65]

The politicization of Islam

The 1980s saw a critical deterioration of the social, economic, political, and military situation in Mozambique. The economy collapsed because of the large-scale flight of Portuguese settlers, problems related to the socialist management of state and society, and the Rhodesian policy of destabilization and related creation of a Renamo guerrilla group that went on to wage an armed struggle that developed into a civil war. The country's political situation became 'militarized' when Renamo's guerrilla war spread across the country after 1984, despite the Nkomati agreement between South Africa and Mozambique having brought an end to most of South Africa's support for Renamo. Furthermore, the social and economic concessions Mozambique made to Western countries, the International Monetary Fund, and the World Bank did not provide the regime with much breathing space.[66] In view of this, Frelimo decided to make a radical change to its political orientation and international alliances. At its Fifth Congress in 1989, it abandoned all references to Marxism and socialism and adopted a liberal, if not neo-liberal, economic and political model.[67] In terms of religion, Frelimo shifted to what many have called a 'pluralist' system, though it might more accurately be called a 'free religious market'.[68] Frelimo gave nearly absolute freedom to religious organizations (freedom of establishment, proselytization, and engagement in health services and education). The only restriction was that religious institutions had to have a minimum of 500 members, had to be present in the whole country, and had to register with the DAR, which was to remain in charge of overseeing the religious sphere.[69] A new phase of relations between religious organizations and the state ensued, all the more so as peace returned thanks to the Rome General Peace Accords, which were signed in 1992 after three years of negotiations.

Frelimo rapidly reaped the fruits of its strategic change in religious policy. First, it brought significant recognition by the international community. In terms of Islam, in 1990 the minister of justice was able to attend a meeting of the Organisation of the Islamic Conference (OIC, now the Organisation of Islamic Cooperation) for the first time, during which he requested Mozambique's formal membership of the organization. The country was given observer status until its admission was approved, and (here too for the first time) the OIC sent sacrificial meat to Mozambique for the hajj season (2,600 carcasses).[70] In 1992, after eight years of negotiations, Rabitat finally signed a definitive cooperation agreement with Mozambique, and in 1993 it opened an office in Mozambique, nominating as its director none other than Ibrahimo Nordine, the adviser for Muslim Affairs at the DAR in the Ministry of Justice.[71] Mozambique became a full member of the OIC in 1994 and of the Islamic Development Bank in 1995.[72] During this period, Frelimo finally succeeded in establishing diplomatic relations with several Muslim countries, such as the United Arab Emirates (UAE), Oman, and Indonesia. It goes without saying that, with such new international recognition, social, economic, and religious cooperation with Muslim countries increased. For example, aid from the Islamic Development Bank rose from a few million dollars annually in the 1980s to tens of millions in 1999.[73] Looking from the Muslim perspective, not only was Islam now recognized by the Mozambican state but it was also promoted, so that Muslims gained an importance and role in the country they had never had since the onset of colonialism.

Frelimo's new religious policy led to a 'religious explosion' in the country, the return of religious competition, and a rise in religious tension and conflict. Once religious freedom was recovered and the civil war had ended, faith organizations quickly engaged in expansion and conversion work. A series of new religious organizations, both Christian and Muslim, came to the country from abroad or were created locally, and a significant number of churches and mosques were rehabilitated or built, while many people converted to new religious credos.[74] Proselytization led many organizations to areas of the country where they had not been before or to which they had been prevented from going: the Portuguese colonial state had worked hard to keep Islam limited to the north of the country and Protestantism to the south, and Frelimo's postcolonial religious policy had not altered this. This expansion led to new tensions and conflicts. Christians saw the 'progress' of Islam in the south (often judged by the construction of mosques) as proof for the numerical growth of that faith (something official statistics do not confirm) and/ or its growing political influence.[75] It did not take long for warnings to be raised about the threat of Islamic fundamentalism. Muslims, in turn, became concerned with the rapid growth and expansion of evangelical and Pentecostal churches, particularly in the centre and north of the country. To oppose this trend, in the 1990s they entered into an alliance with the Catholic Church, which shared the same concern.[76] Internal to Mozambican Islam, fighting emerged or re-emerged between different organizations, the lines of division and conflict remaining mainly between reformist (or Wahhabi) and Sufi (and pro-Sufi) Muslims and between Indo-Pakistani Mozambicans and African Mozambicans. At times, the lines of conflict overlapped, and alliances varied. The Islamic Congress contested and tried to block the progress of CISLAMO (there were even physical clashes, with injuries and arrests),[77] but on other occasions the two bodies worked together to counter Christian organizations or to work against the domination (particularly in financial terms) of the members of the Comunidade Mahometana who were becoming successful post-socialist entrepreneurs.[78]

A third consequence of Frelimo's new religious policy was the politicization of faith after 1989—Cédric Mayrargue argues this was a continent-wide phenomenon in the 1990s that went hand in hand with the pluralization and globalization of religions.[79] Three factors led to this politicization in Mozambique. The first was the state's attempt in the 1980s and 1990s to manipulate faiths. Indeed, the fact of the state entering into an alliance with religious organizations blurred the nature of the state. The state was still officially secular, but an impression developed that favours could be negotiated, and some religious organizations gained advantages by doing so successfully. State attempts at manipulation led to the politicization of faith organizations, and soon accusations not only of politicking but also of 'fundamentalism' were made against some faiths who made demands

THE 'RISE' OF ISLAM AFTER INDEPENDENCE, 1974–94

on the state.[80] The second factor that led to the politicization of Islam related to the fact that, with the DAR, the government put in place a patrimonial system of controlling faith organizations, a system that encouraged religious leaders to engage in politics. Most notably, religious institutions did not have legal status in the country, and they had to work through the DAR on any project that had a legal dimension. Yet, if the DAR was engaging in politics to optimize the returns of the new religious policy, this meant that it also became sensitive to pressure, influence, and political manipulation. For example, the Catholic Church, as the biggest religious institution in the country, successfully lobbied for the administrative burden of its imports to be eased and for its dignitaries to be given VIP status at airports. Similarly, the Brazilian neo-Pentecostal Universal Church of the Kingdom of God received significant support from the state to set up in the country because it promised to support the ruling party at the 1994 elections.[81] The third and last factor in the politicization of the religious sphere relates to the social importance Islam gained, or regained, with liberalization after 1989. The Indo-Pakistani community in particular benefitted from post-socialist economic deregulation and became one of the main private political actors and donors in the country.[82] This emboldened some of its members to engage in politics, especially seeing that this community was assiduously courted by both Frelimo and the opposition for its (financial) support.

The politicization of Islam began soon after 1989 when Muslims started making demands on the government in the name of their faith, such as calling for better representation in state institutions and government. Muslim leaders were only invited to the negotiations between the government and the Renamo guerrilla movement (as mediators) at the end of 1989, years later than their Christian colleagues, and they refused to take part.[83] But they subsequently demanded the right to appoint the directors of several commissions that resulted from the peace accord and gained the directorship of the Commission for Demobilization.[84] In 1993, several Muslim businessmen based in the capital founded a political party, the Independent Party of Mozambique (Partido Independente de Moçambique [PIMO]), to contest the multiparty elections that were

37

due to take place the following year. The launch of this party was controversial because the constitution did not allow religious or ethnic political parties; yet this did not prevent its leaders regularly and publicly replacing the word 'Independent' with the word 'Islamic' when speaking about their party, and the state did nothing about it.[85]

The politicization of Islam increased with the first multiparty elections of 1994. During the electoral campaign, Mozambique's two main parties, Frelimo and Renamo, competed for Muslim support. Frelimo added to its electoral list several influential Muslim leaders or directors of Islamic organizations, such as CISLAMO, the Islamic Congress, the Maputo Muslim Community, and the Muslim League of Zambezia. Renamo added Muslim leaders from Niassa and several important sheiks from Nampula province to its electoral list.[86] In as much as one can talk of a Muslim vote, the results from the first multiparty elections (which were won by Frelimo) revealed that Renamo gained a majority in most Muslim areas in the country's north.[87] PIMO's participation in the election was a failure: it gained a meagre 1 per cent of the national vote, both for the presidential and the parliamentary elections.[88] Overall, via Frelimo and Renamo, Muslims managed to enter the Mozambican assembly as 'Muslims', and Frelimo was forced to include this dimension in the set-up of its government and its approach to governing thereafter. Among other things, it chose to nominate the aristocratic Muslim José Abudo as minister of justice, the ministry in charge of religious affairs.[89]

The politicization of Islam was not limited to elections and the government. In the 1990s, Muslims began to demand, more generally and more fundamentally, a change in certain state practices and institutions. In 1995, Muslim deputies proposed a law to turn the two main Islamic festivals, Eid Ul Fitr and Eid Ul Adha, into national holidays, just like Christmas, which had been a national holiday since independence, even if technically under the name of 'Family Day'. The proposal was submitted to a vote in parliament in early 1996 and was accepted by a majority. This created a major controversy that saw Frelimo accused of fundamentalism (whether Muslim or Christian) and electoral opportunism. Two years later, the Supreme Court decided the law was unconstitutional, upon which

THE 'RISE' OF ISLAM AFTER INDEPENDENCE, 1974–94

the country's president, who needed to confirm the law, sent it back to parliament for annulment or redrafting—this affair is analysed in full in Chapter 2.[90] Another controversy emerged in 2000, this time in relation to a green paper on family law. The green paper was opened for public comments in March and provoked strong reactions from some sectors of the Muslim population who did not appreciate the way the paper conceptualized the family. They considered it too 'Roman Catholic' because it assumed that the 'normal' family was nuclear and monogamous. They also objected to the paper for removing the idea of a 'family leader' and raising the age of consent to eighteen years of age.[91] Again, accusations of fundamentalism were quick to surface, with some Christian intellectuals and politicians claiming that Muslims wanted to push sharia law on to the country and some Muslims arguing that the project aimed to impose alien religious principles on to a majority of the population (Muslims and adepts of African traditions).[92] The controversy led the parliamentary debate over the green paper to be postponed until 2003. The law was adopted in 2004 with some concessions to recognize and manage the existence of polygamous and non-adult marriages.[93]

At the dawn of the twenty-first century

Several tendencies can be noted in relation to Islam in Mozambique at the close of the twentieth century. First, on a general level, the international Islamic presence in the country has continued to grow with the arrival of new organizations such as Munazzamat al-Da'wa al-Islamiyya from Sudan, Muslim Hands from the United States, and the Aga Khan Development Network, and with an ever-greater investment in already existing organizations. AMA, for example, built, fixed, and renovated hundreds of mosques, schools, and boreholes all over the country, with mosques now bearing its name, something that gradually changed the country's landscape.[94] Religious competition continued too, as did religious conflict, both between Christians and Muslims and between or within Muslim organizations themselves. Thus, in late 1999 the state administration was forced to defuse a Muslim–Christian conflict when American evangelicals preached in a mosque in Maputo during Ramadan.[95] In

TOWARDS JIHAD?

2000, an aggressive debate took place within Mozambican Islam, particularly in the newspapers *Domingo* and *Savana*, when a eulogy to Sheik Mágira from the new head of the reformism movement, Sheik Aminuddin, was denounced on the basis that it had criticized Sufism, the practice of Mawlid, and the sanctuary of Nova Sofala.[96] In the same year, a conflict took place during a funeral at Ilha de Moçambique after members of the reformist CISLAMO tried to prevent local Sufis from chanting for their dead. The town's cemetery used to belong to the Ismaili community, but the Ismailis had handed it over to CISLAMO, which seized the opportunity to impose new rules over burial practices.[97]

The relationship between CISLAMO and the Islamic Congress remained tense. Their rivalry continued, and the balance of power remained about the same. The Islamic Congress continued to dominate numerically: in 1992, it represented 5,000 institutions, while CISLAMO represented just over 100. But CISLAMO had more funds and more public visibility, benefitting from the wealth and education of its members and supporters. Most students on scholarships in Sudan, Saudi Arabia, and Egypt affiliated themselves with CISLAMO before or after returning from their studies.[98] Overall, however, the hegemony of these two organizations was starting to decline. With liberalization, old organizations were relaunched, such as the famed Anuaril Isslamo,[99] and new organizations emerged, such as the Islamic Forum, the Associação Muçulmana de Angoche (Muslim Association of Angoche), and the Organizações da Juventude Islâmica de Angoche (Angoche Organizations of Islamic Youth, whose aim was to overcome the divisions between CISLAMO and Islamic Congress).[100]

Ruptures were also emerging within CISLAMO and the Islamic Congress. In 1992, several Islamic Congress members founded the Centre of Islamic Training (Centro de Formação Islâmica [CFI]) in Beira, whose president was none other than Minister of Justice José Abudo. CFI had links with the Islamic Movement that formed in parliament the same year with the objective of organizing a Muslim lobby among the chamber of deputies. CFI was also behind the launch in 2000 of the first Islamic university in Mozambique, the Universidade Mussa Bin Bique in Nampula (named after the last

THE 'RISE' OF ISLAM AFTER INDEPENDENCE, 1974–94

ruler of the Island of Mozambique before the Portuguese took over in 1544).[101] With regard to CISLAMO, a schism appeared in 1998 when several sheiks took a stand against their leaders, whom they accused of getting involved in politics. They called their new organization Ansar al-Sunna; it was still awaiting official recognition in the year 2000.[102] In short, an array of new organizations emerged that undermined the centrality of CISLAMO and the Islamic Congress. By 2001, the Islamic Congress seemed moribund, with rumours circulating that some of its members were thinking of launching a new political party to regain the initiative.

Politically, some significant developments were seen with the second multiparty elections of 1999. First, Frelimo shifted its religious alliance. It either moved Muslims it had co-opted in 1994 to the bottom of its electoral lists or got rid of them completely, replacing them with less well-known figures—Renamo did the opposite. Frelimo's course of action seems to have been the result of the Muslim holiday debacle when Muslim deputies defied the party's voting guidelines. Frelimo also turned more strongly towards the Muslim brotherhoods, successfully co-opting two *tariqa* leaders from the existing eight, including the most prestigious and influential, Sheik Abdurrahman Amuri bin Jimba.[103] Second, and relatedly, Frelimo started to lash out against the powerful Indo-Pakistani community, specifically the Maputo Muslim Community. This started in 1999 when a decapitated human head was discovered in one of Maputo's main mosques. The mosque's sheik called the police but was soon arrested after the person who brought the head to the mosque accused him of having ordered the killing.[104] What followed was a series of articles in Frelimo-controlled print media that attacked the Indo-Pakistani community. They were so vitriolic that the local media spoke of an anti-Muslim campaign, and a journalist stated that the campaign evoked the spectre of Idi Amin Dada's 1972 repression of the Asian Muslim community in Uganda.[105] The ins and outs of the story are far from clear, but it was certain that something important was taking place—I will discuss this in full in Chapter 3. For now, it is simply important to note that, for all its efforts to readjust the alliances between itself and various Muslim sectors, Frelimo did not gain much electorally. While the party won the elections in 1999,

41

Renamo once more achieved a majority of votes in many Islamic areas in the north of the country. In addition, the results of the elections were hotly contested. This meant that the new Frelimo government lacked legitimacy.[106] To resolve what it saw as rising regionalism, Mozambique's president decided late in 2000 to organize, for the first time in the country's history, a meeting of his cabinet outside of the capital. For this, he tellingly chose the historical Muslim town of Angoche, the place of origin of his minister of justice and the former seat of an important sultanate.[107]

Finally, we turn to the terrorist attacks of 11 September 2001 in the United States, which had some important consequences in Mozambique. Most Mozambicans quickly and unambiguously condemned the attacks, as did most of the country's Muslim leaders. Privately, however, some claimed that the United States should not be surprised at such attacks in view of its interventionist policies towards other countries. These kinds of comments were not only made by Muslims: I heard Catholics express similar views, for example, and such beliefs were not uncommon among people holding positions of responsibility in Christian churches. As in other countries, the US response to the attacks led to strong reactions and disputes. Soon after the United States decided to attack Afghanistan in retaliation for harbouring the leaders of al-Qaeda, some Muslims in Maputo organized a demonstration against terrorism. The march went ahead smoothly, but anti-US slogans were displayed and even pro-Taliban references were made. This led some journalists and newspaper readers to call for the demonstrators' arrest.[108] Finally, the 9/11 attacks led the United States to search for al-Qaeda cells across the world, including in Mozambique, with support from the Mozambican secret service. There are reports that the investigation focused on several money exchanges, the former president of the Maputo Muslim Community, and the AMA. Officially, no members or supporters of al-Qaeda were discovered, and no arrests were made.[109]

Conclusion

A shift in the public positioning of Islam in Mozambique took place between 1975 and 2000. Before independence, and even up to 1979, the Islamic faith and its organizations were marginalized and even opposed by the state. By the early 2020s, Islam and its believers occupied a prominent and influential public position that was more in keeping with their numerical strength in the country, with Muslims accounting for at least 20 per cent of the population. Still, this was a new position and one that was contrary to what had been the case throughout most of the twentieth century. This shift began to take place in 1980, when Frelimo ended its anticlerical policy, ushering in a new period when Muslims could regain some social and political activism thanks to newly founded organizations such as CISLAMO and the Islamic Congress, the support of foreign governments and international Islamic organizations, and encouragement by the Mozambican government. Muslims also benefitted from Frelimo's adoption of a free market approach to regulating faith organizations in 1989, which facilitated the expansion and politicization of religion, allowing Muslims to become more visible and socially and politically active. A third important date is 1994, the year of Mozambique's first multiparty elections. Through the elections, Muslims gained access to parliament and the government as Muslims. This set the scene for the next period when Muslims began to make demands about the nature and form of the Mozambican state. The critical date here is probably early 1994, when Muslims made a first fundamental public demand about the Muslim holiday law.

What explains the transformation of Islam's position in Mozambique? Was it due to internal or external factors? Was it a change in Islam itself or a change in political power? The answer is both: the changes in Mozambican Islam intertwined with the changes in Mozambican political power, and the internal causes interacted with the external causes. We can identify five general reasons for the transformation. The first relates to the repression of religion carried out by Frelimo after independence, which alienated Muslims while also leading certain elements in Mozambique and some foreign governments to oppose Frelimo, something the party-state could ill afford in the face of a developing civil war. These pressures soon forced Frelimo to undo its religious policy. A second cause has to do with the Mozambican government's struggle to understand Islam, leading it to make mistakes and gaining few benefits from its change in religious policy. This forced the government to make even more concessions, so that, by the end of the 1980s, DAR's director dared to admit in writing that the government's policy towards Muslims had been a 'fiasco'. A third cause for this shift has to do with the changes within Islam in Mozambique. The development of reformism in the guise of Deobandism and then Wahhabism, and the creation of CISLAMO, led to the parallel (and oppositional) development of the Sufi or pro-Sufi Islamic Congress. Yet, despite the disagreements and rivalry between CISLAMO and the Congress, the two organizations were both effective at liaising and negotiating with the government and making demands—together making a significant overall impact. A fourth reason for the reversal of the government policy has to do with Frelimo itself, the holder of state power, which, after changing its religious policy and then turning away from Marxism in 1989, went on to integrate assertive Muslims in its midst and placed them on its electoral list, providing a platform for Muslims to make political demands. A final cause has to do with international relations and global Islamic institutions, which actively provided help to national Muslim organizations in Mozambique, not least financially, and placed much pressure on the Mozambican government, such as imposing conditions in turn for recognizing the republic in Muslim international organizations.

What was the balance at the end of the 1990s? First, the reformist Wahhabi movement continued to grow in influence, with the help of international organizations and with most Mozambican Muslim students returning from their studies abroad working for CISLAMO after their return. Second, while reformism and Wahhabism had spread until then almost exclusively through CISLAMO, new movements began to appear in the 1990s, such as Ansar al-Sunna, opening up the possibility of diversification and further expansion. This did not look inevitable or irreversible in any way, however. Sufi and pro-Sufi elements and associations organized themselves effectively, with the creation of the Islamic Congress, the launch of CFI (linked to elements in government), and the creation of a Council of Brotherhoods. Third, the period saw the emergence of a political form of militantism—'Islamism'—among Muslims in relation to the state. Already in 1996 Muslim leaders had (unsuccessfully) demanded the recognition of the two Eid festivals as national holidays, and in 2000 contested the green paper on family law, forcing the government into a compromise. By the end of the 1990s, this militantism looked set to continue, particularly considering that Islam was an important religious, social, and political presence in the country and many aspects of the postcolonial state remained 'Christian', with little sensitivity to Muslim traditions. Finally, Mozambique's first Muslim political party, PIMO, eventually failed, not least at the polls in the 1994 elections. After that, Muslims were comfortable enough to continue to work with the country's two dominant political parties, and they showed a renewed willingness to work with, if not for, the government and state administration. At the end of the 1990s, considering the divisions among the Muslim community at a national level, it seemed that this way of doing politics was unlikely to change in the near future.

Map 2. Muslims in Mozambique, 1997

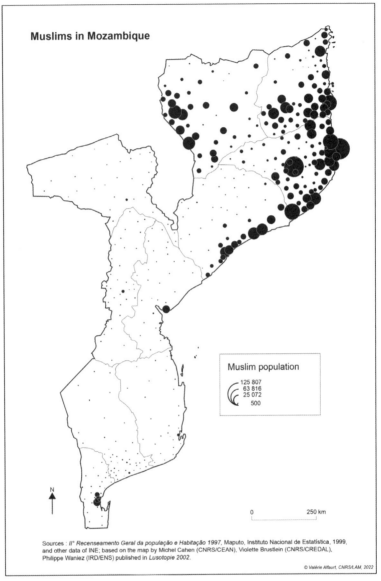

Source: Designed by Valérie Alfaurt (CNRS, Sciences Po Bordeaux)

2

THE 1996 'MUSLIM HOLIDAYS' AFFAIR

In early 1996, a controversy broke out in Mozambique over a proposed law that would turn two Muslim holy days—Eid Ul Fitr (marking the end of Ramadan) and Eid Ul Adha (the festival of sacrifice and return from Mecca)—into public holidays. The law had been drafted by a group of Muslim parliamentarians in 1995, and it had now come before Mozambique's parliament, the Assembly of the Republic. If passed, the law would not only create two official Islamic holidays but also the first religious public holidays in Mozambique since independence. For the proposal's opponents, the law undermined the secular nature of the state. They feared that it could lead to Islamization of the state and even to religious war. For its proponents, the law was an attempt to redress the injustice and marginalization that Muslims had suffered both before and since independence. It was intended to re-establish equality between faiths and thereby contribute to peace in the country. The controversy was heated, and the vote of a majority of deputies in favour of the law in March 1996 did not improve the situation. The controversy continued unabated with pressure shifting from the assembly to the president and the Supreme Court, who each had the power to validate or veto the law. After almost a year, the Supreme Court declared the law unconstitutional. After yet another year, deputies

47

finally shelved the legislation after the president sent it back to the assembly to be revised or cancelled.

Most if not all commentators analysed what came to be known as the 'Eid affair' as being solely about Islam. Arguments took different forms, but most agreed that the controversy had to do with the 'rise' of the Islamic faith. The international and specialized press was particularly explicit in making this argument. It presented Mozambique as a country where Muslim organizations had gained so many converts that Islam was starting to flex its political muscles and becoming a resource over which political parties were fighting.[1] As we have seen in the previous chapter, this line of reasoning is not necessarily incorrect: Islam has grown in political influence to some extent, Muslims have become increasingly involved politically, and political parties have been courting the faith more than ever in recent years. But this line of reasoning is insufficient insofar as it fails to address a number of crucial questions and issues. It does not analyse, first, the development and politicization of other religions, their competition with Islam, and their role in the Eid affair. Second, it does not look at the role of the state in the rise and politicization of Islam, in the development of religious competition, and in the making and unfolding of the controversy. To be precise, it is not that commentators ignored the state or other religions entirely; it is rather that they presented them as passive or reactive forces. The state was usually described as an object of contest or conquest; non-Islamic faiths were presented as merely responding to a situation created by Muslims.

Much of the literature concerned with religious tension and conflict where Islam is involved faces the same problems. Some authors simply ignore the role of other religions in building tensions and conflicts. A typical example is Samuel Huntington's *Clash of Civilizations*, which presents Islam as the only active religious force worldwide and the only potential (or actual) source of conflict.[2] When Huntington considers what Islam is reacting to, he does not mention any other religion (not even those sectors of Christianity that target Islam as part of their evangelization and 'spiritual warfare' programmes)[3] but focuses on Western civilization and modernity.[4] Although other authors may take into consideration the multiplicity of religions, they still underplay their interaction and the role of

THE 1996 'MUSLIM HOLIDAYS' AFFAIR

religious competition and state policies in creating or preventing religious strife. The literature on 'fundamentalism' is a case in point in that it hardly ever considers the interaction between different religious 'resurgences' and rarely considers the role of the state in fostering or preventing the resurgence of these religions.[5] Finally, there is a small but fast-growing literature that deals specifically with religious competition and state mediation. But it does not even consider the possibility of religious tension and conflict: following an economistic and neo-liberal theoretical model, it only looks at how state 'deregulation' fosters competition between faith organizations and, in turn, increases religious freedom, pluralism, and the quality of church 'products'.[6]

This chapter contributes to the debate on religious tension and conflict, particularly where Islam is involved. Specifically, it adds to our understanding of the Eid affair in Mozambique. Contrary to theories about the 'rise of Islam' and politico-religious conspiracies, it tests the hypothesis that conflict around faiths primarily has to do with competition between faiths and the state's mediation of religion—what I call the 'religious regime'. I suggest that the deregulation of religious competition—the creation of a 'free religious market'—and a laissez-faire state role can, and in the Mozambican case did, lead to tension and conflict around faith. The chapter proceeds in three steps: first, it details the affair and its most common explanations. It then analyses the history of religious competition in Mozambique and the history of state mediation up to 1996. Finally, the conclusion draws out some methodological and practical points about church–state relations, religious strife, and the specific case of Mozambique.

The controversy and its actors

The Eid affair erupted almost by surprise. The legislation (see Appendix III) had been drafted in 1995 by a group of Muslim deputies from all political parties, and it had faced no opposition, public or otherwise, at that time. Yet when it reached the discussion stage in the Assembly of the Republic in early 1996, a debate erupted that soon became heated. The law was to create the first two official religious holidays

49

in Mozambique since independence in 1975, and both were to be Islamic. For the project's opponents—Christian churches, opposition parties, and the independent press—the law threatened to undermine the secular nature of the state by favouring one religion over others. Some of its opponents further argued that, considering the number of faiths in Mozambique, the law would undermine national unity and thus ran the risk of destabilizing the country. In a more religious and conspiratorial vein, some actors claimed that the legislation could be a first step towards Islamization of the state and thus religious war. In contrast, the project's proponents (Frelimo and Muslims) argued that the legislation was simply about compensating a religious community that had been discriminated against in both colonial and postcolonial times. They pointed out that the Catholic Church had been favoured under Portuguese rule and that Christmas had been declared an official holiday in 1981 under the secular label of 'Family Day'.[7] The law would thus merely re-establish equality between faiths. As for secularism, proponents declared themselves in favour of a more flexible and pluralist model whereby all religions would have their own official religious holidays, and, to be consistent, they proposed drafting a new law to declare Holy Friday a public holiday.[8]

Despite extensive protest, most deputies voted in favour of the law in March 1996. But contrary to what might have been expected, this did not put an end to the controversy. Rather, it shifted activism and protest from the assembly to the president—who now had the power to either sign or veto the law. To avoid having to take this decision, or to gain time, President Joaquim Chissano sent the law to the Supreme Court to consider its constitutionality. The court took six months to give its ruling, during which the controversy continued unabated. In December 1996, the judges announced that the Eid law was unconstitutional. In their view, it contravened two constitutional principles, namely the secular nature of the state and the equality of all citizens.[9] But the ruling did not end the controversy either. The law still had to be annulled. The president chose not to do so himself but to return the legislation to parliament. The assembly either had to annul the law or reformulate it and vote again, with a two-thirds majority required to pass the law. After almost two years, in late 1998, parliament returned to the legislation. In a new twist,

50

a majority of parliamentarians decided not to discuss the issue but to postpone it indefinitely. The justification given was that deputies would thus be able to consider the law at a later, undefined stage as part of a broader discussion on all public holidays in Mozambique.[10] The motivation for the decision is unclear. It may have been a way for parliament to cancel the law without losing face, or it may have been a way for deputies to shelve the law for a period in the hope of passing it later, once the situation had cooled down. Either way, the decision put an end to the controversy—at least in the short term.

Not surprisingly, churches and other religious institutions were at the fore of the Eid controversy. They had no direct say in parliament, but they were able to make their voices heard quite effectively nevertheless. They pressured parliamentarians, sent letters of support or protest to the assembly, and wrote to and met with the president. The Catholic Church took the most militant stance. Almost all bishops made declarations to the press, and, after the legislation was passed, the Episcopal Conference and various parishes in the south of the country sent letters of protest to the assembly.[11] The nunciature and the Community of Sant'Egidio sent notes of protest to the Department of Foreign Affairs.[12] The Catholic Church argued that the law went against the secular nature of the state because it was a compromise with 'fundamentalist Islam', and that the law and the whole affair could ignite religious conflict in Mozambique.[13] The Christian Council of Mozambique (Conselho Cristão de Moçambique [CCM]) put forward roughly the same argument, though less aggressively. Although CCM and the Catholic Church sent a joint letter of protest to the government, Protestants used a more moderate tone and even seemed ready to compromise. Indeed, while the Catholic Church stood against all religious public holidays, CCM declared before and after the vote that it was ready to accept the law if Protestants were given an equal privilege.[14] For their part, Muslims overwhelmingly favoured the law. All major organizations made declarations in support of the legislation, and no fewer than fifteen brotherhoods and communities in the north of the country sent letters and faxes of congratulation to parliament after the law was passed.[15] As the controversy unfolded, some fissures appeared in the Muslim community over the lack of consultation and political manipulation. Still, hardly anyone dared oppose the law.[16] As for smaller or less prominent religious institutions such as the Hindu temples or the Zionist churches, they either refused to take a stand, remained silent, or demanded equal treatment of all faiths.[17]

Although the Eid law project was launched by a group of parliamentarians from all political parties present in parliament, Frelimo, Renamo, and the União Democrática (Democratic Union) ended up adopting different positions, with the tiny União Democrática opposing the proposal and eventually voting against it. Closely following the Catholic argument (two of its three leaders were former Catholic seminarians),[18] it declared that the country was secular and that the nation should be concerned with issues of work and development rather than religious holidays.[19] Renamo, the main opposition party, held a similar view, or at least did so officially, since its parliamentarians were divided over the issue. Renamo had been saying for many years that it stood for religious liberty for all, yet the law demanded that the party choose between the Eid law, which was supported by Muslims, and strict secularism, which Christians favoured. In the end, Renamo officially chose to oppose the law but did not demand its deputies vote against it in parliament. As a result, Renamo's Christian deputies voted against the proposal while those of Muslim origin abstained. In contrast, Frelimo, the party in power, not only stood clearly and officially in favour of the law but also managed to silence internal dissent. It had a small majority in parliament, which permitted it to pass the legislation in 1996—and to postpone the final decision on the law in 1998 when parliament had to choose on voting again or postponing discussions.

Interpretations of the controversy and its origins

As noted, most if not all explanations of the Eid affair held that Islam was at the root of the controversy. Proponents of this position argued that Islam had grown enormously in Mozambique over recent years. Reliable figures to back such a view did not exist at the time—the controversy took place just before the second population census of 1997 (the first postcolonial census did not ask any questions about religion). Some state projections about religious affiliation

THE 1996 'MUSLIM HOLIDAYS' AFFAIR

were made public just before the vote in parliament, but they were contested and soon shown to be unreliable; they also indicated that the number of Muslims in the country had risen at a similar rate to, if not lower than, that of other monotheist religions.[20]

Similarly, the figures on religion from the 1997 population census, which were released after the affair and were no less problematic,[21] indicated an increase in the Muslim population that was hardly bigger than that of other monotheist religions—all gained between 3.8 and 4.8 percentage points (proportionally, this represented a 19 per cent increase for Catholicism and a 36.9 per cent increase for Islam as well as a 76 per cent increase for Protestantism; see Table 1 below). Still, explanations of the Eid affair assumed that the growth in the number of Muslims in Mozambique had been exceptional, with two lines of reasoning being developed from this 'factual' basis. The first held that the increase in Muslims had made Islam a resource for which political parties would compete—the controversy was thus a struggle *over* Islam as a constituency. The second held that the rising popularity of Islam would enable Muslim organizations to launch a political offensive to gain advantages for themselves—the controversy was thus a struggle *of* Islam, for political power. These two lines of explanation are not exclusive: many analysts saw both dimensions at work at the same time. But for reasons of clarity, I shall treat them separately below.

Table 1. Approximate percentage of population by religion, 1975 and 1997

Religion	1975	1997
Muslims	13%	17.8%
Catholics	20%	23.8%
Protestants	5%	7.8%
Animists and others	62%	50.6%

Source: Compiled from Cónego Francisco Maria Pínheiro, *Na Entrega do Testemunho 1975*, Torres Novas, Portugal: Acção Missionéria Portuguesa em Moçambique, 1992; 'IV Recenseamento Geral da População 1970', in *Moçambique: Panorama Demográfico e Sócio-económico*, Maputo: Instituto Nacional de Estatística, 1995, p. 33; Instituto Nacional de Estatística, 'II Recenseamento Geral da População e Habitação 1997', Maputo: Instituto Nacional de Estatística, 1999.

The first line of explanation of the Eid controversy was that a Frelimo strategy, if not conspiracy, was at the root of the 1996 'Muslim holiday' affair: Frelimo intended to use the affair to undermine Renamo's religious support, and it hoped to bolster its own popularity nationally and internationally.[22] Considering the history of Muslims and Frelimo, it is plausible that the ruling party created this affair deliberately, though it is also possible that Frelimo was merely taking advantage of a situation that came into being by itself. Either way, the argument is that the proposal for the Eid law was used to force Renamo to choose sides between Muslims who supported the law and Christians who opposed it. The law forced a choice upon Renamo that would diminish its religious support in forthcoming elections. Judging by the declarations that Frelimo leaders made during the affair, there is no doubt that Frelimo took advantage of the situation to do just that. One of the main proponents of this argument was Renamo itself. To avoid dividing its constituency, the party chose to denounce the law as a Frelimo trick while seeking to remind everyone that it had fought militarily for religious freedom in Mozambique. In March 1996, for example, Renamo's Secretary General Marcelino Xavier declared that

> if there is some space for religion [in present-day Mozambique], it is because there has been a war. We did not understand why Frelimo was saying that religion did not exist. President Samora [Machel] entered mosques wearing his shoes and he forced Muslims to eat pork knowing that they couldn't. Mosques were not respected. This shift of 360° [on the part of Frelimo] leaves us concerned.[23]

In addition to dividing Renamo's constituency, this line of explanation argues that Frelimo's strategy aimed at bolstering its own support. At the international level, some have argued that the Eid law was intended to improve Frelimo's image in Muslim countries and to attract greater levels of financial support from Islamic states as well as from Western nations concerned with the advance of Islam in Mozambique. Evidence that this was Frelimo's intention never became public. But we do know that Frelimo worked hard for many years to charm Arab and other Muslim states, and we know

THE 1996 'MUSLIM HOLIDAYS' AFFAIR

that much of the party's policy of co-opting Islamic organizations since the early 1980s had this aim.[24] In addition, the minister of foreign affairs made statements linking the law to aid from Muslim international organizations.[25] At the national level, it is often said that Frelimo was trying to please or 'pay back' Asian Muslims who acted as a bridge to Islamic countries (notably the monarchies of the Persian Gulf) and who had been important financial supporters during the 1994 elections. Probably more importantly, it seems that Frelimo attempted to use the Eid law to co-opt the Muslim brotherhoods based in northern Mozambique. According to the leader of an important *tariqa*, the Qadiriyya Baghdad, a group of Frelimo deputies held a meeting with all brotherhood leaders in early 1994 to propose the Eid law in exchange for electoral support.[26] Renamo's president, Afonso Dhlakama, also thought this was Frelimo's strategy and tried to give the ruling party a taste of its own medicine: he denounced the legislation as mere pay-back to 'half-a-dozen extremely rich Indians', who, he argued, had nothing in common with the Muslim majority in northern Mozambique.[27]

The second explanation for the origin and nature of the Eid affair focused on the politicization of Islam and Muslim efforts to gain political power. As a South Africa-based journalist argued at the time, the Eid affair was a result of Islam beginning to 'flex its political muscles'.[28] The main evidence for this reading was that the law was proposed in parliament by a coalition of fifty-six Muslim deputies from across party lines, something never seen before in Mozambique. More generally, commentators pointed out that Muslims had become increasingly involved in public affairs as a religious group. From specific claims in the late 1980s, Muslims had moved on to political activism in the early 1990s. Calls for inclusion in the 1980s had turned into demands by the early 1990s when community leaders insisted on representation in the commissions resulting from the 1992 peace agreement.[29] Finally, demands transformed into political lobbying on the occasion of the first multiparty elections in 1994 when Muslims started to negotiate their support for and inclusion on the electoral lists of political parties, as we saw in Chapter 1.[30] Internationally, the politicization of Islam was said to come from countries such as Sudan, Saudi Arabia, and Iran that

55

supported local Muslim associations, had sent religious NGOs to Mozambique, and had pushed Islam as an issue in their relations with the Mozambican state.[31]

As useful and insightful as they may be, there are limitations to these lines of interpretation. First, they only see Islam at the root of the Eid affair, whether as actor or object of the controversy, and they do not take other religions into account. Yet we have seen that Christianity, for example, was very active in the affair. What was this faith's (and other faiths') role in the affair and in creating the controversy in the first place? Second, these interpretations do not consider the state—as distinct from the party holding state power— yet the state was crucial in allowing the Eid law to be discussed and voted on and, later, in its annulment. Finally, the lines of explanation border on the conspiratorial, with the affair reduced to an Islamic plot to gain political power and/or Frelimo strategizing to increase its Muslim support and undermine Renamo. This is not to say that there was no conspiracy, but rather that this conspiratorial thinking needs to be contextualized and explained. To try to clarify these issues and add to our understanding of the Eid affair, I now turn to the broader context of the controversy and, more specifically, to the issues of religious competition and state mediation up to 1996.

Religious competition in Mozambique

Competition between faiths in Mozambique has gone through different phases that need to be described if we are to understand the dynamics at play, particularly when the Eid affair took place. The first period to consider is the nineteenth century, when both Islam and Christianity expanded as a result of outgrowths of earlier works. Islam spread from the coast, whereas Christianity spread from missions over the border. These developments took place relatively freely and openly: missionaries, evangelists, and proponents of *dawah* (the act of converting people to Islam) could work wherever they wanted, the only limitation being their acceptance or rejection by local people and chiefs. Competition was rarely direct: there was sufficient space and potential converts for every organized faith to work without interfering with another. In fact, most religious organizations at that

THE 1996 'MUSLIM HOLIDAYS' AFFAIR

time (church, religious orders, and *tariqa*) carved out a particular area and people to work with, some of them even entering into 'comity' agreements to avoid overlapping and clashes.

This relatively free and fair competition gradually came to an end after 1920 as Portugal asserted full control over Mozambique and started to impose its own religious regime. As António de Oliveira Salazar secured his hold on power in Portugal in alliance with the Catholic Church, religious policies became increasingly favourable to Catholicism, as we have seen.[32] In 1940, Lisbon signed a concordat and a missionary accord with the Vatican. According to these agreements, the Portuguese state and its administration supported the Catholic Church in exchange for a say in the institution's affairs and the church running the state's social institutions in its overseas territories.[33] Implicit in the accords was the marginalization of, if not opposition to, other faiths. Of course, Portugal could not be officially or openly repressive of non-Catholic faiths since international law and neighbouring imperial Protestant states would not allow it. But it managed to do so indirectly, by taking measures and passing laws that favoured the Roman church and discriminated against Protestant and Muslim institutions.[34] As a result, while the Catholic Church expanded after 1940, the number of believers of other faiths stagnated, and non-Catholic faiths in Mozambique were contained geographically: Islam was locked in the north and on the coast, while Protestantism was blocked mostly into the south.[35] After 1959, some loosening of colonial discriminatory religious policies was seen in anticipation of, and later in response to, the war of liberation.[36] But these reforms were limited and tactical, and they did not change the pattern of (unequal) growth of faiths, as Table 2 shows.

National independence in 1975 did not lead to religious freedom in Mozambique. As discussed in Chapter 1, Frelimo implemented a strongly secular and soon even anti-religious policy. It nationalized all social services (most of which had been in religious hands), limited the movement of religious personnel, and in some areas even forbade religious activities, such as in the former 'liberated zones' (from 1975) and in the vicinity of state institutions (from 1978). Furthermore, it prohibited new religious organizations from entering Mozambique and did all it could to prevent the emergence

57

Table 2. Approximate percentage of population by religion, 1960 and 1975[1]

Religion	1960	1975
Muslims	18%	13%
Catholics	9%	20%
Protestants	2%	5%
Animists and others	71%	62%

Source: Compiled from 'III Recenseamento Geral da População 1960', in *Moçambique: Panorama Demográfico e Sócio-económico*, Maputo: Instituto Nacional de Estatística, 1995; Cónego Francisco Maria Pínheiro, *Na Entrega do Testemunho 1975*, Acção Missionéria Portuguesa em Moçambique, 1992; and 'IV Recenseamento Geral da População 1970', in *Moçambique: Panorama Demográfico e Sócio-económico*, Maputo: Instituto Nacional de Estatística, 1995.

[1] Religious figures in Mozambique are problematic if not unreliable. They should therefore be taken as indications only. In this case, Catholic figures are most probably inflated and the others undercounted—for ideological reasons and because of the method of calculation. The figures for 1960 are for the African population only; non-Africans were mostly Catholic, but they constituted less than 2 per cent of the population.

of new faith organizations inside the country. As a result, the immediate post-independence period saw no religious expansion and no open competition between faiths. With the Africanization of the state bureaucracy and the movement of state personnel all over the country, the religious institutions that had previously been contained in specific areas (such as Islam and Protestantism) saw the spread of some of their believers. These formed new religious communities and often established a presence in some previously 'unreached' areas. Numerically, this was insignificant, but, added to the seeds sown during the religious policy reform of the colonial regime in the 1960s, it created a firm base for later developments. Still, religious expansion was not to come for many years, as state restrictions continued until the late 1980s, and the war of destabilization, started in the late 1970s under the direction of Rhodesia (and later South Africa), developed into a full-scale civil war between Renamo and the Frelimo state.[37]

THE 1996 'MUSLIM HOLIDAYS' AFFAIR

Organized faiths did not give up their plans for expansion in the face of restrictions and war but instead took a long-term perspective, organizing for the day when religious evangelization would again be possible. We can distinguish five strategies that were used to prepare for such an expansion. First, some religious organizations and movements initiated, or reinforced, bases in the provincial capitals of unreached provinces. Most notably, 'mainline' Protestant churches discreetly sent pastors to Beira, Quelimane, and Nampula in the north.[38] Second, some organized faiths gained access to new areas, if not always in Mozambique itself, through the humanitarian arm of their institutions or through confessional NGOs. This was the case, for example, for the Lutheran Church and the AMA.[39] It was also the case for World Vision, which spread its evangelical message into new provinces as it gave humanitarian aid.[40] Third, many if not most religious institutions started to operate in refugee camps in Mozambique and in neighbouring countries. Some churches followed their flock to help them materially and spiritually. But others, more cynically, saw an opportunity to evangelize among a 'captured' and concentrated people who would spread back on their own all over Mozambique after the war.[41] More radically and politically, a few extreme right-wing individuals and churches went to work in Renamo rebel areas (allegedly in coordination with the US Central Intelligence Agency and/or the South African intelligence forces).[42] A final strategy was to step up the training of theologians and evangelists. It is difficult to know exactly how much of an increase in training resulted from this evangelization strategy, but the number of students in religious institutions clearly grew in the 1980s. By 1997, there were 120 students in Sudanese, Saudi Arabian, and Egyptian universities, and more in Algeria, Libya, and Pakistan.[43] There were as many, if not more, students in Christian seminaries and universities in Africa, Europe, and the Americas (Brazil and the United States in particular).[44]

After years of preparation and planning, the end of religious restrictions after 1989 and the end of the civil war in 1992 led to unprecedented competition between organized faiths. The Catholic Church made huge efforts to restart and staff its mission stations. Lacking personnel, it brought in new religious orders (for example,

Maryknoll and Verbi Divini), relied on 'base communities', and stepped up its strategy of educating the elite. It reopened various private secondary schools and, in 1996, inaugurated the third Catholic university on the continent in the city of Beira.[45] In comparison, Protestant churches had few personnel problems. They were quick to put all their energies into expanding into the north of the country. Historic institutions—Methodist, Nazarene, Presbyterian, Baptist, etc.—were helped in this expansion by the arrival in Mozambique of many new evangelical and Pentecostal churches.[46] Islamic organizations similarly had no lack of personnel and chose to expand too, in the south of the country and, more particularly, into previously unreached rural districts. All this expansion led to the building of many mosques and churches in the country and to the conversion of significant numbers of people. Though figures are fragmentary and often unreliable, there is little doubt that, after the civil war, Mozambique saw a restoration of Catholicism, the geographical expansion of Islam, and the spatial and numerical leap of Protestantism.[47]

This sudden expansion of faiths quickly led to tensions and some degree of conflict. Most tellingly, accusations of fundamentalism, false teaching, and wrongdoing increased dramatically in the early 1990s. Among others, neo-Pentecostals were accused of being involved in mere commercial enterprise; reformist sheiks were attacked for breaking with Islamic tradition; and the Catholic Church and some Muslim organizations were charged with introducing or fomenting fundamentalism.[48] More specifically, tensions spread because of two factors. First, radicalization took place within all monotheist religions, a phenomenon noted for the whole of the African continent.[49] Most notably, there was an increase in the number of reformist Muslims under the influence of Saudi Arabia, Sudan, and Iran, and in the number of fundamentalist Protestants supported from, if not by, the United States and to a lesser extent Brazil and South Africa.[50] Second, rivalry emerged because new organizations started working in previously untouched territories, and different institutions started to proselytize in the same areas. Islam expanded in the rural districts to the south where Christianity was strongest; reformist Islam gained momentum in the north,

THE 1996 'MUSLIM HOLIDAYS' AFFAIR

particularly in Nampula province, where a Sufi form of Islam was dominant; and Protestants, notably evangelicals and Pentecostals, spread in the centre and north of the country where Islam and Catholicism had their largest following. Because both reformist Islam and fundamentalist Protestantism established their strongest base in central Mozambique, this became the country's religious hotspot.

The conflicts of the early 1990s had little in common with what was to come with the Eid affair, however. They did not involve the whole nation: they remained local problems that found local solutions. They also did not split religious organizations between Christian and Muslim camps: conflicts and competition were as much intra-religious as inter-religious, and alliances were seen not only within denominations but also across religions. For example, rivalry and even physical fighting broke out between Muslim organizations and brotherhoods in Nampula province in 1991 and 1993 over rituals, the interpretation of scripture, and proselytization.[51] Similarly, serious tensions emerged between Protestants in Zambezia, Nampula, and Niassa as evangelicals and Pentecostals worked at converting Muslims and 'pagans' at the cost of ecumenism and mainline churches.[52] Competition also led to alliances across religious affiliations. Most notably, the Catholic Church made an alliance in 1995 with established Muslim organizations in Nampula to monitor and counter what they saw as an invasion of 'fanatical or fundamentalist ideology'.[53] Though no formal alliance seems to have been established elsewhere, Muslims, Catholics, and ecumenical Protestants converged on various occasions in denouncing 'fundamentalism' (of all origins) and in criticizing, for example, the Universal Church of the Kingdom of God, a controversial Brazilian neo-Pentecostal church that arrived in Mozambique in 1994 that I will discuss further below.[54]

State mediation since independence

As discussed, when Frelimo came to power in 1975, it adopted a constitution committed to secularism and a policy of strong religious control.[55] Since it aimed at establishing socialism, Frelimo's policy eventually went further than merely containing the expansion and competition of religions: it tried to limit faith to the realm of individual choice, prevented religious institutions from working in certain areas, and discouraged people from attending church or mosque. After the party's Third Congress in 1977, at which Marxism–Leninism was officially adopted as the state ideology, Frelimo started to prevent religious institutions from working in or near social institutions such as schools and hospitals, closed some sites of prayer, and initiated an anti-religious propaganda campaign.[56] These actions went well beyond control and secularism; what is important here, though, is that evangelization and competition were prevented. All religious organizations were controlled and attacked, so that religious tensions and conflicts decreased dramatically.

Most authors dealing with religion in Mozambique after independence argue that Frelimo 'shifted' its policy on organized faiths in 1982,[57] following a well-publicized meeting with the country's religious institutions in which it announced that its policy on religion would change with immediate effect.[58] Some changes did indeed take place after 1982: some praying sites were returned to religious organizations, and some foreign missionaries were allowed to return to Mozambique. But the nature of Frelimo's 'policy shift' has been partly misunderstood in the literature, and the extent of the changes overplayed.[59] While it is true that some churches and mosques were allowed to reopen, this applied only to the buildings that were closed in 1978–9, not those nationalized at independence.[60] Similarly, though some missionaries were allowed back into the country, this process was highly selective and tactical, designed to gain publicity and give the impression of radical change. And although it is true that the state put an official and definitive end to the 'anti-religious offensive' it initiated in 1978, Frelimo did not abandon secularism, religious control, and restrictions. Quite the reverse: it not only continued this policy but also formalized a series of restrictions (for example, the interdiction on creating new religious organizations),[61] and it gave the state more means to enforce its policy by creating the DAR with extensions at both provincial and district levels.[62] In other words, although some changes were seen from 1982, the post-independence 'religious regime' of secularism,

THE 1996 'MUSLIM HOLIDAYS' AFFAIR

restrictions, and control remained firmly in place—what I called in the introduction 'strong secularism'.

If something like a policy shift in religious matters happened, it took place in 1989. Before that date, Frelimo had moved closer to organized faiths and made concessions to gain religious support in the face of Renamo's guerrilla war and international hostility.[63] Thus President Chissano visited the Vatican in 1987 and invited the pope to visit Mozambique. To convince the Holy Father that its religious policy had changed, in 1988 Frelimo began to return religious property nationalized in 1975. In a similar move, the state permitted the construction of an Islamic centre in Marracuene in the same year (the first such construction since independence) and invited the ambassadors of Egypt, Libya, Nigeria, and Palestine to the laying of the foundation stone.[64] Still, even if changes were beginning to be made, the turning point in Frelimo's religious policy came only in 1989 with the party's Fifth Congress at which it reversed its policy of religious restrictions and control.[65] With this, it finally complied with the demands of many countries, most notably Western nations.[66] Soon after the congress, Frelimo also abandoned the project of a religious law, which it had discussed at length with all major organized faiths since 1988, a law that was to continue secularism, a degree of control, and some restrictions.[67] In 1990, the government decreed that religious organizations could become involved in education and, in 1991, passed a law allowing organized faiths to work in health too.[68] During the same period, the state began to register and allow almost all religious institutions to work in the country, though this measure was not grounded in any legislation.[69] By lifting all restrictions, Frelimo established what we can call a 'free religious market'.[70]

Mozambique's free religious market regime was mostly without rules, regulations, and rights. As the head of DAR noted in 1992, by merely lifting restrictions, the country eventually found itself without 'any legislation regulating matters related to religious freedom', a situation that does not seem to have changed to this day.[71] Faith organizations were allowed to preach and establish themselves wherever they wanted, no limits were set on their missionary work, and they had the right to work in health, education, humanitarian aid, and development. But at the same time, they were not accorded the status of a juridical person, had to register with the DAR, and were not given any legal rights (notably custom exemptions). This had three immediate consequences. First, as legal non-entities, religious organizations had problems dealing independently with government bodies and private companies and ultimately had to work through the DAR, which thus became an institution of 'tutelage', as its director noted.[72] Second, the absence of legal rights led to inequalities between religious organizations as some managed to gain exemptions and privileges from the state and government circles while others did not. Finally, religious expansion and proselytization was not regulated: state officials could favour some organizations, but they had no tools to prevent conflict.[73]

The growing importance of patronage led to the involvement of religious organizations in politics and that of political parties in religious affairs.[74] Thus, for example, the Brazilian neo-Pentecostal Universal Church of the Kingdom of God entered Mozambique through an alliance with Frelimo. The church supported Frelimo in the 1994 elections, in exchange for which it was allowed to rent a whole floor in the Frelimo headquarters as well as state cinemas as praying sites.[75] In 1994, Mozambique became a full member of the OIC at the same time as Frelimo was making deals with Mozambican Muslims in anticipation of the first multiparty elections (one of the deals being the Eid holiday law, as we have seen). Muslims bargained over their inclusion on electoral lists, and some of them even founded what was officially a non-denominational political party (PIMO), though it made explicit denominational statements despite this being prohibited by law, as we saw earlier.[76] The founding of the party led to no official reaction from the state. No less tellingly, in about 1992 President Chissano became an adept of the Maharishi Mahesh Yogi transcendental meditation sect. In 1993, his government signed a contract awarding this organization charter company-like rights over land and people in two-thirds of the country: 20 million hectares for the building of a 'Paradise on Earth'.[77] Although the deal was eventually cancelled, Chissano still managed to introduce courses of transcendental meditation in the police force, the army, and even among his ministers.[78]

This laissez-faire religious policy, in which politics and patronage played a prominent role, could not but undermine the state's secular identity. Significantly, accusations that the state was becoming Muslim, Christian, or even Catholic—in other words, confessional—increased dramatically in the 1990s.[79] Yet Frelimo did nothing to address these 'side effects' of its policy. It retreated from its most dubious religious deals only when forced to, and even then only in part. This was the case with the Maharishi Mahesh Yogi, as we just noted, and with the Universal Church of the Kingdom of God: while the state stopped renting it some of its cinemas in 1998, it still granted the church the first religious television channel in Mozambique.[80] Further, Frelimo never tried to make a distinction between its deals as a party and holder of state power and the position and options of the state itself. During the Eid affair, for example, the DAR head not only defended his party's support of the law but was very active as a state official in promoting the controversial legislation and countering any opposing view.[81] In short, although officially the religious regime in Mozambique remained secular (if a softer or more passive secularism) and the state continued to be committed publicly to religious equality, by 1996 the government and the administration's day-to-day practice had become unclear. Even if the state did not become confessional, it gave the impression that it could become so.

Conclusion

Taking into consideration the religious competition at the time of the Eid affair and how the state mediated it under Frelimo's guidance, it should be clear why the proposal of a Muslim public holiday raised the spectre of the Islamization of the state. The analysis should make it clear too how such a controversy was able to take place in Mozambique and why it shook the country and the sense of national unity so deeply. The state's religious leanings were unclear, and it seemed like they were about to change. Similarly, religious competition and state mediation help explain how tensions and rivalries, which in the early 1990s were inter-religious as well as intra-religious, suddenly crystallized into a conflict that split

Mozambicans along clear Christian–Muslim lines. Last but not least, these two dynamics elucidate the predominance of explanations that referred to conspiracy among actors in and commentators on the Eid affair. This is not to say that there was no 'rise' or politicization of Islam in Mozambique or that no conspiracy took place but rather that the relative rise of Islam and the conspiring turned into a problem and eventually into a national affair only because all organized religions were heavily competing with each other, and because the state's religious stance had become unclear and seemed up for grabs. Put differently, it is only because Frelimo 'deregulated' the religious market in Mozambique (under heavy external pressure) that organized faiths started to grow again, and it is only because the state did not maintain a clear position on religion that a specific political deal seemed about to change the whole Mozambican religious regime and possibly alter the state's secular nature.

Where did this 'Muslim holiday' affair leave Mozambique in 1998? It certainly left a bad taste in the mouth of Muslim leaders and politicians, particularly those who proposed or supported the law and believed some historical redress for past discrimination was at hand. But it also left behind a degree of uncertainty since the law was never annulled or reformed—its discussion in parliament was shelved indefinitely. This solution left actors uncertain about what the next step would be and wondering whether the issue could be revived at any moment at the whim of the party in power. The original conclusion of this text asked whether a similar controversy could appear again in the future. I originally argued that the Eid controversy was not just the result of a conspiracy or of electoral politics by Frelimo, Muslims, or anyone else but also, and more importantly, of structural changes in the state's religious policies and mediation. If this analysis was correct, I argued, and if we considered how Frelimo resolved the affair (that is, without addressing its structural origins), it was likely that problems and conflicts around faith would continue. Assuming that each conflict increased the intensity of the next, I forecasted not only the persistence of religious tensions and conflict but also the possibility that they could become more severe. Since Christianity and Islam are the most important religions in the country, it seemed quite possible that future problems would increasingly oppose these two faiths, even though the antagonism between them was not extensive in the early 1990s. In sum, it was my judgement at the time of writing this text that conflicts around religion were likely to continue in Mozambique even if the Eid affair was resolved. Religious tensions and conflicts would continue as long as the state maintained a free religious market approach and did not adopt a clear legal position towards religion—something we will discuss further in the following chapters.

More broadly, beyond Mozambique, what does this analysis of the Eid affair tell us? First, it shows that many if not most arguments and theories about 'fundamentalism' and about the 'rise of Islam' (or the rise of any other religion) offer a limited explanation of religious tensions and conflict. They omit other faiths, the competition between faiths, and the state's role in mediating and regulating their growth and competition. Put differently, they do not consider the religious regime that is in place. Second, the Eid affair tells us something about relations and conflicts between faiths. It shows that religions, and most notably Islam and Christianity, are by no means doomed to 'clash', as Huntington and his followers would have it. All depends on relations between religions on the ground, as well as the religious policies enforced in a nation-state—and internationally. Finally, the affair tells us something about the relationship between religious regimes and religious tensions and conflicts. It shows that a policy of religious deregulation (the creation of a free religious market) increases competition between organized faiths but that such increased competition brings not merely greater religious freedom, pluralism, and improved religious 'products', as neo-liberal sociologists would like us to believe. It also brings tension and conflict, especially when deregulation goes too far and/or when the state does not have a clear or secular position.

3

A PROSPECT OF SECULARIZATION?
MUSLIMS AND POLITICAL POWER, 1994–2004

The position of Islam in Mozambique underwent a transformation between the early 1990s and the 2020s. An oppressed, and at certain times repressed religion since the beginning of the twentieth century, Islam became socially and publicly important in the 1990s, even if it remained a minority religion. Chapters 1 and 2 looked at these changes, their causes, and their chronology. The current chapter examines the effects of this transformation. What was the impact of this turnabout in the public place and role of Muslims, in particular on civil society and political power? How did Muslims make use of their newfound status? What was the reaction of those in power? Were Muslims integrated into the elite in power, and has the national hegemonic bloc therefore been reconfigured? If so, according to what modalities and with what consequences? If not, how is the relationship between political power and the Muslim community now articulated? How have the different segments of the community reorganized outside of state power and what relationships have they developed with the rest of civil society?

I began this investigation with the research hypothesis that Muslims in Mozambique were being integrated into the national hegemonic bloc and that this bloc was consequently reconfiguring itself. I based this on a series of clues. Several Muslims had been added to Frelimo's parliamentary list; Muslims had been appointed to important positions in government and civil service; and an attempt had been made to pass laws that took Muslim interests into account. But my field research in the second half of 2004 called this hypothesis into question. The alliance concluded in 1994 between Muslims and Frelimo had at least partly collapsed in the period since; the most prominent Muslims on Frelimo's electoral list and in municipal governments had lost their seats; and a law that was hotly contested by influential sheiks was passed by parliament. Did this mean that the alliance between Frelimo and Muslims was over? Did Frelimo only enter into a momentary tactical alliance with Muslims instead of integrating Muslims into its power bloc? Reality turned out to be more complicated and subtle. This chapter shows that Frelimo broke its political alliance only with certain elements of the Muslim community, replacing individuals whom it marginalized in parliament or in local governments with other elements of the community after 1999. In other words, Frelimo redeployed its alliance with the Muslim community in Mozambique. This chapter explains how, why, and with what consequences.

The chapter is based on research conducted in Mozambique over a period of two months in 2004. At the national level, I did documentary research and interviews in the capital, and I did fieldwork in the province of Nampula, the most important region in the country as far as Islam is concerned. The methods used were, yet again, historical and sociological: archival research combined with numerous interviews with political and religious actors. The investigation took place just before an election, which imposed certain limits—leading politicians had little time to be interviewed, for example—but also permitted the observation of certain dynamics that are normally not as visible, such as political alliances. The research results are presented in three sections. The first evaluates the integration of Muslims into the national hegemonic bloc, focusing on the public political sphere. The second examines the policies Frelimo developed towards Muslims from the 1980s onwards in order to ensure its own hegemony. We will see how Muslims were informally co-opted and how Frelimo broke this

A PROSPECT OF SECULARIZATION?

alliance at least partly after 1999. Finally, the last section examines the evolution of the Muslim community since this partial break with Frelimo and the community's most recent socio-organizational developments and strategy for the future. The conclusion places the results of this research into comparative and historical perspective.

An integration of Muslims into the 'hegemonic bloc'?

The state in Mozambique has a twofold Christian origin. First, the colonial administration put in place by the Portuguese was both Christian and secular. Thus, while secular in its form, the state was deeply influenced in its functioning by Catholicism, which was considered an integral part of Portuguese identity, particularly after António Salazar's accession to power in 1926. Muslims were treated with hostility (alongside all other faiths that were not Catholic), and Islam was at times repressed, its laws and tribunals relegated to the domain of customary law. Second, after independence, the Mozambican state was run by leaders and agents who were primarily of Catholic and Protestant origin. It is true that Frelimo, inspired by socialism, broke with religious institutions, in particular with the Catholic Church, which had been organically linked to colonial rule. But it did not change the secular nature and form of the state, and it did not seek to redress prior injustices, thus leaving Islam in a subordinate position. When Frelimo embarked on a liberal path after 1989, party members were again allowed to show their religious affiliation, and most of the party's leaders re-joined their churches, generally Protestant or Catholic. This occurred just as Islam was becoming increasingly powerful socially and politically. This section investigates how Frelimo reacted to this new situation.

I have not succeeded in finding minutes or reports of discussions after 1989 within the leadership of Frelimo or the state over what should be done in light of the public rise of Islam. However, we know that in 1988 and 1989 the government drafted a law on religious freedom, which, despite much consultation, was never passed.[1] The government also passed laws and decrees after 1989 that allowed religious institutions to operate in the domains of health and education.[2] Similarly, we know that in 1998 the minister of justice, with the assistance of students, conducted a study of the religious situation in the country. One of the entries on the questionnaire addressed the dangers of the 'proliferation of Muslim organizations', and another asked about the best way of managing Muslim organizations. There were no equivalent questions about Christianity, which led one journalist to enquire about possible religious discrimination.[3] Be this as it may, the law project and decrees showed that Frelimo was concerned with religion, and the 1998 questionnaire revealed that after 1989 the administration was preoccupied with the place of Muslims in Mozambique. Before I began my field research in 2004, it seemed to me that Frelimo had decided to integrate Muslims into the nexus of power. This led me to formulate the hypothesis that Muslims had been integrated into the hegemonic bloc and that this bloc had consequently been reconfigured. I wanted to know how the elite had reorganized itself and study the reformulation and the national imaginary it revealed. But my hypothesis was partly contradicted by the results of my study. I first review the criteria that led me to formulate the hypothesis as a basis to determine the situation of Islam and politics in Mozambique at the turn of the century.

The ministers

In the early 1980s, Frelimo began to concern itself with the Arab and Muslim world, as we saw earlier. With this, it tried to counteract the poor image it had acquired through its religious repression and to combat the real or potential support that Renamo was obtaining from Arab and other Muslim countries. Frelimo also hoped to obtain humanitarian aid to help it address the limits the Mozambican state was facing with a civil war that was spreading across the country. The DAR, formed in early 1983, had the task of working with religious institutions to improve the image of the People's Republic of Mozambique abroad and recruiting support from coreligionists there.[4] Initially, the leaders of the country's principal Muslim organizations, the Islamic Congress of Mozambique and CISLAMO, travelled to the Gulf monarchies, Iraq, Iran, and other countries, but the results were not conclusive—according to the government, this was because of the competition and division between these two organizations.[5] In June 1984, the government appointed the lawyer Ussumane Aly Dauto as minister of justice and informally put him in charge of relations with the Arab and broader Muslim world. Aly Dauto worked together with the two national organizations and with Frelimo as well as with Muslims who were members of Frelimo or close to it (for example, Sharfuddine Khan, Carimo Vazirma, and Mohamed Mogne). Although progress was initially slow, the strategy ultimately paid off. In 1987, Aly Dauto became the first ever member of the Mozambican government to make an official visit to Saudi Arabia.[6] In 1990, he announced Mozambique's formal application to join the OIC. In 1994, the year in which he left the government, Mozambique was accepted into the OIC. Aly Dauto thus managed to have Mozambique recognized as an Islamic nation even though no more than 20 to 30 per cent of the population was Muslim.[7]

After the first multiparty elections in Mozambique in 1994, José Ibraimo Abudo, another lawyer, assumed control of the Ministry of Justice and of relations with the Arab and Muslim world. Abudo was quite different from his predecessor. He was a practising Muslim and an active member of his community. Before being appointed minister, he was very active in Muslim circles in Beira, and in 1992 he had created the CFI, whose goal includes the establishment of mosques and schools and the distribution of humanitarian aid. After his appointment, the CFI was instrumental in establishing the country's first Islamic university.[8] Abudo also had a more important internal political role than Aly Dauto. He had close ties with Sufi circles and was a member of the reigning family of the old Sultanate of Angoche—his wife came from an important family of Ilha de Moçambique, where all the Sufi orders are headquartered. In other words, Abudo's appointment was intended not only to help Mozambique establish relations with the international Muslim world but also to promote the government's relationship with Muslims domestically. For this reason, the shift of power from Aly Dauto to Abudo marked a qualitative change. Whereas Aly Dauto was a representative of the government in Muslim circles, Abudo was also a representative of the Muslim community in government. This qualitative change can partly be explained by changes in the country's situation: in 1989, it became possible for members of Frelimo to be religious. But it also represented a political choice. When Abudo was reappointed to his position in 1999, several newspapers commented that he had been retained principally because Frelimo wanted to secure the votes of Muslims in Nampula province and to conclude agreements for several financial projects with Arab countries.[9] To summarize, Abudo's presence in the Frelimo governments between 1994 and 2004 reflected Frelimo's full recognition of and concern for the Muslim section of the nation.

The Muslim presence in government after the 2004 election was roughly equivalent to that of previous years, with between two and four ministers and vice ministers of Muslim origin. Nevertheless, there no longer seemed to be any representatives of the Muslim community in the government. All ministers and vice ministers appointed in the 2000 election had a secular leaning or belonged to minority Muslim groups such as the Indo-Pakistanis or the Ismailis (by 'secular', I mean that they had no links to national Muslim organizations, that they obeyed party discipline, and that they did not attempt to bring elements of their faith into politics). In addition, the minister of justice no longer seemed responsible for relations with the international Muslim world. At the time, it looked possible that the role had fallen to another minister. But it is more probable that the role had been entrusted to someone of lower standing, such as the director for Middle Eastern or Asian relations at the Ministry of Foreign Affairs. This would be logical since relations with Muslim countries had now been normalized. Whatever the case, one should note that with the 2004 election the minister representing Muslims and in charge of Islamic international relations had left the government and did not seem to have been replaced by a person of a similar nature, and all Muslim ministers and vice ministers who were in government now had secular leanings.

The representatives

One of the principal novelties of the 1994 multiparty elections was the appearance of a Muslim factor in the institutional political arena. This was made possible both by the end of one-party rule and

A PROSPECT OF SECULARIZATION?

Marxism–Leninism and by Frelimo's decision to no longer demand that its members not be religious. As a result, many religious people joined the electoral lists of the ruling party and the opposition, and an openly Islamic party was founded in 1994, as we saw.[10] The result was that in December 2004, many people entered parliament 'as Muslims': sheiks, ordinary believers, Sufis, and reformists; some of them were Asians, others Africans, yet others were people of mixed race; some were for Frelimo, others for Renamo, some appeared on a party's electoral list without being a signed-up party member. I counted about forty Muslims out of a total of 250 representatives, a proportion slightly lower than that of Muslims in the country. For Frelimo, among the most important representatives elected were:

Ussumane Aly Dauto, former minister of justice (1986–94);
Abdul Carimo, former counsellor of the minister of justice (1990–4);
Nazir Lunat, entrepreneur and head of the Council of Islamic Theologians;
Hassan Ismail Makda, president of the Islamic Congress;
Abdul Kha Leck, an influential member of CISLAMO;
Ismail Inusso, entrepreneur and president of the Muslim community of Quelimane;
Amade Chemane Júnior Camal, major entrepreneur; and
Abdul Amide Mahomed, general secretary of the Muslim League of Zambezia.

The most important newly elected Muslim representatives for Renamo included:

Rachid Mustafa, president of the Islamic community of Niassa;
Jorge Adriano Nampula, traditional chief of the city of Nampula;
Paulo Mautamurro Nampuio, traditional chief of the province of Nampula.

The arrival of these Muslims in parliament had several consequences. First, they managed to have the first Muslim president of parliament elected along with a Muslim vice president. Also for the first time, representatives asked and were allowed to be sworn in on the Quran. Second, Muslim parliamentarians organized themselves into the Movimento Islâmico de Moçambique (Islamic Movement of Mozambique) and rapidly proposed a law to make the Eids into national holidays, as we saw in Chapter 2. Among other things, the affair illustrated how the entry of Muslims (as Muslims) into parliament created a new dynamic that initially seemed to favour Frelimo but that later created complications from which the party in power had difficulty extricating itself.

In early 1999, there were signs of change in the alliance between Frelimo and Muslims. The first public indication came with the strange affair of a decapitated head found in one of the principal mosques of the capital, Babu Salam, whose steering committee included two influential activist Muslim members of parliament. As mentioned in Chapter 1, a man had brought a human head to the mawlana (man in charge of a mosque, from the Arabic mawlâ, 'master') who was an Indian recently arrived in the country. The mawlana called the police, only to find himself accused of ordering the beheading for magico-religious purposes. The person who had brought him the head, however, was left at liberty. Newspapers linked to the regime—in particular the Maputo weekly Domingo—used this bizarre story to launch an anti-Muslim and even explicitly anti-Asian campaign.[11] Several months later, the relationship between the party and certain Muslims—including the two members of parliament who were members of the Babu Salam steering committee—completely broke down. Frelimo removed many Muslims who had been elected in 1994 from its list of candidates to the National Assembly in the 1999 elections (or else placed them at the bottom of the list); in contrast, Renamo largely put forward the same Muslim candidates as at the previous election. These marginalized men (all those listed above except for Aly Dauto and Abdul Carimo) were Islamic 'activists' who had refused to vote along party lines on the question of the Eids and/or members of a group of Muslims who had negotiated their inclusion on the Frelimo electoral lists with President Chissano without actually joining the party.[12] The break was selective in that Frelimo only eliminated 'activist' Muslims from its list of representatives.

76

A PROSPECT OF SECULARIZATION?

This allowed the party to propose a family law the following year without receiving any criticism from within its own ranks. The law was accepted without a hitch by parliament in 2004, although several sheiks protested that the text was fraught with imported, secular, and Christian principles.[13] In short, Muslim activism and criticism was no longer a factor in Frelimo after 1999.

Municipal governments and assemblies

We now turn to the situation at the local level. Were Muslims also integrated into municipal governments? If so, did this occur in the same proportion as at the national level, and did the same marginalization of certain types of Muslims take place after several years? More generally, what local relationships can one see between Muslims and power (or Muslims and the party in power)? The question is all the more relevant because Mozambique held municipal elections in 1998 and 2003. At least theoretically, the electoral process opened the door to better representation of Muslims in positions of power. Elections were held in thirty-three towns, officially chosen because of their socio-economic development. The choice of these towns was hotly debated, and their number was supposed to be increased in 2003, but this did not happen, officially for technical reasons. Whatever the case, local elections did take place, and some of them were held in areas with a Muslim majority, for example the towns of Angoche, Ilha de Moçambique, Nacala, and Pemba.

As the published results of the 1998 municipal elections do not mention religion, it is difficult to be precise on this subject. But it should be noted that these elections were boycotted by 85.5 per cent of the population, in large measure due to a call for a boycott by the principal opposition party and its allies, which did not even field candidates.[14] Thus the election results cannot be considered representative of the will of the people. But they remain interesting in that they demonstrate the policy of the political party in power at the time. Nearly all elected candidates had been nominated by Frelimo; a few had been put forward by two small parties and four citizens' groups. Five Muslim presidents of municipal councils (mayors) were elected, three in Islamic areas (Abacar Abdul Satar

77

Naimo in Ilha de Moçambique, Camissa Adamo Abdala in Mocímboa da Praia, and Assubugy Meagy in Pemba) and two in non-Islamic areas (Suleimane E. Amuji in Vilankulos and Faquir Bay Nalagi Faquir Bay in Xai-Xai). All had been nominated by Frelimo.

Many Muslims were also elected to municipal assemblies in towns within the country's Islamic zone. But in proportion far fewer were elected to these assemblies than are present in the local population. For example, only half of those elected to the assembly and the municipal council of Angoche were Muslim, although the town is 90 per cent Muslim.[15] The same was true in Nacala and Ilha de Moçambique. On the other hand, Frelimo, which controlled municipal councils, appointed several Muslims as *vereadores* (municipal ministers) in non-Muslim towns. Some of them were not even members of the party, such as the influential CISLAMO Sheik Cassimo David in Maputo and the president of the Maputo Muslim Community, Abdul Latif (a member of the citizens' group Juntos pela cidade [Together for the City]).[16] In other words, as had been the case in the national elections of 1994, the ruling party made a clear effort to propose Muslim candidates in the 1998 municipal elections.

The elections of 2003 unfolded with fewer problems than those of 1998, with all political parties participating in the process, even if there were many accusations of fraud and a high abstention rate. The results can therefore be considered as largely expressing the popular will. PIMO fielded ten candidates (for 857 seats) and won three seats, one each in the assemblies of Cuamba, Angoche, and Nampula.[17] The party remained quite marginal, but still succeeded in getting candidates elected.[18] Second, the majority of elected officials in the Islamic towns of the north of the country remained non-Muslim despite most of the population of these towns being Muslim. The proportions were quite similar to 1998, which is not surprising if one remembers that Renamo, which won a majority in Muslim areas, is as much a product of Christian and secular influence as Frelimo is. These results speak more to the historical marginalization of Muslims in the country than to a conspiracy on the part of one political party or another. Third, the number of Muslim mayors remained almost the same. Pemba and Xai-Xai no

A PROSPECT OF SECULARIZATION?

longer had Muslim mayors, but Angoche acquired one, leaving their number at four: Gulamo Mamudo in Ilha de Moçambique, Camissa Abdala in Mocímboa da Praia, Suleimane Amuji in Vilankulos, and Alberto Assane in Angoche. The first three were nominated by Frelimo, whereas Assane was nominated by Renamo.

Finally, there is a major difference between the 1998 and 2003 elections. As it had done for the National Assembly, Frelimo eliminated activist Muslims from its electoral lists and the municipal administrations under its control. Thus Cassimo David lost his position as *vereador* in 2003, while Abdul Latif was not re-elected (though this was because his party did not obtain as many votes as it had in 1998).[19] In sum, in the field of religion, the results of the 2003 elections were similar to those of 1998, even if the conditions were radically different (no opposition boycott and fewer abstentions). The most important point though is that, just as in the national elections of 1999, Frelimo eliminated activist Muslims from its municipal political alliances in 2003.

The Muslim policy of the party in power

In summary, Frelimo entered into an alliance with Muslims in 1994, but this alliance partly collapsed between 1999 and 2004. While Frelimo incorporated Muslims of all origins into its lists in the first multiparty and first municipal elections, after 1999 and 2003 it only added non-activist, secular, or secularized Muslims— in other words, men and women who were not linked to national Muslim organizations, who obeyed party discipline, and who did not attempt to introduce aspects of their religion into politics. Why, then, did Frelimo (partly) break its alliance? If a rapprochement had been necessary or useful earlier, why was it no longer so after 1999? Or was the price of this alliance no longer acceptable? Similarly, how did Frelimo compensate for this rupture, to minimize the political costs of the loss of this alliance? Specifically, how did Frelimo succeed in winning elections in Muslim areas for the first time in 2004 even though it had broken its alliance with the activist religious elite? To answer these questions, we need to understand Frelimo's policy towards Islam in general and the place

79

of Muslims in the national hegemonic bloc, particularly outside the institutional political arena.

The first element to note about Frelimo's policy is that over the years it established an effective system to control the country's religious institutions. It is true that a religious 'free market' has existed in Mozambique since 1989. But this free market and its rules are not anchored in legislation, and religious organizations are not legal entities. Rather this free market, though in practice never threatened, depends on the regime's goodwill. Moreover, religious institutions that wish to operate in Mozambique are still required to register with the National Directorate for Religious Affairs (Direcção Nacional dos Assuntos Religiosos [DNAR], which succeeded the DAR), which imposes certain minimum conditions and serves as an intermediary in the institutions' legal affairs, as we have already seen. As DNAR's director noted in 1992, the DNAR thus functions not only as a mediator but also as a 'supervisor'.[20] DNAR can recognize (or refuse to recognize) religious institutions and facilitate (or hinder) the purchase of buildings, the obtaining of travel permits, and so on. This allows the state to control—or negotiate, if need be—the entry of new religious institutions into the country, the emergence of new national organizations, and the general functioning of all religious institutions in the country. Overall, state practice has been and remains liberal, so that every organization that meets the necessary requirements has been accepted.[21] This latitude is shown by the fact that, according to lists established by DNAR in 1991, 1995, and 2004, the number of recognized religious institutions doubled from 1991 to 1995 and again from 1995 to 2004, reaching 617 institutions in the country in 2004.[22] Locally, the situation was similar: in the province of Nampula, the number of institutions grew from seventy-four to ninety-two between 2000 and 2004.[23] But it is still true that this freedom is under surveillance and that the government exercises a form of control that can be described as patrimonial.

Within the existing legal framework, Frelimo has deployed a strategy of co-opting Islam. As shown in Chapter 1, this began in 1982 with the creation of national Muslim organizations (CISLAMO and the Islamic Congress) that Frelimo used to oversee the faithful and to regain favour among Arab and Muslim countries. From the

80

A PROSPECT OF SECULARIZATION?

late 1980s, Frelimo's strategy expanded and became more complex, with social, religious, and economic liberalization. In a strategy of 'preservation through transformation',[24] the Frelimo elite privatized many companies to the benefit of public enterprises, of companies Frelimo had created, and those of trusted individuals. Several Muslims close to the party were associated with—or instrumental in—this policy, which integrated them into the hegemonic bloc (although in a relatively subordinate position). At the same time, the Frelimo elite created new enterprises, including several in partnership with elements of the Indo-Pakistani community who had access to international credit and import–export networks and who re-established traditional links of exchange, disrupted during the Marxist–Leninist period, with the Muslim world (India, Pakistan, UAE, Bahrain, etc.).[25] These business alliances knitted links between Frelimo and the Indo-Pakistani community, links that permitted the integration of these Muslims into the country's economic elite and that partially explain the political agreements concluded in 1994 between Frelimo and certain Muslims concerning the national elections—but only partially since there were other individuals besides Indo-Pakistanis in the alliance. This political alliance, as we have seen, was partly broken in 1999. But this break did not stop the two sides from doing business. Apparently, the expulsion of activist Muslims from formal politics was above all political: Frelimo did not feel at ease with them or was afraid of losing control as they refused to follow party discipline.

Another dimension of Frelimo's policy after 1990 was the attempt to co-opt Muslim Sufi masses and elites from the north of the country. This policy is reminiscent of Portuguese policies at the end of the colonial period. Frelimo attempted to appear ostentatiously favourable to Islam. In the late 1980s, the president of the republic began to express official good wishes for the Eids, to inaugurate mosques in person, and sometimes to pose for the press in Muslim dress.[26] From the late 1980s, the regime started to allow trips to Mecca again and—with the help of the Saudis—even financed them, just as the Portuguese had in the 1960s, and it finally began to give permission for the construction of new mosques in the country. In the early 2000s, Maputo, the capital, thus found itself

81

with two new, imposing mosques in the centre of town. The regime attempted also to co-opt Muslim elites, in particular the heads of Sufi orders, who, even if they had not joined the opposition after independence, were still hostile to or reticent towards the regime in power. We have seen that the leaders of the reformist Muslims were co-opted in 1981 and the Indo-Pakistani leaders from the late 1980s; the co-optation of Sufi leaders came in the 1990s through the offering of trips to Maputo and Mecca, the promise to take the wishes of Muslims into consideration (especially concerning the law on Muslim holidays), and helping *turuq* find trustworthy foreign donors. Thus Frelimo regained the confidence and support of Sheik Abdurazzaque Jamú, head of the Sadat brotherhood (from which other branches of the Qadiriyya issued), by acknowledging his status and by accepting his proposition before the 1994 election to proclaim the Eids as public holidays.[27] Shortly afterwards, Frelimo co-opted Sheik Abdurrahman Amuri bin Jimba, head of the Liaxuruti brotherhood (from which all other Shadhiliyya branches issue), by putting his Association of Friends of Ilha de Moçambique in contact with reliable donors (the European Union, a Portuguese NGO called OIKOS, and a Swiss Protestant NGO called EPER) and by including him in official activities; Minister Abudo, a member of the order, played an important role in this regard.

Despite this co-optation, Frelimo did not succeed in winning elections in the Muslim parts of the country until 2004. Apparently, one could co-opt the heads of orders without co-opting their members—or Islam was not a sufficiently strong mobilizing element (there was no community 'in itself' to use a concept discussed in the introduction). Indeed, in interviews Sheik Amuri bin Jimba was realistic, perhaps even cynical, about his own rallying to the party in power and its effect on his followers in the *tariqa*. It should be highlighted here that most Muslims continued to live in extreme poverty, and in 2000, provinces with a Muslim majority remained among the poorest in the nation.[28] These economic inequalities were so significant that in the later 1990s several Western countries decided to reorient their development aid in favour of the centre-north of the country: the United States, the Netherlands, and Switzerland all chose the province of Nampula as the new focus of their attention.

A PROSPECT OF SECULARIZATION?

After 2001, the Americans devoted even more attention to this province in order to gain access to the strategic port of Nacala (the deepest on the East African coast) and to keep a foothold in, and an eye on, the mostly Muslim (and what it thus considered the most 'dangerous') region of the country.[29] Anticipating, coordinating, or following this shift, Frelimo also devoted effort to these provinces, notably by accelerating administrative decentralization, which it saw as a means of diffusing social tensions.[30] Frelimo's electoral defeat in this region in 1999 further spurred the government's activism: shortly after the election, as the results were increasingly disputed, the government for the first time held a Council of Ministers outside the capital, in the historical Muslim town of Angoche. A bit later, in 2000, the government appointed Abdu Razak Mohamed as governor of the province, the first Muslim native of the area to hold this position. Under his direction, the administration undertook extensive analysis and social and political work in cooperation with anthropologists. In 2003, Frelimo launched the Aguebas movement to support the candidacy of Armando Guebuza (popularly known as 'Gueba'), who would become president in 2005.[31] For Angoche, Nacala, and Ilha de Moçambique, towns where Frelimo lost the municipal elections of 2003, the party even created special commissions of the Aguebas movement, the Zero Brigades, consisting of Muslim leaders 'mentalized and mobilized' to convince or denounce opponents.[32] As a result, the party finally won the province of Nampula in the 2004 elections. But this came at the cost of a climate of intimidation and a record abstention rate (only 27 per cent of eligible voters participated).[33] Irrespective of Renamo's shortcomings, Frelimo's eventual electoral victory in Muslim areas in 2004 was clearly not due solely to the force of its arguments.

In short, Frelimo's policy towards Islam bore its first fruits in the late 1980s in the field of foreign relations. Internally, however, it had to wait until the elections of 2004 to win Muslim areas in the country, and it only did so by neutralizing the opposition vote. As I have shown, in several respects Frelimo's policy eventually came to resemble the Portuguese colonial policy of the 1960s. It consisted of ostentatious respect for Islam, socio-economic co-optation of its religious leaders, and the neutralization of opponents.

83

In an interesting parallel, Donal Cruise O'Brien talks about the Kenyan regime's policy towards Islam as made of 'some adroit symbolic politics as well as the routine advantages of patronage and coercion'.[34] This noted, it remains that the position of Muslim elites in the nation of Mozambique by the mid-2000s was nothing like it was under the colonial regime. Secular Muslims had gained access to power and some even held prominent positions, whether in parliament, the government, or the economy. It is true that the proportion of Muslims in the administration, the government, and especially among the national and local elite was still lower than that in the national population. But this seems to have been the result of history and past policies rather than the regime's policies. If there still was some discrimination against Muslims, it occurred at the political level in that Frelimo seems to have made it a necessity for a candidate to be secular in order to accede to a position of higher responsibility. Frelimo no longer wanted men and women who did not obey party discipline and who attempted to bring their faith into politics. In this light, the prior co-optation of activist religious Muslims in the national and municipal assemblies and executive bodies could be explained as having been an 'error', a term Frelimo likes to use. More plausibly, it can also be seen as a tactical alliance by the party in power in its attempt to win Muslim support at a time when it was entering into a difficult and uncertain period, that is, the end of the civil war and the transition to multiparty rule.

What future for Islam?

The government co-opted many secular Muslim leaders but marginalized activist religious leaders from institutional politics. This might lead one to think that Muslim elites had simply become cooperative, that Islam had been 'institutionalized', and that one could expect stability in the future.[35] But the situation was not so simple. First, history is rarely linear, and the 'end of history' had not been reached in Mozambique. Second, activist Islamic leaders were far from content with their marginalization, as we will see. Third, the idea of a secular government was more Christian than Muslim, leading Muslims perhaps not to reject it but to at least question it. When considering the present and the future of Muslims in Mozambique, we need to consider what they were thinking, expecting, and hoping at this point in the mid-2000s. A key question is: How did activist leaders understand their political marginalization, and how did they respond to it? What dynamics were visible in the Muslim community at this point? Last, in what direction did the dynamics of the relationship between Islam and political power point to?

The Muslim leaders who were removed from parliament were neither satisfied with their removal nor with the state of the National Assembly after the 2004 elections. Nazir Lunat, who negotiated the agreement with President Chissano to include Muslims on Frelimo electoral lists, explained during an interview in 2004 that he had engaged in negotiations because Muslims had always been marginalized in Mozambique. It was necessary to redress the situation, he said, which he attempted to do in collaboration with various Muslim colleagues in parliament. Retrospectively, Lunat considers that up to 2004 Muslims in the National Assembly did not accomplish much, except to demonstrate that they existed. The reason for their failure, he argued, was that Frelimo did not want to change its secular approach (it is a question of generations, he suggested); even more, Frelimo's party discipline did not allow parliamentarians to defend any interests except those of the party. Because of this, even the family law was passed with no opposition from Muslim members of parliament. Looking ahead from this election, Lunat believes that Muslims did not have the means to create a successful political party and that overall the community was socially, economically, and educationally behind the rest of the country.[36] As one of his colleagues, Sheik Cassimo, remarked, Muslims were lagging for historical reasons (marginalization and opposition from the Portuguese) and because aid from Muslim countries had not been productive. Many young men who left to study in Muslim countries, notably in Saudi Arabia and Sudan, were not trained in anything but religion and because of this could find no work on their return to Mozambique—a situation that was generating frustration, did nothing to promote the welfare of the community, and created intergenerational conflict.[37]

What could be done? According to these men, members of the new *ulama* with reformist and possibly Wahhabi leanings, it was necessary to effect changes in three domains. First, Muslims in Mozambique should be better educated. This was not a simple task. In the mid-2000s, there were six large Muslim centres of secondary education in the country and one Islamic university. But, according to some sources, more than half the pupils in these high schools, and even students at Mussa Bin Bique University, were not Muslim. Muslims seemed to have trouble earning a secondary school education, the obstacles probably stemming from the socio-economic position of their families.[38] Moreover, as already mentioned, men who travelled to study abroad often returned with only a religious education, which made it difficult for them to re-enter their home society. Second, there was a need to foster unity among Muslims in the country. The Muslim elite was small, and it was divided along various axes: religiously, between Sufis and anti-Sufis, as well as between different Sufi movements; socially, between rich and poor, and between 'Indians' and Africans; and politically, between Muslims in the party in power and those in the opposition. Consequently, Muslims were easily manipulated by the party in power, which divided and ruled or simply exploited divisions to impose its own hegemony. Third, the country's Muslim population needed to become more advanced economically. Most Muslims were living in extreme poverty and were facing serious obstacles to education. It should be borne in mind that these opinions were expressed by members of the new reformist *ulama*, with particular leanings. But the other Muslim sectors in Mozambique seemed to share these goals, at least in general terms. For example, the pro-Sufi former minister of justice, José Ibraimo Abudo, attached a great deal of importance to education, and he had worked tirelessly to open the country's first Islamic university. If there were disagreements and tactical struggles, I suggest that they were over who would lead (and how), not about the goals to be achieved.

A nationwide Muslim effort to reach these goals began in 2000, after the removal of Muslim activist representatives from the institutional political sphere in 1999 and the death in 2000 of Sheik Mágira, the leader of the reformists. Sheik Mágira had been highly

A PROSPECT OF SECULARIZATION?

impulsive and confrontational, not hesitating publicly to attack Sufis and those favourable to them, including the then minister of justice. This generated animosity and much conflict and undermined any attempts at unification. His successor, Sheik Aminuddin Muhammad, appointed in 2000, was a modern, more open-minded, and conciliatory man.[39] This change of leadership in the reformist movement reduced tensions between the reformists and other Muslims, rapidly leading to a general decline in intra-community conflict, and soon even to the appearance of an 'ecumenical' movement. Thus, in 2002, the União Muçulmana de Moçambique (Muslim Union of Mozambique) was founded in Nacala, intended to include local leaders of both the Islamic Congress and CISLAMO. By 2004, the Muslim Union was attempting to establish itself at the national level.[40] More importantly, on the initiative of the Muslim Association of Sofala, the First National Islamic Conference was held in Beira in September 2003. This conference had as its principal goal 'the reinforcement of Islamic unity, humanitarian action, and the education of Muslims'.[41] Spread over two days, the conference saw the participation of representatives of all religious currents from all over the country. The topics discussed at the conference included Muslim history, law, education, health, and *zakat*. There were twelve workshops at which as many resolutions were passed (see Appendix IV for a list of the resolutions).[42] The conference decided to establish an executive committee and define criteria for determining the beginning and end of Ramadan that depended on the sighting of the moon 'on national territory' rather than in Mecca.[43] Provincial commissions were formed to assure unity in this matter. This momentarily put an end to one of the principal disputes between the country's main Muslim religious leaders, a dispute that had prompted the creation of a Council of Ulama of Mozambique (Conselho de ãlimos de Moçambique) in favour of the sighting of the moon in Mecca to define the date of the Eid to counter the Council of Muslim Theologians (Jamiatul ulama de Moçambique), which was in favour of the sighting of the moon in Mozambique.[44]

It was far from certain in 2004 that this strategy would bear the anticipated fruits. On the one hand, the community in Mozambique remained profoundly divided socially, politically, and religiously. Its resources remained limited and unequally distributed, especially along social and ethnic lines (Indo-Pakistani vs African). The competition between partisans of the party in power and those of the opposition remained heated. Religiously, certain Wahhabis refused to make even tactical concessions to Sufism, and some even managed to alienate the reformist leaders of the country.[45] Tellingly, in 2004, a few isolated mosques in the capital and in Ilha de Moçambique scheduled their Eid Ul Fitr celebrations, marking the end of Ramadan, according to the moon's appearance in Mecca, although the majority still complied with the decision of the Beira conference to rely on the sighting of the moon in Mozambique. But it must also be said that the ruling party in Mozambique did not change its Muslim strategy of divide and rule; on the contrary, it intensified it—this was clear with the electoral campaign in 2004. This would not necessarily prevent Muslims in the country from uniting and advancing, but it would make achieving their goals more difficult and the path to realizing them more tortuous. Frelimo's new policy also opened up the question of whether its strategy of co-opting only secular Muslims into politics would lead to a secularization of the whole community and whether it would reinforce the distinction among Mozambican Muslims between the Kingdom of God and that of Caesar. In the wake of the retreat of Muslim activists solely to social and religious matters, it seemed like activist Muslims had given up their direct political ambitions and were, by the mid-2000s, engaging more directly in civil society, whether in the struggle against HIV, in civic education, or the supervision of elections.

Conclusion

The decade from the mid-1990s to the mid-2000s witnessed many changes in the relationship between Islam and the government in Mozambique. The first change was the entrance of numerous Muslims into national and municipal assemblies in 1994, thanks to the adoption of multiparty elections and the end of Marxism–Leninism. Muslims attempted to unite in parliament to promote their interests, which cost the most activist among them their place on Frelimo's electoral lists after 1999. After that date, it seemed

A PROSPECT OF SECULARIZATION?

that Frelimo would only accept secular Muslims in positions of political power; activist Muslims were ousted from local power after the 2003 municipal elections and from government after the 2004 national election. The second transformation concerns the policy that Frelimo established with respect to Islam. Although it had been adopted in 1982, it did not attain its intended goal until 2004, when Frelimo achieved an electoral victory in the Muslim regions of the country. Thanks to its policies of ostentatious support, co-optation, and coercion, Frelimo succeeded in marginalizing the opposition and winning over Muslim provinces, if only with a low level of voter participation. Finally, Muslims were not passive in the face of their political marginalization. Profiting from the death of Sheik Mágira and the appointment of a more conciliatory successor, Muslims attempted to unify differing tendencies as well as work for the social, educational, and economic improvement of the community as a whole. In the mid-2000s, it was doubtful that this attempt would achieve rapid results. But it was a new development that deserved notice and was seen as possibly leading to more changes in the relationship between Islam and the government, if not an increased secularization of Muslims in the country.

My hypothesis at the outset of the research was that Muslims were in the process of being integrated into the national hegemonic bloc and that the latter was reconfiguring itself. At the end of my 2004 study, it was possible to state that the hypothesis did not hold up, or more precisely that it did so only partially. Although Muslims were integrated into the Mozambican elite in power in reasonable proportions (slightly less than the proportion of Muslims in the country as a whole), they were not integrated on an equal footing, and it had not led to a reconfiguration of the hegemonic bloc. It was possible that small but significant transformations occurred and that these could have long-term consequences. Nevertheless, the integration of Muslims into the national elite was taking place on Frelimo's terms. Muslims had to accept secular principles and exclude their religion from politics while the state structure—of Christian-secular origin—was never called into question. Little was said about the opposition, in particular Renamo, in part because Frelimo held a majority in parliament and thus prevented the opposition from furthering an alternative, oppositional politics in any effective manner, and partly also because Renamo, the main opposition party, shared the same Christian origins as Frelimo, and it, too, seemed to favour secularism. In short, then, Muslims were integrated into Mozambique's 'hegemonic bloc' but only on condition that they kept the nature of that bloc from being called into question—and the same can be said about the state, the nature of which could change over the long term, as a result of imperceptible changes introduced by secular Muslims or the constitution of a Muslim faction within the ruling party, but not in the short term, given the ongoing divisions within the Muslim community and the ruling party's ability to exploit them.

The relationship between Islam and politics in Mozambique around the turn of the millennium was typical of countries where the state is Christian-secular and Islam is a minority religion (Kenya, Tanzania, etc.). The political party and most of the elites in power were the product of a Christian background, although their practice of power was secular. What was unusual about Mozambique was that the same party had been in power for thirty years and had done a complete turn-about regarding its policies: from Marxism–Leninism to the 'free religious market', and from confrontation with Islam to the co-optation of its elites, if not yet of its masses. This tells us a lot about Frelimo and its capacity to transform itself in order to survive. Also unusually, Muslims in Mozambique managed, in the face of many obstacles, to emerge from their marginalization since independence. Nonetheless, as they approached the centres of power, members of the Muslim elite discovered the limits of their political possibilities as a religious community. They saw that there was never any question of changing the form of the state, even just to make two Muslim holidays official—although this may have seemed possible between 1994 and 1999. Probably because the opposition was no different from the party in power in this regard, Muslims seemed to turn in on themselves, concentrating on unity and the social advancement of their community. The results of this change were hard to anticipate. I argued in the original text that they could prove to be a tactical retreat so as to move forward or even take the offensive in the future. They could also prove to be a more definitive change, creating more unity and strengthening the community. They could also foster a new, more secularized Muslim political culture, as Muslims acknowledged and came to accept that the party in power would only admit individuals who kept their faith separate from the realm of Caesar. What I did not see at the time of writing was that these changes could also have fostered some elements that would begin to reject a state they perceived as impossible to reform or unworthy of it.

4

GROWTH AND RADICALIZATION?
ISLAM AND POLITICS AFTER 2004

In early 2011, a controversy arose in Pemba, the provincial capital of Cabo Delgado province, over the burqa, a particular form of Muslim veil some women wear as dress, in public institutions. Early in the year, a pupil began to wear a burqa to school, and the teachers and school principal refused to teach the young woman unless she removed it. After visiting Pemba, the minister of education supported the school administration and formally banned the wearing of the burqa at schools across Mozambique in the name of the secular nature of the state. This was backed by the minister of justice, who declared that religious freedom did not mean one could impose one's religion on the state. In the following days and weeks, the leaders of the country's main Muslim organizations publicly condemned the measure and described it as a form of discrimination against Muslims. Months of tension ensued, oscillating between threats and attempts at reaching a compromise. It became the country's second major crisis over Islam, twenty years after the Muslim holiday affair (see Chapter 2). Was this new incident a sign of Islamic fundamentalism and, more importantly, of the radicalization of Mozambican Muslims?

Since the mid-2010s, and particularly since the emergence of the jihadi insurgency in northern Mozambique in 2017, there has been a sustained discussion about Islamic 'fundamentalism' and the 'radicalization' of (some) Muslims, alongside an older idea that the country had seen a significant 'growth' of Islam. A number of questions follows. Could it be that the secularization hypothesis (advanced in Chapter 3) was wholly mistaken, and that (some) Muslims had set out on another path, more critical if not confrontational, perhaps towards jihad? What happened to Muslim politics and institutional life in the 2010s, and what is meant by 'growth', 'fundamentalism', and 'radicalization' in the Mozambican Muslim context? Indeed, is growth an issue of a rise in the number of believers or a return to a more rigorous religious practice? Is extremism a more rigorous religious practice by religious followers or the deployment of religious views into politics, or the readiness to use force to achieve objectives?

Little research has been conducted on the growth and radicalization of (parts of) Islam in Mozambique. Worse, there is little critical engagement with the subject within the various sectors, be they popular, journalistic, political, or academic. Most authors and commentators posit 'radicalization' and 'extremism' as a given, particularly since 2017, when a discourse on extremism crystallized to feed and sustain an institutional view and an emerging cottage industry around 'countering extremism' and 'countering violent extremism'. The research for this chapter has been carried out over many years, during various field trips to, and years of living in, Mozambique, with many interviews with state officials and Muslim leaders, and some participant observation. On that basis, and against the popular view that Mozambican Islam has seen growth and radicalization, the chapter starts by investigating the dynamics of this faith, based on an analysis of the existing national censuses. It then discusses the idea of a rise in radicalization in the country, focusing on one particular moment that is considered as the epitome of radicalization, and then analysing the views of Muslims in the country in the first decade of the twenty-first century. It wraps up with an exploration of the evolution of Muslim institutions and politics in the 2010s, with an eye to continuity and change within the community.

GROWTH AND RADICALIZATION?

Religious growth

In earlier chapters, we saw that the dynamics of religions in Mozambique changed significantly after 1992, when the country returned to peace and the government liberalized its control of faith organizations. This resulted in new dynamics across all religions and all regions of the country. It led to competition, tensions, and conflict, within as well as between faith traditions, and opened up space for new areas of collaboration between and within faiths.[1] On occasion, these new dynamics led to the emergence of conspiracy theories, expressing fears that one religion or another might be trying to take control of the state and dominate society. In those moments and ever more since then, politicians, analysts, religious figures, journalists, and citizens have often referred to a general 'religious growth' in Mozambique and particularly to the 'growth of Islam'.[2] The idea that Islam was growing in Mozambique crystallized over a number of years; by the 2010s, it had become common knowledge. The idea was rarely, if ever, contested, least of all by Muslim leaders who felt they were still being discriminated against and not accounted for adequately in the national censuses. With so much talk about the growth of Islam in the country, we need to ask: Did Islam really grow in Mozambique after the end of the civil war, and if so, how much?

Before engaging in any analysis, we must acknowledge that the term 'religious growth' (or 'religious upsurge') is polysemic. It is used by various people to mean different things, including an increase in the number of believers, the geographical spread of a religion, the establishment of new religious institutions, the appearance of new religious currents or practices, the establishment of new sites of prayer, or a gain in public visibility. All these aspects differ from each other but are not exclusive. Some can unfold in parallel and complement each other, to different degrees and in different ways. At times, elements may steer in opposing directions (for example, a loss in visibility but an increase in believers). Considering this multifaceted reality, we must not only look at each of these aspects but also unpack the articulation between them and how they unfold on the ground. I do so here by analysing the three national censuses that were conducted in 1997, 2007, and 2017 and then reading the results critically against information gathered in archival documents, newspapers, and interviews, and through participant observation.

Censuses in Mozambique, like elsewhere, contain their share of issues. In terms of religion, they asked citizens to self-identify their religious orientation. They could either choose from a list of categories or they could enter their own description. For Christianity, the categories changed over time (where, for example, the 1997 census offered the option 'Protestant/Evangelical', the 2007 census listed 'Protestant/Pentecostals' and introduced the new category 'Anglican'). I have tried to systematize the categories across the years to make the censuses comparable (see Table 3). In relation to Islam, research shows that in 1997 some census takers in one region read the census question to mean that only people who pray five times a day could count as 'Muslims'.[3] The extent to which census takers applied this interpretation during the 1997 census remains unclear, as does whether it reoccurred in subsequent censuses. A similar if reverse problem was seen with the category 'Catholics'. Official figures give twice as many Catholics for Cabo Delgado province and more than twice as many Catholics for Nampula province than the church itself counted.[4] The main reason was presumably that the church counted only those baptized (minus those who had died or left the church), while the census had asked for self-identification. There are other minor issues, but the point is that it is important to triangulate information, for example positing church data against the census results, and to include a margin of error. The Pew Research Center in the United States triangulated religious data on Mozambique from four statistical sources: the national census, demographic and health surveys, results from research conducted by the Afrobarometer research network, and its own research (questionnaires in ten provinces). It found that about 20 per cent of the population was Muslim (with a range between 18 and 23 per cent).[5] Where different surveys use different methods and ask questions differently, and thus achieve varying results, the Mozambican National Institute of Statistics—which sets the national census—tends to use the same methodology and the same criteria, if not the same questions, in its surveys. It is thus likely that there

GROWTH AND RADICALIZATION?

is a smaller margin of error in the shifts that are evident in the data across the censuses.

With these caveats, we can now turn to Table 3, which captures the figures for how Mozambicans self-identified their faith in the years 1997, 2007, and 2017.

Table 3. Religious self-identification on a national basis, 1997, 2007, and 2017

Religion	1997	2007	2017
Muslims	17.8%	17.9%	18.9%
Catholics	23.8%	28.4%	27.2%
Protestants and other Christians	11.3%	12.2%	17.0%
Zionists	17.5%	15.5%	15.6%
Without religion	23.1%	18.8%	13.9%
Others and unknown	6.3%	7.3%	7.3%

Source: Instituto Nacional de Estatística, 'II Recenseamento Geral da População e Habitação 1997: Indicadores socio-demográficos—País total', Maputo: Instituto Nacional de Estatística, 1999; Instituto Nacional de Estatística, 'III Censo 2007 Geral da Geral da População e Habitação', http://www.ine.gov.mz/operacoes-estatisticas/censos/censo-2007, accessed 17 February 2022; and Instituto Nacional de Estatística, 'IV Censo Geral da População e Habitação 2017', http://www.ine.gov.mz/iv-censo-2017, accessed 29 November 2019—both censuses are now available at: https://web.archive.org/web/20230316012026/http://www.ine.gov.mz/operacoes-estatisticas/censos/censo-2007

What these statistics reveal at a general level is, first, that the main monotheist faiths in Mozambique grew between 1997 and 2017. 'Protestants and Other Christians' grew most (by 5.7 percentage points), followed by Catholics (who grew 4.6 percentage points by 2007 before dipping 1.2 percentage points in 2017) and then Islam (which grew by 1.1 percentage points). The main losers were the category 'Without Religion' (which presumably included the so-called 'animists'), who decreased by 9.2 percentage points, and the Zionists, who dropped by 1.9 percentage points. 'Others and Unknown' grew by 1 percentage point. Overall, this means that over a period of twenty years Islam grew only modestly (1.1 percentage points or +6.2 per cent) which is much less than its monotheist competitors (+14.2 per cent for Catholicism and +50.4 per cent for Protestantism). The difference is significant and quite surprising. Could it be that in some areas the numbers of Muslims were rising more quickly than in others, or there were areas with decrease, so that there was only a modest overall increase? Indeed, many believe that Islam grew particularly in the country's south.

A look at the census data by province (see Table 4) reveals steady but marginal growth in the number of Muslims in the south and centre of Mozambique between 1997 and 2017: 1.4 percentage points in Maputo city, 1.5 in Maputo province, 0.4 each in Gaza and Inhambane provinces, 0.8 in Sofala, and 0.5 in Tete province. It also reveals a marked decrease in central and northern Mozambique: 2.1 percentage points in Manica province, 0.8 in Zambezia, 2.1 in Niassa, and 1.9 in Cabo Delgado. Nampula is the exception in the north with an increase of 1.3 percentage points, though the low value means that this figure could be a statistical artefact. Yet, if we take the latter to be factual, then we can say that there was minor growth in the number of Muslims in southern and central Mozambique but an overall loss in the north, except for Nampula province. Some provinces offer odd constellations: while Islam lost 2 percentage points in Cabo Delgado and Protestantism 10.1, Catholicism grew by 16.3. Nampula is also odd: where Catholicism gained 10.6 percentage points and Islam 1.3, Protestantism lost 5.5. Some local analysis will be needed to confirm this data and understand these dynamics. In the meantime, we can tentatively conclude that Islam grew a little in the south of the country and decreased a little in the north. More definitively, we can conclude that there was no major 'Islamic growth' in Mozambique, locally or nationally, over these two decades, especially when compared with the numbers for the other faith communities in the country.

If there was no significant numerical growth or geographical spread of Islam between 1997 and 2017, could it be that the faith instead grew in visibility over this period? Here the answer is clearly in the affirmative. In 1989, the government in Mozambique

Table 4. Religious self-identification by province, 1997, 2007, 2017

Province	Religion																	
	Muslims			Catholics			Protestants and other Christians[1]			Zionists[2]			Without religion			Others and unknown[3]		
	1997	2007	2017	1997	2007	2017	1997	2007	2017	1997	2007	2017	1997	2007	2017	1997	2007	2017
Maputo City	4.4%	5.3%	6.0%	20.8%	23.0%	20.0%	9.3%	22.9%	30.5%	39.4%	25.2%	23.3%	16.5%	14.3%	11.0%	7.4%	0.9%	0.9%
Maputo province	1.7%	2.5%	3.3%	14.0%	16.5%	14.7%	8.3%	18.1%	25.7%	49.5%	39.8%	30.9%	14.9%	13.7%	8.2%	6.4%	0.9%	0.7%
Gaza	0.6%	0.9%	1.0%	12.4%	15.4%	13.7%	7.3%	18.8%	27.8%	37.4%	37.5%	24.7%	36.8%	19.8%	12.5%	5.6%	7.6%	6.0%
Inhambane	1.0%	1.2%	1.4%	20.7%	24.0%	21.8%	18.2%	11.6%	18.1%	34.3%	35.8%	39.6%	7.6%	15.0%	9.2%	1.3%	12.2%	9.7%
Manica	3.2%	0.9%	1.1%	10.9%	9.6%	8.2%	3.5%	19.7%	24.2%	26.7%	30.6%	36.6%	54.3%	30.3%	36.3%	36.0%	2.8%	4.8%
Sofala	1.9%	2.4%	2.7%	16.3%	18.5%	15.0%	10.1%	24.2%	30.8%	17.8%	18.9%	20.4%	46.2%	33.2%	24.9%	7.6%	4.6%	6.2%
Tete	0.4%	0.8%	0.9%	22.7%	21.5%	20.1%	8.0%	12.5%	18.2%	17.5%	17.0%	17.4%	43.5%	38.7%	32.8%	7.4%	9.4%	10.4%
Zambezia	9.7%	9.7%	8.9%	38.2%	40.0%	39.5%	16.7%	11.1%	22.7%	12.0%	8.6%	9.9%	19.9%	15.1%	13.1%	3.0%	15.4%	15.3%
Nampula	38.3%	37.5%	39.6%	27.2%	39.0%	37.8%	12.6%	5.7%	7.0%	1.3%	1.5%	2.0%	17.1%	14.0%	10.2%	0.9%	2.7%	3.2%
Niassa	61.1%	60.8%	59.0%	23.3%	26.0%	26.3%	9.8%	7.7%	8.6%	1.9%	2.6%	2.7%	2.9%	0.9%	0.7%	0.8%	1.8%	2.0%
Cabo Delgado	54.5%	53.8%	52.6%	19.6%	36.0%	35.9%	12.3%	1.5%	2.2%	0.4%	0.3%	0.4%	11.8%	7.6%	7.4%	1.2%	0.7%	1.4%
Mozambique: Total	17.8%	17.9%	18.9%	23.8%	28.4%	27.2%	11.3%	12.2%	17.0%	17.5%	15.5%	15.6%	23.1%	18.8%	13.9%	6.3%	7.3%	7.3%

Source: Calculations based on the censuses of 1997, 2007, 2017. Instituto Nacional de Estatística, 'II Recenseamento Geral da População e Habitação 1997: Indicadores socio-demográficos—País total', Maputo: Instituto Nacional de Estatística, 1999, p. 33; Instituto Nacional de Estatística, 'III Censo 2007 Geral da População e Habitação', http://www.ine.gov.mz/operacoes-estatisticas/censos/censo-2007, accessed 17 February 2022; and Instituto Nacional de Estatística, 'IV Censo Geral da População e Habitação 2017', http://www.ine.gov.mz/iv-censo-2017, accessed 29 November 2019—now available at https://web.archive.org/web/20230316012026/http://www.ine.gov.mz/operacoes-estatisticas/censos/censo-2007

[1] The categories in the 1997 census were: Catholic, Zionist, Protestant/Evangelical, Undetermined Christian, and, in some provinces, Jehovah's Witness. The 2007 census categories were: Catholic, Zionist, Evangelical/Pentecostal, and Anglican. I have thus kept the census categories that remained the same across all censuses and collected all non-Catholic and non-Zionist Christians in the single category called 'Protestants and Other Christians'. Similarly, I brought together the census categories 'Other' and 'Unknown', as both are non-descriptive; and, for 1997, I added in the census category 'animist'.

[2] 'Zionism' is an established religious category in Mozambique, commonly used to describe local Afro-Pentecostal churches.

[3] The 1997 census contained the category 'animist', but this has been ignored here. It was statistically marginal, at 2 per cent nationally, and was no longer used in subsequent censuses. My impression is that so-called animists are contained in the category 'Without Religion'. Indeed, the figure for the latter is high, and people in Mozambique do not consider the worshipping of ancestors as a religion. Yet in reality almost everyone, whether Christian, Muslim, or other, celebrates the spirits of ancestors, in one way or another and to some degree or another.

changed its policy towards religion, shifting to a form of 'free religious market' as we saw in earlier chapters.[6] This and the end of the civil war in 1992 led to a return of religious proselytization and demonstrations of religious affiliation in the public sphere and the construction of new religious buildings. Religious processions returned to the streets of cities, towns, and villages throughout the country. For Islam, this took place in particular during the festivities of Mawlid and the two Eids, with mass prayers and marches, sometimes attended by politicians from the government and the opposition alike. Similarly, there was a massive increase in the construction of mosques, Islamic schools, health posts, and boreholes all over the country, often financed by Muslim NGOs such as AMA (rebranded Direct Aid International in 1987, though the old name continues to be used in Mozambique).[7] Major new mosques were also built in the centre of Maputo, the capital, leading to a tangible sense among citizens that Islam was growing—a perception generated socially, visually, and audibly (with the muezzin's call to prayer five times a day).

Another element of Muslim 'growth' in Mozambique from the 1990s to the 2010s related to the development of new religious movements. Unfortunately, the generic statistical category of 'Muslims' in the census does not capture the rise of movements within the Muslim community, for which we have to rely on qualitative information. On that basis, the biggest rise of a religious movement seems to have been the establishment and expansion of Wahhabism, embodied in CISLAMO. The numbers might have been significant, but just as importantly, this new current represented a new way of practising faith, dressing, and posturing socially and politically. It became visually very noticeable, at times even making the headlines of newspapers.[8] Many of the new mosques they built and staffed, usually financed by international partners, were identical, in the same style, and of the same size (100 square metres),[9] and were markedly different from traditional mosques, often mud-brick structures. This generated a widespread impression that Wahhabi Islam (and Islam in general) was experiencing significant growth, and this in turn might have helped foster the perception that 'radicalization' was taking place.

Radicalization

The topic of 'radicalization' is complex, with many (sometimes conflicting) definitions of the term and various approaches to the issue (at the micro, meso, and macro level and socially, politically, or economically).[10] In much of the literature on Mozambique, it is assumed that if radical jihadists are at work in the early 2020s, it is because a process of 'radicalization' happened beforehand. But this assumption has neither been researched nor problematized.

What is radicalization? Does it refer to the taking-up of arms, or to a change of ideas so that armed conflict is seen as acceptable, or to religious or political thinking that has shifted away from the mainstream? Is thinking that deviates from the religious mainstream also radicalization even when no violence is considered? Who undergoes radicalization: individuals, social groups, the youth, society as a whole? How do individuals or social groups radicalize? And what are the causes of radicalization? The topic is complex, and this chapter cannot do justice to it, whether in general or in a specific situation. What I aim at doing instead is to focus on two specific aspects of the question to start revealing a first level of complexity about a topic that badly needs serious, extensive, and critical research. I first consider an affair that some decried as an example of radicalization, and then attempt to evaluate the level of 'radicality' of Muslim views about society in Mozambique in the twenty-first century.

First, then, the affair: in early 2011, an incident took place that involved the burqa, the most concealing of female Islamic veils. The affair was widely covered in the media, which did much to crystallize the idea that radicalization was taking place among Muslims in the first decades of the new millennium. The incident happened in Pemba, Cabo Delgado, when a female pupil, the wife of a CISLAMO *hafiz* (a Muslim who has completely memorized the Quran), was suspended from school for wearing a burqa, a dress that was prohibited by school regulations. Other pupil were happy to wear the burqa when outside of school only, but this pupil insisted it was her right to do so within the school grounds as well. Some teachers refused to teach her, which meant not teaching the entire class, so that the school principal felt obliged to suspend her. The dispute continued over several weeks, with the AMA, which owned the school, siding with the pupil and local state officials trying to mediate (seeing that all teachers, whether in public or private schools, are state employees). At the end of May, the minister of justice travelled to Pemba and confirmed the pupil's suspension. The minister explained that religious freedom was the right to practise one's religion but did not include the right to impose it on to others:

> It cannot be accepted that each student invokes and shouts their religion in the loudest tones in schools ... Our country has many people who profess this same religion, but they don't wear burqas in the schools where they study.[11]
>
> Imagine if a person who professes the religion of the Zionists needs to wear strings in school—and so on [with other faiths], where will we end?[12]

The minister's position on the issue was not well received and escalated the matter. On 27 June 2011, three Muslim leaders from Nampula province, Wahhabi and Sufi, explained in an interview with the media that ninety more pupils in the province had been excluded from school for wearing a burqa. They argued that these exclusions violated Article 24 of the country's constitution, which holds that '[i]n the Republic of Mozambique, education shall be a right and a duty of all citizens'. They stated that they were open to dialogue but warned that they would engage in protest and withdraw their vote at the 2014 election if matters were not resolved rapidly. It took a whole year until, after some negotiation, the government decided on a compromise by permitting the wearing of the burqa during Ramadan, but only then. This was not well received by Muslims either, and the same three leaders made a public statement directed at the government: 'Enough of the humiliation, discrimination, and instrumentalization of the principals of public schools to exclude Muslim students. We hope you will work with us on the issues we submitted to central government for prompt resolution so that Muslim minds can be put at ease.'[13] A few days later, CISLAMO's commission of Islamic scholars, the Alim Commission, published its position on the affair: it threatened to end all cooperation with the government if serious action was not taken and demanded that the government 'apologise via the media to all Muslims'.[14]

After further negotiations with Muslim leaders, the government finally found a solution acceptable to all in August 2012. It distinguished between veils that hide the wearer's face and those that do not (see Figure 1) and banned the former while permitting the latter. This meant that it banned both the burqa and the niqab from schools. At a press conference, the minister of education explained that the government always preferred dialogue: 'What is most important is that the meeting led to a consensus, namely: that Muslim women can use the veil. We are talking of the veil only, and not the burqa—let us be clear.' The Muslim leaders at the press conference echoed the minister's words by declaring that dialogue was key to resolving problems.[15] The incident thus ended well, with a compromise acceptable to all. Within a year, the issue of the burqa resurfaced twice, first in relation to a hospital in Pemba that banned the burqa after a fully veiled woman kidnapped a child, and second when some Muslim women requested that their identity cards carry photos of themselves where they were veiled. In both cases, the incidents were resolved quickly thanks to the new understanding, channels of communication, and approach that had been established to resolve the school incident.[16]

Figure 1. Types of Muslim veils

Source: BBC News, https://www.bbc.com/news/uk-45112792, accessed 18 January 2023

The burqa affair needs to be understood from a historical and legal perspective.[17] After independence, Frelimo had banned the use of all religious symbols in the public sphere. In the late 1970s, the prohibition included religious teaching, religious festivals, and all religious dress, including the *cofió*.[18] Frelimo reversed its anti-religious policy in the 1980s, and the state became more tolerant of religious dress and public displays of religiosity more generally. But no regulations or principles were formally established setting out how one was allowed to dress in what context and on what occasion. Hence, while wearing the burqa may be seen as proof of radicalization, the burqa affair can also be interpreted as a negotiation between the Muslim community and the state over the limits of the use of religious dress in public. For all the drama and threats, Muslim leaders always negotiated, and wanted to negotiate, with the state, and they were happy to ban the use of the burqa (just not all veils). The affair, thus, does not reveal that the leaders of the Muslim community had been radicalized towards political extremism, violence, or terrorism. Rather, they respected the state, did not question secularism, referred to the constitution, and ultimately agreed to limits on wearing the burqa. In effect, what they demanded was better integration within society and respect from the state.

If there was no significant radicalization from above in the 2000s and 2010s, what was the situation from below? As will be discussed in Chapter 5, there was some radicalization taking place in Cabo Delgado and adjoining areas with the development of a religious sect in Cabo Delgado that rejected the state in all its forms, so as to operate only according to sharia law—in 2017, the sect shifted to violence. In a similar if unrelated development, Christian Laheij has described a situation in Nampula town in the 2010s where a sheik called for the application of sharia law and the (partial?) rejection of the state, commanding his followers never to go to the police, whatever their problem.[19] There were undoubtedly other sheiks in Mozambique who rejected the state and wanted to follow sharia law in part or in full, but they remained in the minority and did not belong to any legal Muslim organization, i.e. they were marginal.

What about the majority of Muslims in the country? What were their views? The only existing data about the views of Muslim citizens in Mozambique dates from the 2000s. There is no comparative data, so no possibility to analyse whether a process of radicalization can be detected over time. But the data can tell us something about what the Muslim population in Mozambique thought at that time, and so offer an idea of how 'radical' (or not) their views were. Existing data comes from a survey carried out in 2008–9 by the Pew Research Center on 'Tolerance and Tension' among Muslims and Christians across sub-Saharan Africa.[20] The survey was carried out in Mozambique among 1,500 individuals, of which 340 were Muslim. This is statistically significant but not sufficient to be properly representative of all Muslims in Mozambique. Tellingly, the authors of the Pew report introduced a margin of error of 8 percentage points for the survey's results.[21] In other words, the survey can indicate a tendency but is not definitive or precise.

One of the first questions dealt with by the survey related to the veil. It asked interviewees whether 'women should ... have the right to decide whether to wear a veil' or not. In their answers, 40 per cent of Muslims thought women should have this right while 58 per cent thought that society as a whole should decide. This compared, at the one end, with the Democratic Republic of the Congo (DRC), where only 29 per cent of Muslims thought women should be able to choose and, at the other, with Senegal, where 58 per cent of Muslims thought women should have the right.[22] Asked about gender, 36 per cent of Muslim Mozambicans supported 'restricting religious leadership roles to men', similar to the 34 per cent of Christians who felt the same. This was quite different from the 73 per cent of Muslims in the DRC and Ghana and a high 83 per cent in Ethiopia and Cameroon.[23] In short, Mozambican Muslims were, apparently, relatively liberal on the issue of gender and the veil.

Asked if they would support 'making sharia, or Islamic law, the official law of the land in our country', 65 per cent of Mozambican Muslims were in favour of the proposition while 31 per cent were opposed (2 per cent did not answer). The country with most people in favour of sharia law was Djibouti, with 82 per cent, while Tanzania had the fewest, with only 37 per cent.[24] When asked the parallel question whether they would support 'making the Bible the official law of the land in our country', 63 per cent of Christian

GROWTH AND RADICALIZATION?

Mozambicans supported the idea and 31 per cent opposed it—almost the same percentage as Muslims wanting sharia.[25] It is worth noting here that there has never been a public debate in Mozambique about introducing the sharia or the Bible as official law. The closest to it was the debate about family law in 2000,[26] when a member of parliament proposed the partial reintroduction of sharia law for Muslims in relation to family affairs.[27] When the interviewers asked about the details of sharia law, the interviewees' answers became even more nuanced. A majority of those in Mozambique who had supported the introduction of sharia law rejected the death penalty for those leaving Islam (70 per cent), rejected whipping and the cutting off of the hand for theft or robbery (63 per cent), or stoning for adultery (67 per cent).[28]

Another important question asked by the survey related to 'the return of the Mahdi, the guided one who will initiate the final period before the Day of Resurrection and Judgment'. In Mozambique, 63 per cent of Muslims expressed a belief in this messianism and 69 per cent said they thought the Caliphate would be re-established during their lifetime.[29] This was among the highest rate in Africa, a surprising and somewhat concerning result since the Islamic State professes these ideas and promotes itself as realizing this prophecy, not least with the insurgency that began in Cabo Delgado in 2017. A parallel belief existed among Mozambican Christians, however, with 63 per cent believing that 'Jesus will return to earth during [their] lifetime.'[30] This rate is equally surprising and puzzling since no one in the public realm ever discussed such a scenario, whether on the Muslim or the Christian side. To mitigate against a narrow political reading of this finding, it is worth noting that only 26 per cent of Muslims and 25 per cent of Christians in the survey agreed with the idea that 'the use of violence against civilians can be often/ sometimes justified' in the defence of one's religion.[31] Some 18 per cent thought it was 'rarely' justified, and 46 per cent answered that it was 'never' justified. Interestingly, the percentage of those opposed to violence was marginally higher among Muslims than Christians.[32]

To complicate matters further, the Pew survey revealed that a clear majority of Muslims in Mozambique firmly supported democracy and religious freedom. In fact, more Muslims (73

107

per cent) than Christians (69 per cent) believed that 'we should rely on a democratic form of government to solve our country's problems'.[33] Similarly, 96 per cent of Muslims supported religious freedom.[34] In turn, 25 per cent of Muslims were concerned with 'religious conflict' as opposed to 33 per cent concerned with ethnic conflict, 69 per cent with crime, 72 per cent with corrupt political leaders, and 80 per cent with unemployment.[35] As to religious extremism, the same proportion of Muslims and Christians were concerned: 25 per cent of each community were greatly concerned, and 27 per cent of Muslims and 25 per cent of Christians were moderately concerned.[36] There was also no significant difference in their perception of Muslim and Christian extremism: 19 per cent of Christians were concerned about Muslim extremism and 21 per cent with Christian extremism, while 21 per cent of Muslims were concerned about Islamic extremism and 20 per cent with Christian extremism.[37] These proportions tended to be similar across the continent, though some countries saw much higher percentages as in Guinea Bissau with rates between 54 per cent and 58 per cent of the population concerned about Muslim extremist groups.[38]

It is worth reiterating that many of the issues covered in the survey were not topics of public debate in Mozambique during the 2000s and 2010s. The question of fundamentalism, extremism, and violence was discussed on occasion, but only in the most general terms and with a particular slant—most often as an accusation. At the First National Islamic Conference in 2003, for example, PIMO[39] proposed a debate on a paper it had penned about the 'Phenomenon of Fundamentalism'. The paper stated that fundamentalism is about following the Quran faithfully, and it accused the West not only of labelling the faithful as fundamentalists but as 'terrorists'. The paper argued that 'to condemn Islamic fundamentalism is the same as condemning indirectly the mission of the Holy Messenger of Allah, the prophet Muhamad (S.A.W.) [in Arabic, subhanahu wa ta'ala]'.[40] Less polemical and more thorough was an article on fundamentalism published in the independent Islamic magazine *Al Calam* in 2003, which argued that the West's definition of Islamic fundamentalism as a rejection of modernization and a dogmatic mentality was close to Muslims' own definition of fundamentalism. The problem with the

Western definition, however, was that the West historically associated fundamentalism only with Islam and focused exclusively on the Islamic faith, when the West not only faced its own fundamentalism but was intricately linked to Islamic fundamentalism, which it fostered through its double standards.[41] In turn, in 2015, CISLAMO president Sheik Aminuddin dedicated an opinion piece to the subject of 'terrorism and the "media"'. He began by stating that

> terrorism and, before that, fundamentalism are myths created systematically by some Western intellectuals ... Using these terms, their objective is to distract people from the true problems confronted by society ... Those who practice terrorism, whatever their religion, are criminals who need to be imprisoned and severely punished, as stated in the Al-Qur'án ... The best way to combat terrorism is to respect the fundamental liberties and apply justice to the World.[42]

In short, Muslim intellectuals in Mozambique were clearly concerned about fundamentalism, but much of their (public) energy was not spent discussing the situation in Mozambique but what they perceived to be an accusation coming from 'the West' that good Muslims are fundamentalists.

Finally, it is worth asking whether the elements discussed so far amount to a rise of Islamic fundamentalism and radicalization in Mozambique in the 2000s and 2010s. The answer depends in part, of course, on the definition of radicalization that one adopts. Relying on Zaheer Kazmi's distinction between three 'definitions' of radicalization,[43] one can say the following. If, first, radicalization is to mean a shift towards political violence and terrorism, then these years saw no radicalization. No Muslim leader in Mozambique defended the use of violence, of any sort, and neither did the overwhelming majority of the country's Muslims. At best, a few individuals began to distance themselves from, if not reject, aspects of the secular state. If, second, radicalization is taken to mean a shift towards resistance to domination, then we can identify more wishes for, and action in favour of, integration than opposition and resistance to the state, particularly on the part of the Muslim elite. If, third, radicalization means a shift towards religious revivalism, then we can say that the 2000s and 2010s did see signs of religious renewal (including scripturalism), but with limited political consequences; indeed, scripturalists in Mozambique (not least CISLAMO) are fervent supporters and allies of the state. The most problematic case related to the use of the burqa, the political consequences of which were successfully contained by a coalition of Wahhabi and Sufi Muslim leaders. All in all, then, there was little radicalization in Mozambique in the first two decades of the twenty-first century. Or, if radicalization did take place (in relation to the rejection of the state and a possible move towards the use of violence), this was a fringe phenomenon, in fringe groups and mosques, such as the al-Shabaab sect.[44]

Continuity and change in Muslim organizations

If there was no significant growth of Islam and only some fringe radicalization, what can we see in the development of Islamic organizations in the 2010s? Broadly speaking, the dynamics witnessed in earlier decades continued on the same trajectory as before. CISLAMO continued to expand organizationally and geographically, with the support of international organizations, foreign governments, and the Mozambican state. With the return of dozens of students from Saudi Arabia, Sudan, and Egypt, most of whom joined CISLAMO after their return, the council gained ever more staff to work in its provincial and district delegations, to take control of or serve in new mosques (whether purposely built and handed over by the AMA, or seized legitimately or forcefully from Sufi organizations), and to serve in all sorts of institutions, organizations, and NGOs. The council's top leadership similarly engaged ever more strongly with the state and politics. In 2013, the CISLAMO secretary general became the head of the National Electoral Commission, where he served until 2020. His term was controversial, but his position gave CISLAMO great visibility. Geographically, CISLAMO expanded across the country with its objective of having a mosque and a primary school in each district and a secondary school in each region. After its first secondary school opened in Matola, providing for youth in the south, CISLAMO built a second school in Nacala (Nampula province) in 1993 and a third in Lichinga (Niassa province) in 1997. Consolidating its presence in the north, it opened yet another secondary school in Pemba (Cabo Delgado province) in 2014. In 2011, CISLAMO also opened its first international school in Matola, near Maputo. In terms of training, in 1994 the Hamza Mosque in Matola began training *hafiz*, who were often appointed as imams after their training; its first six students graduated in 1998 and were sent to work at CISLAMO mosques around the country. By 1998, Hamza Mosque had eight professors teaching 100 students—two professors sent by Al-Azhar University in Egypt, two from India, and four Mozambicans.[45]

In the 2000s and 2010s, CISLAMO became less assertive and aggressive, particularly in relation to Sufism. This resulted from the change of its leadership after the death of its first president, Sheik Mágira, in 2000 and the appointment of his successor, Sheik Aminuddin. The new president moved away from his predecessor's confrontational approach and adopted a more conciliatory stance, with the objective of reaching goals in the medium, if not the long term. This shift was also determined by a call for constructive engagement with Sufis, promoted by some CISLAMO members and some Kenyan missionaries (present in Mozambique since 1988).[46] While this stance helped CISLAMO's public image, it did not prevent internal disagreements and divisions. In Cabo Delgado, younger Islamists founded an organization called Ansaru Sunna to contest the leadership of the provincial CISLAMO delegation over issues of age, race, and money. Under the leadership of Ame Chande, the organization was recognized by the provincial government in 1995 and was active until Chande became CISLAMO's provincial director in 2002.[47] In Nampula, a similar organization, called Ansar al-Sunna (or Ahl al-Sunna), appeared in 1998 with broadly the same aims, but it is not clear whether it was recognized by the state and how long it continued to be active, or whether it was just a branch of the Cabo Delgado organization.[48]

If conflict between Wahhabis and Sufis declined, organizations supporting Muslim *turuq* and their leaders continued their efforts to counter Wahhabi expansion. In Cabo Delgado in 2018, the elders of the local Pemba Sufi Islamic community were still trying to regain control of the central Paquitiquete mosque that had been taken from them by force. In 2012, they had written to the provincial Department of Justice, asking for the suspension of the mosque's new leadership on the basis that the building was in a poor state of repair and elections were required as per the mosque's statutes. The state did not respond to the Sufi request, and by 2018 the elders had largely given up on the issue, even more so because most Pemba Muslims had come to consider the Paquitiquete mosque as a CISLAMO site of prayer. Organizationally, the once super-representative pro-Sufi Islamic Congress of Mozambique[49] collapsed in the 2010s and all but disappeared. To a large extent, this was because of the emergence of other pro-Sufi organizations, notably the Beira-based CFI, which emerged in 1992 and began to be noticed on a national level in 2000 when it opened the first Islamic university in the country, Mussa Bin Bique University, in Nampula. In 2001, CFI dissenters founded the Comunidade Islâmica de Moçambique (CIMO), also in Beira.[50] CIMO opened regional delegations (north and south) and an education centre in Beira, and did various social and religious works, particularly in the centre and north of the country (where most Muslims reside). By 2022, it was finishing the construction of a large secondary school and a technical school in Beira, and a primary school, health post, and sports complex in Nampula city.[51] In the early 2010s, ten years after CIMO broke away, the CFI was affected by a major conflict over the direction of its university. The conflict went national in 2012 when different factions nominated different rectors for the university.[52] José Abudo, a CFI co-founder and influential former minister of justice (by then judge of the Supreme Court), lost control of the organization and decided to leave. The CFI never recovered, and thereafter CIMO became the main pro-Sufi organization in the country.

Various other associations and Sufi groups continued to operate, independently or under the umbrella of national organizations such as CIMO. Sufi *turuq*, whose headquarters are still based at Ilha de Moçambique in Nampula province, functioned discreetly, rarely making the headlines in any of the national media. Their reach is hard to evaluate, both numerically and regionally, some having a presence throughout the country (for example, Qadiriyya Sadat), others limited to the north if not solely to the province of Nampula (for example, Qadiriyya Saliquina and Qadiriyya Jailane). In 2013, Qadiriyya Baghdad claimed it had 800 mosques in the province of Nampula alone.[53]

Turning to Pakistani and Indo-Mozambican organizations (also Sufi), the Maputo Muslim Community continued to operate autonomously, organically tied to the Pakistani and Indo-Mozambican business community of Maputo. It related to other Muslim communities in the main towns of the country, for example the Associação Muçulmana de Tete and the Associação Mahometana de Nampula. In Beira, the Muslim Association of Sofala was somewhat different, less diasporic (or ethnic), and with an African element in its leadership that gave it more grounding and visibility.[54] These Pakistani and Indo-Mozambican organizations were well endowed, many members being major traders and industrialists, with a few influential criminal elements. They gave financial support to all political parties, but especially the party in power, while also financially supporting the main Sufi organizations to counterbalance the support CISLAMO received from the party in power, the state, and international donors.[55] Internally, these Pakistani and Indo-Mozambican organizations disagreed over politics, finances, and nationality. A good example is the Maputo Muslim Community, whose president, Momade Bashir Sulemane, had to step down in 2010 after the United States accused him of being a 'drug baron'.[56] In his place, the community elected the Pakistani businessman Saleem Karim, who, by the end of the decade, was also challenged by a Mozambican-born faction that questioned how he had acquired Mozambican nationality and accused him of being involved in dubious business practices.[57] The 2010s saw, finally, an increasing number of kidnappings and assassinations in the Indo-Pakistani community, particularly in Maputo and Beira, and at times abroad, in South Africa or Pakistan, reflecting increasing criminalization of this sector of the Muslim community involved in international drug trafficking.[58]

Regarding the Shia community, it has an old presence in the country too, but almost disappeared after the departure of most of the Ismaili community between 1973 and 1976.[59] In the late 1990s, after the civil war had ended, the community looked into returning in some form. In 2000, the Ismaili Aga Khan Development Network entered Mozambique with a number of business and educational programmes. The community invested in hotels, opened private schools, and engaged in humanitarian aid. After restoring its main *jamaat* (mosque) in Maputo, the community built a new *jamaat* on Ibo island in 2003. The community of believers did not grow much, but its presence strengthened. In 2007, the community's world spiritual leader, the Aga Khan, paid his first visit to the country. He was received officially with pomp and honour by the authorities.[60] More discreetly, the tiny Shia Ithna-asheri (Twelvers) community, based in Nampula, also grew during the same period. In 2001, it established a second *jamaat* in Maputo where several Lebanese and Iranian families had recently settled.[61] In 2011, it built a *jamaat* in Nacala and at that time claimed to have 365 registered members (up from 235 in 1986).[62]

Apart from mosques, education facilities, and businesses, different sectors of the Muslim community invested in the media in the 2000s and 2010s—much like organizations from other faiths were doing.[63] In 1995, Muslims founded two newspapers, *Bilal* and *Crescente*, in Maputo and later several magazines such as *Djá-Al Hak* (based in Beira) and *Al Calam* (based in Matola), while CISLAMO re-started the magazine *Sautul Isslam* (which had ceased publication in 1992). Muslims also invested in radio stations. In 2002, a Muslim shortwave radio station called Voz do Islam was launched in Matola city, near Maputo, and in 2005 CISLAMO founded Radio Haq in partnership with the Sudanese NGO Munazzamat al-Da'wa al-Islamiyya. At first, Radio Haq broadcast only in Nampula province; by 2013, it had expanded to Cabo Delgado, by 2014 to Zambezia, and by 2022 to Sofala and Tete provinces.[64] In the 2000s and 2010s, many Muslims also invested in the Internet. Organizations and radio stations created their own web pages or websites,[65] thus reaching ever more people, and rapidly engaged with social media, particularly Facebook. CISLAMO opened a Facebook page in 2011, the Sufi Qadriyya Baghdad in 2013, and CIMO in 2015.[66] Many committed individuals opened pages and discussion groups to talk about and promote their faith.[67] This multiplication of public media

114

led to an increased visibility and outreach for organizations, though also to some occasional confusion, as for example when a Wahhabi community called its blog 'O Minarete', which was the name of the official publication of the (by then all but defunct) Sufi Islamic Congress.[68] It goes without saying that if social media projected Mozambican Muslims on the web, it also gave them access to people around the world through the latter's websites, social media, and discussion fora. No study exists on this form of cross-influence in Mozambique, but there is little doubt that new ideas made their way into Mozambique in this way, not least new Islamist and jihadi ideas.

In the eyes of the law, Muslim and other religious organizations were equal. This principle did not change in the 2000s and 2010s; the policy deployed by the party in power in Mozambique continued to be one of secularism (in its softer or more passive version). In practice, however, among the Muslim organizations the state was biased towards the Wahhabi CISLAMO, as we saw in previous chapters. Part of the reason for this had to do with the educational level of the CISLAMO leaders and members, which made them good partners to politicians and useful allies for international diplomacy. This point is important because during these decades Frelimo was still battling to regain full and advantageous relations with Muslim states, particularly with the 'reactionary monarchies of the Middle East' (as the head of the DAR called them in 1989), namely countries such as Saudi Arabia, the UAE, and Qatar. A turning point was reached in 1994 when Mozambique joined the OIC and established diplomatic relations with most of these countries.[69] But little happened after that, and by the 2010s relations were still not as productive as the Mozambique government had hoped for. In 2010, Mozambique's president visited Qatar, upon which the semi-official newspaper *Notícias* noted that '[s]ince 1994, when diplomatic relations were established between the two countries, bilateral cooperation has not progressed much. Mutual relations have been limited to the diplomatic field, characterized solely by exchanges of delegations.'[70] The relationship with the UAE was apparently not much better. It was only in 2015 that a diplomatic representation for the UAE was finally opened in Mozambique, twenty-one years after Mozambique joined the OIC.[71]

Conclusion

This chapter was concerned with developments in Muslim politics in the first two decades of the twenty-first century. It looked, first, at the issue of religious growth, then the issue of radicalization, and finally changes among Muslim organizations in the country. What the chapter revealed is, first, that there was some limited growth of Islam over this period, with a small rise in the number of converts, increased visibility, and the appearance of new religious approaches, though the rise in numbers was significantly less than that of other monotheist religions. The south, where some growth took place, differed from central and northern Mozambique, where stagnation or even regression was witnessed, according to national statistics, with the exception of the province of Nampula (though the numbers for the latter could fall within the statistical margin of error). All in all, there was not the massive growth that some commentators have maintained.

Second, the chapter revealed that radicalization affected only some fringe groups and a few individuals. National Muslim leaders clearly supported the secular state, actively engaged with it, negotiated and compromised with it, while still demanding more respect and some adaptation to their needs and customs. Among the broader Muslim population, we saw complex ideas in favour of sharia law and the return of the Mahdi but also strong support for gender equality, religious freedom, and democratization. What was visible is not so much radical ideas as complex views and dynamic engagement with the existing society and state.

Finally, we saw that transformations among Muslim organizations were minor, that the broad dynamics of Sufism vs Wahhabism continued, and that the state's alliance with Muslims remained, as before, primarily an alliance with Wahhabism, rather than one with Sufism, as in Tanzania. This is in line with the dynamics and politics of the previous decades. Added to the previous points, this stands in stark opposition to the increasingly popular conception (we can now say misconception) that many, if not all, Muslims in Mozambique underwent major changes or even a form of 'radicalization' in those years.

5

2017
THE BIRTH OF A JIHADI INSURGENCY

For more than five years, the province of Cabo Delgado in northern Mozambique has faced an armed insurgency. It began in October 2017 when insurgents occupied the town of Mocímboa da Praia for forty-eight hours and stole armaments, only fleeing to the bush when police reinforcements arrived. Since then, the insurgency has grown into a typical guerrilla war. At first, the attacks took place at night, against small villages. In 2018, the insurgents began to stage their assaults during the day. In 2019, they began targeting small towns, army outposts, and transport on roads. By early 2020, they had overrun district capitals and circulated videos articulating a clear jihadi agenda (see Appendix V). In July 2019, they pledged allegiance to the Islamic State of Iraq and the Levant (more commonly known as ISIS). With this, ISIS began to take responsibility for more and more of the attacks in Mozambique. The government reacted by sending troops to the north of the country, securing towns and villages, and hunting down insurgents. In 2019, it hired mercenaries, and an international intervention followed in 2021. While this did not end the insurgency, it managed to degrade it and contain it to a geographical area covering about half of Cabo Delgado province (around 30,000 km^2). As the insurgency continues, in a renewed guerrilla format, many wonder what is coming next. This requires that we understand who the insurgents are and what they want.

There is much debate about the causes, origins, and nature of the insurgency in Mozambique. A first dimension of the debate relates to the religious nature of the conflict. Various commentators and authors, such as Joseph Hanlon, argue that the cause of the conflict is material deprivation, particularly poverty, marginalization, and a lack of opportunities among the youth, with religion functioning only as 'rallying point' or cloak.[1] These authors highlight that Cabo Delgado is one of Mozambique's poorest provinces and one of the areas where considerable discoveries of gas have created unmet expectations as international companies are still in the process of building an LNG industry in the area. Other authors, such as Saide Habibe, Salvador Forquilha, and João Pereira, argue the opposite, namely that Islam is a key, if not the central factor behind the insurgency. They posit that young Muslims in Mozambique have been radicalized under the influence of preachers from Kenya and Tanzania.[2] Some point more widely to Wahhabism and the Mozambican students who studied at Saudi Arabian, Egyptian, and Sudanese universities.[3]

A second dimension of the debate relates to gauging the external nature of the insurgency. Many authors see it as originating from inside Mozambique, some arguing, as we have seen, that it relates to local poverty, inequality, and marginalization. Others argue, however, that it either came from the outside or is the result of a foreign influence. The International Crisis Group, following the UN Monitoring Group, makes the case for an external origin in that it sees the insurgency as the work of Kenyan militants, who, repressed by the government of Tanzania where they had taken refuge, fled to Mozambique.[4] David M. Matsinhe and Estácio Valoi, in turn, argue only for an external influence when reporting an interviewee saying that jihadist thinking was 'imported' from abroad; similarly, Habibe, Forquilha, and Pereira point to the ideological influences of foreign preachers, such as Sheik Abu Rogo.[5] In the face of these divergent arguments and approaches, the research for this chapter began from the premise that we need to know who the insurgents are, where they come from, and what they say they want to achieve before we can engage in any discussion of the religious or foreign nature of

118

their actions. To achieve this, I began research with the first attack on 5 October 2017 to identify who was involved.

The perspective of this chapter is historical and sociological, aiming at analysing, as Raufu Mustapha put it, 'the internal dynamics and historicity of African Muslim societies'.[6] Following Ngala Chome, the text also gives due consideration to the ideas of insurgents and the evolution of their thinking on Islam and politics.[7] Research was conducted during two stints of fieldwork in Cabo Delgado in 2018 and 2019. With the help of local research assistants, I conducted over fifty interviews with Muslim leaders, state officials, workers at NGOs, people affected by the insurgency, and two former insurgents. Different actors and government officials involved in Cabo Delgado also shared written materials. In view of the sensitivity of the situation, I decided to anonymize all names of interviewers and interviewees, and the locations and dates of the interviews. On the basis of this research, the chapter is organized into three sections. The first looks at the nature of the group behind the insurgency; the second investigates the origin and early history of the insurgent group; and the third explores why the so-called al-Shabaab shifted to armed violence after years of relatively peaceful existence and what internationalization it has undergone since. It argues that behind the insurgency lies a religious sect, one that began around the year 2007 and that shifted from Islamism to violent jihadism in the mid-2010s.

Nature of the insurgency in Cabo Delgado

The first attack in Cabo Delgado took place on 5 October 2017 in the town of Mocímboa da Praia. Media reports, interviews, images, and videos all suggest that most of the insurgents were from the town of Mocímboa da Praia itself. The majority had grown up there, some were from other districts of Cabo Delgado, and a few had 'foreign accents', but most of them had been living in the town before the attack. Many local people recognized the attackers and reported that they belonged to what they called the al-Shabaab religious sect. According to these accounts, the sect had a mosque in the town's Nanduadua neighbourhood and was in the process of building another new mosque adjacent to the first one. For several days after the attack, the police tried to deny this, but then they destroyed the mosque as well as buildings associated with the sect in other towns. Some lower-level state officials also made private and public claims confirming that a religious sect was behind the attack, as did members and lower officials of religious institutions. The head of the Islamic Council in Mocímboa da Praia explained, for example, that 'the presence of individuals with ideologies of a radical tendency has been noticed in recent times and had been reported to the authorities'.[8] The administrator of Mocímboa similarly declared that 'some of them are our children from various neighbourhoods and villages. It is a mixture of citizens who got involved in this confusion.'[9] The Maputo newspaper *O País* (which dispatched journalists to Cabo Delgado on 6 October) reported on 9 October that 'the truth is that all the residents of this town have absolutely no doubt that the attacks were carried out by members of the al-Shabaab sect'.[10]

If there was no doubt locally about who was behind the attacks of 5 October 2017, there was some disagreement over the name of the sect behind the insurgents. Some thought it was called al-Shabaab, while others called it al-Sunnah Wal-Jamâa. A few journalists reported the name Swahili Sunnah, a term taken up by the influential independent newssheet *mediaFAX* (Maputo) and the linked weekly newspaper *Savana* (Maputo). But I was unable to confirm this name on the ground, and the scholars Habibe, Forquilha, and Pereira, who did extensive research on the insurgents in Mocímboa da Praia, do not even mention the term.[11] The population on the ground used al-Shabaab to refer to the sect. It means 'youth' in Arabic (most sect members are young, locals explained), and the men behaved like the al-Shabaab organization in Somalia, that is, forcefully, if not violently. By 2018–19, this had become the most popular name for the insurgency, in Cabo Delgado and nationally, among the population and in newspapers, on television, and in other media. It is also the name the insurgents have been using themselves, orally and in written notes. As to the term 'al-Sunnah Wal-Jamâa', researchers Habibe, Forquilha, and Pereira posit that the sect tried to appropriate it because it means 'adepts of the prophetic tradition and the consensus', which is the name by which the mainstream Muslim majority in Cabo Delgado (and elsewhere) calls itself.[12] In other words, it seems the insurgents tried to use this name to present themselves as the legitimate holders of religious orthodoxy. This name-giving failed, however, because Muslim leaders and the population rejected their use of 'Al Sunnah Wal-Jamâa' and instead called them 'al-Shabaab'—a term the insurgents eventually re-appropriated.[13]

What did the insurgents and their sect intend with their attack on 5 October 2017? Contrary to what the national police spokesperson claimed on the subsequent days, they did not attack people indiscriminately with the aim of 'sowing fear and terror to the population and installing public disorder'.[14] Rather, they were very selective and purposeful in their attack. A citizen reported to a journalist that he came across the leader of the al-Shabaab sect and four armed men as he and some friends were walking to the mosque at around 5.00 am on the morning of the attack. The leader told the men that they were not at risk as he and his armed men were only going after the state's armed forces; they would not attack civilians unless they denounced them to the police.[15] Another Mocímboa resident explained: 'They had a machete, a knife, and a machine gun and one told me not to be afraid because they were only after the police.'[16] An old woman encountered the insurgents early in the morning too, upon which they instructed her to go back into her house; another testimony declared: '[O]n the first attack, they crossed my path and informed me not to run and to go back home.'[17] A district administrator confirmed this in an interview in 2018, saying: 'On 5 October, they focused on the police force. They were not preoccupied with civilians, else it would have been serious. They tried to weaken the position [of the armed forces] in the town, but thanks to the help we received, we rapidly managed to chase them away.'[18]

Many of Mocímboa's inhabitants explained that the insurgents and their sect rejected the secular state and wanted to introduce sharia rule. The administrator of the district of Palma (also affected by the nascent insurgency) said that it was a 'group which fights against the government or lawfulness, they do not want children to study, and they enter mosques with their shoes'.[19] A resident of Nanduadua explained further:

> If I were to have problems with my wife, then I should not go to the police station, it has to be to these *monhés* [sic][20] of marriage issues, not the [police] station. [If there is] a problem with crime, one should not go to the police, one should use Islamic law. That is what they wanted. They demanded that the statues of Samora Machel and Eduardo Mondlane be removed in town as well as the Christian crosses at the entrance of town, because this is an area dominated by Muslims and there should be no Christian symbols.[21]

Investigative journalist Lázaro Mabunda, who began researching the group before October 2017, explained in a similar vein a few days after the first attack that

> [t]hey do not accept that children go to school because to them the only acceptable school is the Muslim one. There is no other [school] they accept. They do not recognize state schools. Their food habits have to be in line with what they believe too. Besides, the group says there is only one Supreme Being on earth: Allah, and no one else.[22]

The interviews conducted during my research in 2018 and 2019 confirmed these elements and revealed more characteristics about the sect. Members had a distinctive dress code: women had to wear the burqa while men wore shortened trousers, a scarf around their (shaved) head, a beard, and a knife. This dress was worn by many of the men caught, killed, photographed, or filmed on 5 October 2017. Concerning prayer, the sect saw men praying with arms folded across their chests, not wearing the *cofió*, keeping their shoes on inside the mosque, and praying only three times a day instead of the usual five times for Sunni Muslims. The prayer element seems to indicate the sect is scripturalist and maybe even Quranist. An informant explained that there were two groups in al-Shabaab before 2017, and in one they 'pray with their shoes in the mosque, and they only follow what is in the Quran; they don't want to know the sayings of the Prophet'.[23] The group also forbade women to do any work

122

outside the home, including agricultural work (traditionally done by women). They denounced the existing political and religious order as corrupt and pronounced all those involved in these structures as infidels. They refused to greet or respond to greetings from people they considered infidels and did not hesitate to denounce such people in public, particularly those who worked for the state administration. An Islamic teacher declared in an interview:

> They had attitudes and gestures that were foreign to our religion, for example the prohibition of children to study in schools, the prohibition to vote, marriages which did not follow the law, teachings in which they recommended to insult misbelievers and not respect parents, the government, and [other] religious leaders.[24]

We can draw two conclusions from these descriptions. First, these men identified as Islamists, that is to say as individuals who reject the secular state and want to apply sharia law.[25] They did not simply follow Islamic religious principles but wanted to establish a sharia-based political order. As Bassam Tibi puts it: '"Islamism is not Islam", even if the two are connected. Islam is a religion while Islamism is a political ideology, a form of "religionized politics", aiming at establishing a sharia-based political order.'[26]

Second, these individuals constituted a religious sect. Instead of trying to change the political order, they withdrew from it and cut themselves off from society so as to apply sharia rule for themselves. They demanded that their members not engage with the secular systems of justice, health, and education; instead, they offered these services within their mosques, thus developing a 'counter-society'. By definition, sects are newly formed religious groups that protest elements of their parent religion and society. They operate in high tension with these, denouncing them as 'corrupt' while claiming to represent a return to the 'true religion'.[27] The group we know as al-Shabaab in Mozambique meets this definition: it was an Islamist sect until 2017 (when it decided to stop withdrawing from society and went on the attack in order to change society).

Tellingly, the state and most Muslim leaders in Cabo Delgado understood al-Shabaab as a 'sect' before 2017. They referred to it in

TOWARDS JIHAD?

those terms and described it with the very characteristics just listed. Most exhaustively and tellingly, mainstream Islamic leaders discussed al-Shabaab at their national Islamic Conference held in Nampula on 10–13 November 2016. The leaders, mostly from CISLAMO, discussed three themes, one of which was 'emergent sects' in the country. Their focus lay on Shia Muslims and the 'Al Shabab' (sic), whose presence they discussed in relation to the north-eastern provinces of Zambezia, Nampula, and Cabo Delgado. Shia Muslims were considered a problem in all three provinces, al-Shabaab only in Cabo Delgado. In a presentation on Cabo Delgado, the following points were made about al-Shabaab:

- they discourage formal education in public institutions (school, university, etc.);
- they do not respect Islamic principles;
- they allow weddings without the consent of the girl's parents;
- they carry knives, which symbolize jihad;
- they do not accept dialogue;
- they incite violence and dissatisfaction against the teachers of ISLAM;
- [they promise] attacks against the Ahle Sunnat Wal Jammat [i.e. the mainstream Muslim community].[28]

This is congruent with the descriptions given by Mocímboa residents and with details uncovered by my research. In sum, it is clear that the men who attacked Mocímboa da Praia in October 2017 were from an Islamist sect present primarily in Cabo Delgado and known as al-Shabaab. The sect existed before 2017, and Muslim leaders and others had already discussed its existence, and what should be done about it, before it began to engage in armed violence. I now turn to the question of where the sect came from.

Origins of the al-Shabaab sect

My investigations in the south of the province of Cabo Delgado identified the first manifestation of the sect in the district of Balama in 2007. The sect might have emerged there and then, but it could have begun earlier and in a different district. I say this because I was

124

not able to do research in other parts of Cabo Delgado and because a Muslim leader reported that a similar movement had appeared earlier on, in 1989–90 in Nangade district. The adepts of that earlier sect claimed to be followers of Moses, a prophet in the Muslim tradition. They had a dress code similar to that of the members of the present-day al-Shabaab. The sheik explained: 'They were young, they cut their trousers, they cut their hair, [they wore] a beard, and [they walked with a] wooden stick. In the mosque, they prayed woman, man, woman, man.'[29]

This description reveals that the Nangade group had unusual views and practices, several of which correspond to those of al-Shabaab—haircut, beard, short trousers, and a different way of praying in the mosque. At the time, mainstream Islamic organizations in Cabo Delgado considered the group a risk, and in 1990 the sheik interviewed was tasked with going to Nangade to help the administrator 'contain' the religious group. They talked to some members of the sect and arrested others. Eventually, 'by force, the group faded', the sheik explained. Because the Nangade group acted like the contemporary al-Shabaab, the sheik speculated that the members of the 1989–90 group could be the same as those of the sect today, though he could not point to any specific element that would prove a direct relationship between the two sects.[30] More research will be needed on this point. In the meantime, we can conclude that either the al-Shabaab sect is quite old or that it has connections with an older sect, or it is part of a broader sectarian dynamic; in any case, we need to think of the al-Shabaab sect as part of a broader dynamic and history of Islamic sects in northern Mozambique.[31]

My research in 2018–19 found the earliest manifestation of al-Shabaab in the district of Balama in 2007. This was the year in which a young man, Sualehe Rafayel, of Makua ethnicity, returned to his birth village of Nhacole (also known as Muapé) (see Map 3) after spending several years in Tanzania. He joined the local Wahhabi mosque, recently built by the AMA, an NGO from Kuwait. He had a different approach to the Islamic faith than other believers, rejecting several existing practices and ideas as *haram* (proscribed by Islamic law). He tried to convert members of this mosque as well as other mosques to his ways. Tensions rapidly rose between Sheik Sualehe

TOWARDS JIHAD?

and other Muslims in Nhacole, including CISLAMO. Sheik Sualehe therefore withdrew from the Wahhabi mosque and went to build his own site of prayer, approaching the authorities for authorization on 3 May 2007.[32] There he put his own ideas and principles into practice with a group of male and female followers. The person who was the official head of Nhacole village at the time described their ideas and principles as follows:

> When Muslims finish their prayers, they always clean their face and wash their legs or feet. Yet there [in Sualehe's mosque], you could not clean either your face or your feet before and after prayers. If you did, these practices were considered *haram*. The believers would not use the Muslim *cofió* of CISLAMO, but the men had to wear a cloth around the head; although some actually did not do that either. What they did is not wear the *cofió* of CISLAMO. Women's dress, we know and we could see that they covered the whole body with a black dress, and we asked ourselves: do women not suffer from the heat with this sort of dress? Men dressed with short pants, which were not full pants in the real sense of the term.[33]

Although Sheik Sualehe had withdrawn to his own mosque, tensions between him and other Muslims continued, particularly with CISLAMO. There were many points of contention between Sheik Sualehe and the mainstream (and overwhelming majority of) Sufi Muslims of the area; for the Wahhabi sheik, the main point of disagreement was the believer's relations with the state. While Sheik Sualehe rejected the state categorically, CISLAMO worked with it closely. This led to a clash between Sualehe and CISLAMO as Sualehe denounced those who worked with the state as *kaffir* (unbelievers). After an exchange of letters and at least one meeting (on 16 May 2010) to resolve their differences,[34] CISLAMO decided to go to the state and formally raise a complaint against Sheik Sualehe. The district administrator looked into the issue and eventually decided to imprison Sualehe and some of his followers. On 21 March 2011, the administrator held a meeting with the imprisoned Sheik Sualehe and his followers to explain that the state would not allow anyone preaching the rejection of the (secular) state and preventing their children from going to school. The sheik decided to leave the district, and he and some of his followers went to Tanzania.[35] Sheik Sualehe returned to Nhacole for a short visit (or possibly two visits) before establishing himself elsewhere in the province. No interviewees could say where exactly he went after leaving Nhacole. This is an important question that needs further research, first, to ascertain whether Sheik Sualehe could be the founder of the al-Shabaab sect and, second, to trace whether and how he disseminated his ideas and practices in the province.

What we know is that Sualehe did not flee to the district of Chiure. Here the sect began in 2014 (possibly in 2013), and the founder of the group was a man called Abdul Carimo. Born in Chiure, of Makua ethnicity, Abdul Carimo is said to have been influenced by a sheik from Mocímboa da Praia, where the al-Shabaab sect was established one or two years earlier.[36] After joining the sect, Carimo began to clash with believers at his regular mosque in Chiure. To further his views and practices, Sheik Abdul decided to set up his own mosque at his home in the neighbourhood of Namuita. Some people followed him, and Sheik Abdul turned his house into a compound with a madrasa and several other houses.[37] Later an affiliated mosque opened in the neighbourhood of Nhamissir. As with Sheik Sualehe in Balama, other Muslims were unhappy with the presence of this sect, and on several occasions CISLAMO tried to get Sheik Abdul and his followers to abandon their efforts.[38]

On 4 October 2015, the sect came to the attention of the Chiure authorities when members verbally vilified an official ceremony taking place in town for Peace Day. The following year, sect members protested again, shouting that the Peace Day ceremony was *haram*.[39] A month later, in early November 2016, things turned bad when sect members in Intutupué, in neighbouring Ancuabe district, clashed with other Muslims and killed one of them. Six of the men who were involved in the killing fled to Chiure town, where the police immediately arrested them. The following day, on 3 November 2016, the residents of Chiure were instructed by the local administration to destroy the al-Shabaab mosque in Nhamissir neighbourhood just as thirty-six sect members armed with knives and machetes besieged the local police station, demanding the liberation of their arrested colleagues from Intutupué. Violence erupted in Nhamissir on the following day as sect members demanded the return of the building materials from their destroyed mosque, which the authorities had confiscated. When a believer threw a machete at the police, they fired back, injuring Sheik Abdul. The police arrested twenty-one men, who were rapidly put on trial and condemned to a fifteen-month prison sentence. In turn, the police sent the Intutupué men back to Ancuabe district, where they were placed on trial and also sentenced to jail terms. The injured Sheik Abdul, for his part, was sent to hospital before going to jail, but he and a colleague escaped from the hospital as soon as their health improved. He was recaptured during the course of 2017 and is reported to have died in jail in 2018.[40]

Despite these difficulties—and sometimes because of them—the al-Shabaab sect expanded across the province of Cabo Delgado through the 2010s. The National Islamic Conference that took place in Nampula in 2016 concluded that, by the end of that year, the sect was prevalent in four districts of Cabo Delgado province, namely Palma, Nangade, Mocímboa da Praia, and Montepuez.[41] There were also signs of its presence in Macomia and Quissanga, where problems arose in 2015 and 2017. In other words, by 2016 al-Shabaab had a presence in at least five districts of Cabo Delgado and had been expelled from another three, namely Balama, Ancuabe, and Chiure (see Map 3). Other researchers have more recently identified the sect as having had a presence in Mecula, Niassa province, and Memba, Nampula province.[42] It is not clear whether the sect had any headquarters by 2016, but if they did, it was probably in Mocímboa da Praia: its leaders lived in Mocímboa, and by 2016–17 the sect had two mosques in the town. The history of the sect in Mocímboa da Praia is not yet fully clear. Researchers Habibe, Forquilha, and Pereira suggest that it started there as early as 2013 or 2014.[43] An account by a Sufi sheik I interviewed suggests an even earlier date: the sheik declared he travelled to Mocímboa in 2010, and again in 2011, to resolve conflicts between his Sufi community and the al-Shabaab sect, suggesting that the sect had begun there in 2010.[44]

128

Map 3. Presence of the al-Shabaab sect in
Mozambique before 2017

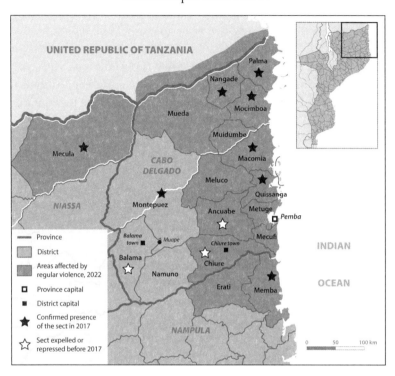

Source: Designed by Dorian Ryser (CERI, SciencesPo). Map updated in 2022

Shift to violence and international links

What induced the al-Shabaab sect to engage in violent action in October 2017? While verbally aggressive, in its initial years the sect seemed intent on withdrawing from and functioning separately from society. What brought about the shift from building a counter-society under sharia rule to waging jihad to transform the state and society? Habibe, Forquilha, and Pereira refer to the militarization of al-Shabaab in 2015, but they are silent on why this happened.[45] My research assistants and I interviewed several individuals in Cabo Delgado who said that, from the very beginning, the sect had a military dimension—that its members had always received military training.[46]

This seems improbable. For one, why would they have trained for ten years without engaging in any armed action? For another, several police authorities told us clearly that up to 2017 they never found any proof for the distribution of arms among sect members; all that the sect members had were locally bought machetes and knives.[47] It might thus be that the military dimension is read into the sect's past in light of the recent violent action. Following on Habibe, Forquilha, and Pereira and other interviews, it instead seems to be the case that the sect shifted to a violent approach in or around 2015. Building on data gathered from different sources, I suggest that the sect shifted its overall strategy after being opposed by mainstream Muslim organizations and increasingly being repressed by the state—with the tipping point reached around 2016.

While on various occasions mainstream Muslim leaders dealt with the sect on their own by trying to engage them in dialogue and debate, from the very start of its existence they also lobbied the state to act against the sect. In Balama district, this led to the sect's expulsion in 2011. In many, if not most other districts, however, state administrators refused to intervene. Like the governor of Cabo Delgado, they saw the conflict as an intra-Muslim affair and reckoned that it was not the role of a representative of the secular state to intervene in a disagreement over religious interpretation and practice.[48] This understanding changed in 2015–16, however, when the sect engaged in a series of violent clashes with state authorities. Violence began at the latest in November 2015 when al-Shabaab members forcefully tried to prevent the sale of alcohol in the village of Pangane, district of Macomia. Bar and shop owners called the police for help, thus inflaming the situation; a member of the sect eventually stabbed a police officer to death; in turn, the police injured two sect members.[49] Though it is not clear whether the government acted in response to this attack, it deported two Kenyan and Tanzanian sect members (possibly leaders) from Mocímboa da Praia in the same year.[50] Then, in November 2016, violence took place in Intutupué (Ancuabe district) during which one man was killed and several sect members fled to Chiure. This led to violence in Chiure town, during which the town's sect leader was shot, twenty-seven sect members were jailed, and the town's al-Shabaab mosques were destroyed, as we saw earlier. This list of events is probably not exhaustive, but we know that repression continued, if not increased, in 2017 with the state detaining many al-Shabaab men in Quissanga and Macomia districts for calling on the population not to respect the secular state.[51] The police in Macomia district explained their actions against the sect in June 2017 in the following manner: 'These three citizens are creating disinformation, calling on the population not to respect the existence of the Government, calling for disrespect to the authorities, non-attendance of schools, and the use of cutting objects such as knives and other instruments for self-protection.'[52] In other words, not only was there an increasing number of incidents in 2015–16 but by late 2016 the government was actively countering the sect and arresting men for belonging to it. It is probable that the sect leaders concluded thereafter that building and living in a counter-society was no longer possible. This may have been the point at which they shifted their strategy of achieving their goal of living in a sharia-based political order from one of withdrawing from society to one of attacking the state, in order to change the way society operated. They would have thus shifted from Islamist sectarianism to armed jihadism.[53]

The emergence of the al-Shabaab sect and its shift to armed jihadism around 2016 did not happen in a vacuum. When the sect emerged in the 2000s, the province of Cabo Delgado was one of the poorest in Mozambique (a situation that has not changed in the meantime). It was and remains an area deeply divided between Muslims and Christians, not so much because of religion per se as because religious divisions are superimposed on to ethnic, social, political, and power divisions. These are not essential divisions, but social and historical constructs that have crystallized over time.[54] The result is that the coastal Makua (Makua-Meto) and Mwani communities form a Muslim majority while the minority Makonde, Christian by religion, hold the social, economic, and political power in the province. Both the Makua but even more the Mwani resent this domination in light of their own 'glorious' precolonial Islamic and Swahili past (albeit as slave traders). The Makonde have always been a backbone for the ruling Frelimo party (with a Makonde elected as its president in late 2014), while the Mwani have historically aligned themselves with the opposition Renamo party (particularly since the multiparty elections of 1994).[55] Tensions are particularly strong in certain towns. In Mocímboa da Praia, which is divided along sectarian lines, ethnic riots erupted in 2005 when Renamo rejected the results of the national election and sectarian looting and killing took place.[56]

The 2000s were also uncertain in economic terms. An illegal economy flourished with smuggling, illegal mining of minerals, poaching, and drug trafficking, while a liberal (and relatively weak) local government allowed the immigration of many individuals from Tanzania and other African countries.[57] Even in the religious sphere things were changing fast and becoming more uncertain. Intra-Muslim tensions developed with the introduction of Wahhabi institutions in Cabo Delgado in the 1990s and 2000s, led by CISLAMO and AMA.[58] There was also competition from new Christian organizations that moved into the province in the 1990s and 2000s to convert the last 'un-churched' communities in the world, namely the Mwani and Makua-Meto of Cabo Delgado.[59]

Despite this evidence, many intellectuals, religious actors, and politicians refuse to accept that the armed violence has anything to do with the dynamics of the Muslim society of Cabo Delgado. They believe instead that the insurgency is a conspiracy. Various theories exist, ranging from a conspiracy by a foreign power (for example, the US Central Intelligence Agency)[60] or private interests (oil companies aiming to control Mozambique's natural resources),[61] to a Muslim conspiracy (jihadists 'moving down' the eastern coastline of Africa) or a political conspiracy from within Mozambique (a Frelimo faction aiming to undermine the country's Makonde president).[62] Underpinning many of these arguments is a view that the insurgents have 'no face' and their political religion is a cloak or smokescreen for objective material or political interests.[63] The problem with such arguments is that we know the origins and details of the insurgency, thus that the al-Shabaab sect emerged in the mid- or late 2000s in Cabo Delgado. Yet this time frame was before gas was discovered off the Mozambican coast, before jihadi violence became serious in Tanzania, and long before a Makonde became president in Mozambique. That does not mean that there cannot be a conspiracy in relation to this insurgency, but that, if there is one, it either had to be fomented before 2007 (which is unlikely) or had to take place at later stages through infiltration or manipulation, something that is quite different from a full conspiracy. A related argument is that the al-Shabaab insurgency originated from outside the country, linked to a 'jihadi international'.[64] As the present research shows, the insurgency built on a Mozambican religious sect whose leadership was primarily Mozambican. It thus seems difficult to sustain an argument for an 'external invasion' or even an 'import' that caused the insurgency. There are of course external influences, connections, and collaborations (the extent and nature of which still need to be investigated properly and systematically), but this is different from an import or invasion. What happened in northern Mozambique is either the internationalization of a local religious sect or the development of a sect in interaction with regional/international elements.

Looking at the issue in more detail, we must ask: What are the insurgents' regional links today? Politicians, analysts, and researchers agree there are many links, particularly with Tanzania, Kenya, the DRC, Uganda, and Somalia. The connections with Tanzania are clear and well established: the sect's supreme leader is reported to be a Tanzanian (AbuYasir Hassan),[65] and several key figures areTanzanians, for example, Amisse Mucuthaya, Abdul Azize, and Faraji Nankalava (also known as Njorogue) (the latter killed in combat).[66] As Tanzania borders Mozambique, some of the insurgent leaders visited, studied, and lived there for a time, as did Sheik Sualehe Rafayel and Abdala Likongo—Likongo was an entrepreneur from Mocímboa da Praia who went abroad to study and became, on his return, one of the top leaders of the sect and now of the insurgency.[67] Like Ibn Omar, Likongo also seems to have travelled to Kenya for training and/or to attempt to reach Somalia. Concerning Kenya, many references are also made about audio recordings of the Kenyan Sheik Abu Rogo's sermons circulating in Cabo Delgado.[68]

The DRC is another important link for the Mozambican jihadi group. We know that some Congolese are fighting in the insurgency in Mozambique; some men jailed by the Mozambican police proudly claimed to be jihadists, and a woman who was captured but managed to flee the insurgents revealed she was married forcefully to a Congolese jihadist while in the bush.[69] There are also persistent rumours that one or two leaders are Congolese (a certain Sheik Muhammud and Mafuriko have been mentioned), though this has not been confirmed. Finally, the UN group of experts on the Congo claimed in June 2023 that jihadi fighters and leaders had repeatedly travelled between the Congo and Mozambique (two visits for the top leaders of the Mozambican insurgency) and that the Congolese jihadis saw al-Shabaab as answerable to them because they had made their pledge to ISIS through them, something the Mozambicans contested and that was ultimately resolved in early 2022 with the creation of an autonomous Mozambique province of ISIS.[70]

As to Somalia, the same UN group of experts saw e-mail correspondence from captured computers revealing that in 2021 the al-Shabaab leadership sent extensive reports to ISIS-Somalia showing that the insurgents recognized this group as its superior. A previous report from the same UN group indicated that a Somalian jihadist had travelled to Mozambique in 2020, presumably to train Mozambican jihadists.[71]

Finally, the picture of the relationship with Uganda is confused but important to discuss to remind us of the uncertainty of sources and the necessity to triangulate information. Studies looking at Ugandan connections with the Mozambican insurgency all rely on a single story about a certain Abdul Rahim Faisal who is said to have been a leader of the insurgency in Mozambique until his arrest in 2018.[72] The story came to the attention of scholars in January 2019 after the man and two accomplices were arrested and presented to the public in Nampula, including on national television. Journalists critically assessed the government's claim and soon uncovered that Faisal and his two collaborators had in fact already been arrested a year earlier and presented to the public in another town in Cabo Delgado.[73] The 2018 arrest had been announced on the very day that the president of Uganda arrived in Mozambique for an official visit (17 April 2018).[74] At the time, officials revealed that Faisal had been the leader of the radical Usafi mosque in Kampala, allegedly linked to the jihadi Allied Democratic Forces in the Congo, which the Ugandans had raided three weeks earlier. After an investigation,

Ugandan newspapers revealed a strong suspicion that Faisal was a government spy planted in the Usafi mosque to catch 'radicals' (a claim the Ugandan police publicly denied).[75] The chronology of Faisal's move to Mozambique also raises questions: the Mozambican authorities declared that he left his mosque in Uganda just before it was raided in April 2018, yet he was arrested in Mozambique in January 2018.[76] One Ugandan newspaper claimed that one of Faisal's companions disappeared from his home in Uganda on 29 December 2017.[77] Could Faisal have travelled with him? Whether on that date or a little earlier, the issue remains that there was only a few weeks between him leaving Uganda and being arrested in Mozambique, so the question emerges of whether Faisal could have travelled to Cabo Delgado, joined the insurgency, and risen through its ranks to become a key leader within that period of time. Is this possible? Odd police announcements, offbeat dates, and the accusation that Faisal was a Ugandan state spy should make all scholars wary of this case. This is not to say that there are no Ugandan connections, but rather that Faisal is at best a problematic example and should not be used as proof for links between Uganda and al-Shabaab. Other evidence is needed to sustain scientifically that there is a link between the insurgents.

At this point, it is worth discussing the insurgents' connections to ISIS. When did they connect to the Islamic State? Drawing from the chronology in Table 5, we can say with certainty that the Mozambican insurgents pledged allegiance to ISIS before August 2018, that is, before the ISIS supreme leader al-Baghdadi made a reference, in a publicized speech, to the creation of an ISIS Central Africa Province (ISCAP) that included the DRC and Mozambique.[78] Al-Baghdadi's statement implied that the Congolese and Mozambican jihadists had already made a pledge and that ISIS had agreed to it, if only to the point of creating a *wilayat* (province) for them.

It is not clear when exactly before August 2018 the insurgents made their request to join ISIS. In late January 2018, the insurgents circulated a video clip (see Appendix V) where they stated that they were not receiving help from anyone and had started out without any outside help. This seems to indicate that the question of external help had become an issue and possibly that there was disagreement over it. Then in May 2018 a photograph circulated on the Telegram account of an ISIS sympathizer of (mostly foreign) insurgents in the bush of Cabo Delgado (with a handmade ISIS flag), with a note that al-Shabaab would soon pledge its allegiance to ISIS.[79] This implies the issue had been agreed upon and a pledge was about to be made. Consequently, it looks like an allegiance request was made after May 2018 and before August 2018, that is, in June or July 2018. The request was provisionally accepted in August 2018, when ISCAP was created, and formally and publicly accepted a year later, on 24 July 2019, when ISIS circulated a video showing the renewal of the pledge of allegiance (thus making it official). This means the final acceptance probably took place a little earlier, possibly in May 2019, since ISIS claimed its first attack in Mozambique on 4 June 2019.[80]

Table 5. Key dates for ISIS in Mozambique

End of January 2018	Short video by insurgents stating 'We do not need help from anyone because we are not capable [sic]. But since we have started like this, *Inch Allah*, we trust in Him, Allah will always always [sic] look at [after?] us.'
31 May 2018	Photo circulates on an ISIS sympathizer's Telegram channel showing four insurgents, with a caption saying an allegiance to ISIS would come soon.
22 August 2018	ISIS leader al-Baghdadi mentions a Central African province (no details).
4 June 2019	ISIS claims its first attack in Mozambique.
24 July 2019	ISIS announces the renewal of the pledge of allegiance from the Central African province (Congo and Mozambique).

There is a debate over what this connection and pledge of allegiance to ISIS mean. A Portuguese pundit wrote in 2020 that the Mozambican pledge had led to a major influx of foreign fighters and commanders into Cabo Delgado (he speaks of no fewer than forty commanders) and to the 'friendly acquisition' of al-Shabaab by ISIS in the DRC.[81] In contrast, an influential British-based journalist argued in April 2021 that ISIS still had no influence on the strategic direction of the insurgency.[82] Researchers of ISIS in Africa at large offer another key to understand what is happening. They argue that ISIS does not seek to exert direct control over the groups and organizations with which it affiliates, and hence there is not, nor would there normally be, any acquisition or taking of control by ISIS of the strategic direction of al-Shabaab. Instead, the Islamic State associates itself with insurgents and allows them much autonomy in their daily operations. Many authors talk of a 'franchising' system.[83] Jason Warner and colleagues talk of provinces as 'sovereign subordinate[s]' where 'nominally subordinate organizations, in practice, retained significant operational autonomy'.[84] They explain that there is a difference between the situation before the pledge, when the organization approaches ISIS and makes a pledge and ISIS then evaluates and validates the credentials of the candidate, and after the organization's pledge has been accepted. In the case of Mozambique, there has been much doubt among scholars about the existence of a substantial connection to ISIS until 2020. But by the second half of 2021 most observers agreed that ISIS had become important for al-Shabaab. The battle of Palma town, near the LNG plant, in March 2021 (almost two years after ISIS had accepted the pledge of allegiance) was a turning point for analysts. Military specialists saw the attack on the town as particularly sophisticated, and this convinced many that ISIS had advised and possibly trained the Mozambicans. Additionally, by the second half of 2021, ISIS's attack claims had become frequent, rapid, and precise. By 2022, most researchers agreed, therefore, that the connection between the Mozambican insurgents and ISIS had become substantial, involving not just communication and branding but also military advice and training, and possibly the provision of foreign fighters. There are few triangulated details, but it is worth noting that the links between al-Shabaab and ISIS continued to strengthen: in early 2022, ISIS made public that it had created a *wilayat* for Mozambique alone, separate from the Wilayat Central Africa (which continues to exist), something that certainly reflects an intensification of the relations between al-Shabaab and ISIS, and looks like a promotion of the group based in Cabo Delgado.[85]

To conclude, how can we think of the future relationship between the al-Shabaab insurgency and ISIS? It is likely there will be a further strengthening of ties between them or at the very least, we can expect that ISIS will maintain its present level of engagement. It should not be assumed that this will happen, however. Hard data about the present situation is scarce, and the future is, as always, uncertain. Two elements need to be considered when thinking of the future. The first is that there remain important differences between al-Shabaab and ISIS—differences that could become a source of tension, if they are not already. First, most al-Shabaab insurgents are black Africans, while ISIS is mostly Arab. This is not just an issue of race but one of a difference in historical trajectory, with the problem of slavery and Arab racism potentially built into it. There are also issues of identity, with most insurgents being locals and speaking in local tongues, Swahili or Portuguese, rather than Arabic. Al-Shabaab training manuals and attack plans that the Mozambican army captured in 2021 were all written in Portuguese, and the lingua franca of the insurgency is Swahili.[86] In 2021, there were also videos circulating outside of the ISIS communication network, with speeches and singing in Swahili, and references to an East African jihad rather than the Central Africa province that was in place then.[87] There are also possible differences in faith and religious practice. We know some insurgents have Quranist beliefs and practices that may not sit easily with ISIS orthodoxy. Second, the future cannot be expected to be linear. The relationship between ISIS and al-Shabaab may continue as it is, may strengthen or weaken, but it may just as well change fundamentally, if not come to an end. If the Nigerian experience is anything to go by, the al-Shabaab sect could diverge if not break away from ISIS, as well as change allegiance. In Nigeria, Boko Haram connected to al-Qaeda in the Islamic Maghreb in 2010 but then switched allegiance to ISIS in 2015. A year later, this led the movement to split in two, one faction retaining its connections to ISIS while the other returned to its original identity and autonomy—a situation that continues to this day.[88] In Mozambique, we have not seen any dissidence, but we have seen al-Qaeda claiming responsibility for an attack in 2020 and we have seen the surprising creation of the Mozambique *wilayat* in early 2022.[89]

Conclusion

This chapter focused on the origins, nature, and beginning of the insurgency in Mozambique. It revealed that the insurgents, commonly referred to as al-Shabaab, built on a religious sect that emerged around 2007. By definition, sects withdraw from society, and this was the case in Cabo Delgado as al-Shabaab leaders and members built their own mosques and distanced themselves from state institutions and the wider society. The sect was Islamist, thus aiming to establish a counter-society ruled according to Islamic law (sharia). The sect had nothing to do with the Sufi Muslim majority of Cabo Delgado nor the Wahhabi CISLAMO, both of which opposed the sect from the outset. While both CISLAMO and the sect shared scripturalist ideas, they differed on several points, the most important being their social make-up and their view of how Muslims should relate to the secular state.

Over a ten-year period, the sect established itself in at least eight districts of Cabo Delgado before turning to violence in 2017. In 2016, the sect was active in Palma, Nangade, Mocímboa da Praia, Macomia, Quissanga, and Montepuez districts in Cabo Delgado province, and in Memba in Nampula province as well as Mecula in Niassa province; it previously had a presence in Balama, Ancuabe, and Chiure districts. The chapter argues that the sect probably shifted to armed jihadism because of the repression it experienced from the mainstream Muslim organizations and, later, from the state—the latter's involvement possibly tipping the sect into abandoning its approach of withdrawing from society.

The chapter considered alternative explanations for the insurgency's origins and development, including the insurgents' link to the Islamic State. It argued that, while international factors were important, they need to be kept in proportion. There have certainly been external influences and manipulations, and al-Shabaab has definitely linked up with ISIS, but it is doubtful that these factors did more than influence or shape the insurgency. The chapter argued it is best to think of the al-Shabaab insurgents in terms of their historical trajectory, developing from an Islamist sect into a violent jihadi armed group, and undergoing a process of internationalization that might develop or evolve in various ways in the future.

CONCLUSION

In 2019–20, the Mozambican government drafted a law for freedom of religion and worship. The law aimed to be the first legislation since independence to regulate religious organizations and practices in the country. Indeed, in 2019 religious matters were still governed by a colonial law of 1971. The new law was extensive, with fifty-five articles. It started by laying down the principles of equality, secularism, legality, cooperation, tolerance, and religious pluralism—in line with the country's constitution. It then established the principle of religious liberty and its guarantees and limitations; the limits for the practice of faith; taxation and exemptions; the requirements for faith organizations to be recognized by the state (with a separate section for foreign organizations); and the duties and qualities required from a religious leader.[1] The core principles were (a) that only registered religious organizations would benefit from freedom and state protection, and (b) that faith institutions could have any doctrine they wanted as long as it did not 'contradict the Constitution of the Republic and many applicable laws, and does not offend customs' (Article 14).

According to the minister of justice and the head of its DNAR, the new law aimed at placing order on the religious world, reigning in abuses and illegalities, and bringing religious 'proliferation' under control.[2] Two concerns were particularly salient in society at the time the law was drafted, namely an increasing number of neo-

Pentecostal churches and other Christian prophets who were seen as more interested in making money than doing good or following their God's teachings, and the jihadi insurgency in northern Mozambique that began in 2017 and showed how faith groups could turn violent. The issue of religious proliferation emerged publicly in Mozambique right after the violence in Cabo Delgado began and was related to the issue of law and secularism. In an interview with the influential newspaper *O País*, Mozambican philosopher Severino Ngoenha argued that the insurgency in northern Mozambique resulted from a rising tide of intolerance and a certain indifference to what happened within religions. He explained: 'Many times, we do not bother with what others are doing, what they do in churches, large churches or mosques, in Maputo or in the North. We are indifferent to what takes place there.' Yet, he continued,

> secularism cannot be understood as indifference in relation to religious organisations. That is true not just for Islam in the north. Even in churches in the south, there are practices that often seem to contradict what should be a practice in line with the rule of law, and we have an interest, as citizens, as a country and as a people, in being attentive to what happens within the walls of these institutions that operate in our country and that have a duty to respect the principles that direct civilian activities of Mozambicans.[3]

This was not the first time the Mozambican government had proposed a law on religion. It did so in 1989, with a shorter law (nineteen articles) that the state discussed with all main religious institutions, but, for a reason I have not managed to uncover, it was never sent to parliament for debate and approval.[4] The 2020 law was debated publicly in 2020, then sent to the Council of Ministers, who approved it and sent it to parliament in early 2022—where at the time of writing in 2023 it was still waiting for debate and final approval. Before and during the public consultation, complaints about the law emerged, particularly in relation to the requirements for having any religious organization officially recognized, in particular in relation to the numbers of signatures required. The law determined 15,000 signatures were needed for state recognition of

CONCLUSION

any existing faith organization and 60,000 for a new organization. An Anglican bishop argued this was too high and would lead many churches to remain illegal until they reached this number, something that might be counterproductive. For the same reason, in 2022 a representative of 150 small Christian churches declared that the law was 'unconstitutional, irresponsible, irrelevant, not reflecting the country and not representing the religious class'.[5] Despite the criticism, the Council of Ministers approved the law and parliament is expected to debate and approve it in 2023. When, and indeed if this happens, one will see the end of the existing religious regime and the emergence of a new one, involving a shift from soft secularism back to strong secularism.

As the current religious regime comes to an end, we need to ask: How can we describe the chronology and trajectory of state policy towards religion and secularism up to 2022? First, after independence, the government deployed an anticlerical stance that lasted from 1975/7 to 1980 and saw the closure of sites of prayer, the banning of religious festivals, prohibitions on the wearing of religious clothing in public spaces, the destruction of some religious materials, and the deployment of anti-religious and atheist propaganda. A second period began in 1981 (made official in 1982) and was characterized by a strong secularism where churches were not opposed but tightly limited and controlled, not least in their movements. By the late 1980s (and officially from the year 1989), a third period began that saw the government shift to soft secularism and a policy of a free religious market (controlled by the patrimonial DAR). Faith organizations regained freedoms and resumed holding public religious ceremonies, engaging in the construction of new sites of prayer, and religious expansion. The policy led to the politicization of some faiths, triggering some turbulence, particularly around elections. In 1999, this turbulence led Frelimo, the party in power, to impose a strong secularism again, though only for itself (as a party). The 2020 Freedom of Religion and Worship Law that should be adopted in 2023 will extend this return to a strong secularism from the party in power to the state and the whole country. Doubtless, the strong secularism that will ensue will be different in form from the secularism of the 1980s.

143

Interestingly, secularism (soft or strong) has not been at issue in the relationship between Muslims and the state in Mozambique. Most Muslims accommodated themselves to the secular state, including the members of the Wahhabi Islamic Council, who were happy to work with and integrate the state administration (in the hope of Islamizing it). Two particular moments of tension between Muslims and the state were identified, in relation to the officialization of Muslim holidays and the new Family Law. These tensions, however, were not so much about secularism per se as the perception that the state was not being neutral, recognizing Christian holidays and not Muslim ones, or making official a Christian model of the family but ignoring the Muslim one or, conversely, recognizing a Muslim holiday or family model that some thought might enable the rise of Islamic fundamentalism. Both these affairs were eventually overcome, and secularism continued, appreciated overwhelmingly by all parties and sections of society. The case of the burqa affair in 2011–12 was similar in its dynamics and resolution. At the level of the population, we saw that the survey of a sample of the Muslim population in 2000s indicated strong Muslim support for secularism, democracy, and religious freedom. Ideally, one should discriminate between Muslim views on soft and strong secularism. Given a choice, some Muslims, like the Wahhabi, might prefer a soft secularism to better Islamize institutions. But weak or strong, it seems that most Muslims are willing to adapt to the secular state as long as it remains neutral and fair. Tellingly, the Muslim politicians who were expelled from Frelimo in 1999 because of their militantism accepted the decision and adapted their strategy accordingly. It will probably be the same with the new strongly secular religious law when and if it is passed in 2023: most Muslims will simply adapt. It will leave only the jihadists fighting in the country's extreme north to oppose secularism fully, frontally, and violently—in all its forms and degrees.

For all the Muslim acceptance of secularism, the relationship between Muslims and the Mozambican state has not been easy since independence. The key trauma was the repression of religion immediately after independence. From the end of 1980, Frelimo worked to neutralize the bad publicity this initial policy had caused worldwide, a task that extended up to 1999 when the country was

CONCLUSION

finally recognized by international Muslim organizations and the 2010s when it managed to build fruitful relations with the Gulf states. The relationship with Muslim nationals was more easily and more quickly recuperated, with relations improving fast after a 1982 public meeting between Frelimo and faith organizations that publicly marked the end of the repression. The end of the civil war and the start of multiparty politics saw Muslims engage fully with the political realm and come into being as a political entity. Political parties reached out to, and tried to gain the favour of, the adepts of Islam, a Muslim political party was set up (with all the associated problems), many Muslims joined political parties as Muslims, and a Muslim forum was set up in parliament. One could say therefore that the relationship between Muslims, the state, and politics became fully normal (even if not unproblematic) with the elections of 1994. After 1999, the strongly secularist stance of the party in power did not prove to be particularly problematic, and it is possible that the same will happen with the new Freedom of Religion and Worship Law. Considering, however, that the insurgency in northern Mozambique has created the basis for a new debate about Muslim law (which the insurgents demand in full), one might see in the near future some Muslims demand a partial introduction of sharia law on the pretext that fire is best fought with fire. This could ignite a new controversy about Islam, though it could also open a healthy discussion about Muslim law—a discussion that has never taken place publicly.

The Frelimo leadership's relationship with Muslims and Islam is relevant here and is a topic that needs more research. In previous pages, we saw that Frelimo has historically had very few members of Muslim origin in its leadership (the few Muslims it did attract were secularized and/or from a minority group such as the Ismaili), and this led the party to make mistakes, such as Samora Machel walking into a mosque without taking off his shoes, pigsties being built in Muslim areas, and a lack of Muslims working in the DAR until 1989. The problem was presumably resolved over time and particularly after 1994 when Muslims gained a full and public voice in society and within Frelimo. This allowed for open discussion in public, in parliament, and in the party. But since Muslim membership was reduced again in the 2000s, the party's problems with understanding

Islam have returned, as was evident in the convoluted resolution of the burqa affair. It was also apparent in Frelimo's problematic handling of the Islamist sect in northern Mozambique that transformed into a jihadi insurgency in 2017. The party and the state struggled to grasp what this sect was, what it aimed at, and how it should be dealt with. Since 2017, a majority of Muslims (and certain Christian figures too) refuse to accept that the insurgency has anything to do with faith (or the corruption of faith). They argue that sacred texts oppose violence, so jihadis cannot be considered religious. Large parts of the party in power have adopted this argument, and, as a result, the government struggles to explain what is happening in northern Mozambique and develop an encompassing and effective counter-insurgency policy.

If Frelimo's relationship with Islam has been ambiguous, the place of Muslims in Mozambican society has evolved clearly and significantly since independence. New Muslim elites have emerged since 1975 with, first, the arrival of Wahhabism and the growth of a social group around CISLAMO. Singularly and contrary to what happened in Tanzania, the Wahhabi elite in Mozambique grew in the shadow of the state that it works closely with, if not for. A pro-Sufi elite emerged in a similar way, if with looser links to the state, with the emergence of the Islamic Congress of Mozambique, then CFI, and now CIMO. Interestingly, it was the pro-Sufi CFI (under the leadership of a former minister of justice with roots in a revived old pre-colonial Muslim elite) that launched the first Islamic university in Mozambique, an institution from which thousands of students have graduated since its foundation, leading to the education of an ever-broader Muslim elite. Over the years, the Mussa Bin Bique University project has revealed that the separation between pro- and anti-Sufi Muslims is not clear cut, however. On this project, like others, pro-Sufi Muslims and CISLAMO (as well as the old Muslim elite) have come to work together, and by the early 2020s many Wahhabi and other types of Muslims were employed by the university. Finally, a third strand of Muslim elite emerged in the 1990s within the Indian, Pakistani, and Indo-Mozambican community whose power and wealth came from trade and business in a neo-liberalized economy (some of it criminal). This elite intervened in politics, but, being small, it has tended to support the Sufis to gain gravitas through

CONCLUSION

numbers (they are Sufi themselves). They made momentary or partial alliances with other groups too, of course. All in all, a significant Muslim elite has emerged in the country since independence whose various strands may not always be on good terms but have learnt to work together when needed or when it suits them.

Finally, we return to the question posed in the introduction about whether Muslims in Mozambique moved 'towards jihad' after independence. The chapters showed that this was not the case. Most Muslims were and remain opposed to violence, and all their leaders were happy to work with the state. When the al-Shabaab sect emerged in the early 2010s, both Sufi and Wahhabi leaders tried to resolve what they saw as a problem. It is true that the jihadis were scripturalists like the Wahhabi, but the methods of the two groups were contrary to each other, the two groups differed socially, and there were significant tensions between them from the very beginning. The jihadi insurgents began as a sect, opposed to other Muslims, the state, and society at large. This indicates that the jihadis emerged in rupture with other Muslims and with society, and particularly in rupture with the historical trajectory of Muslim relations to politics and the state. Their project and actions are against the existing state and against the overwhelming majority of Muslims who accommodated themselves to this state. That is the key lesson in relation to the issue of jihad in Mozambique. The question that follows is not only whether the jihadis can sustain their insurgency in such a context (against almost everyone) but also whether their armed action could change the way the majority of Muslims think of themselves, relate to the state, and imagine their future. There is indeed a risk here: the insurgency could change Muslims, expectations in relation to the state (wanting more Islamic law, for example), while it could, conversely, change (if it has not already changed) the state's expectations in relation to Muslims (the state demanding more from Muslims to prove their allegiance, for example). In other words, the conflict and its jihadi nature put in question the relationship that exists between Muslims and the state in Mozambique. To maintain a good rapport, if not to resolve the insurgency, the state and the Muslim majority will have to work together with renewed dedication to avoid misunderstandings and the emergence of new grievances, and to imagine and design a collective future where all Muslims and all Mozambicans feel included, treated equally, and inspired, leaving no place for a jihadi critique and project of any kind to gain traction.

APPENDICES

APPENDIX I
FOUNDATION OF THE ISLAMIC COUNCIL OF MOZAMBIQUE (CISLAMO), 1981

The Mozambican government created the Islamic Council in 1981 after a meeting with the Muslim World League. On advice from the Saudi organization, it gave control of the organization to Wahhabi Muslims, who, as the information sheet below illustrates, lost no time in attacking Sufi Muslims in the country. The text below—translated from Portuguese—gives some details about CISLAMO's foundation and reveals, in its tone, the spirit of its leaders. Note that Sheik Abubacar Hagy Mussá Ismael had, just like some Sufi leaders, worked with the Portuguese colonial authorities and even with the Portuguese political police that he later so vehemently denounced.[1] It should be noted also that the original Portuguese text contained a number of errors, something the translation could not wholly fix.

> Conselho Islâmico de Moçambique, Information Sheet no. 1, n.d. [1981]

> The Coordinating Commission of this Council decided at a meeting on 15 February 1981 to compose and distribute this information sheet across the whole country....
>
> Associations and puppet brotherhoods were created [during the late colonial period] to divide Muslims. They recruited members from the Muslim community but were infiltrated with

151

spies from the former PIDE/DGS [colonial political police] and waged a campaign of terror, with threats of imprisonment and reprisals expressed against all Muslims who did not adhere [to their views].

Fortunately, after the independence of our country, the political situation changed for all of us. After a phase of astonishment and doubt, and after a number of meetings among Muslims lucid and aware of the responsibility inherent in the liberty that our government conceded, [followed] the creation of an Islamic Council of Mozambique, led by *alims* from the *ulama*.

The authorization [to establish the organization] was given during conversations at a historic meeting with the World Muslim League on 16 June 1980. And [then] the imams met on 27 January 1981 at the [Maputo] provincial government [headquarters] under the supervision of representatives of our government.

At this meeting, the representatives of the government and the party [Frelimo] talked about the unity that Muslims need, and the fact that the government aims to establish good relationships with the Islamic community and with other religions.

Thereafter, they [government representatives] talked about the contacts and agreements that His Excellency, the Minister of Justice, and the Governor of the Bank of Mozambique had with a delegation of the World Muslim League on 16 June 1980. This delegation was led by the Minister of Justice of Saudi Arabia, Sheik Muhammad Aly, and some representatives from the same [World Muslim League] in South Africa.

The delegation asked our government for the creation of the Islamic Council in Mozambique, the training of religious leaders, the construction of mosques, and the permission to import free religious books for Muslims.

The Muslim World League is an international organization; it is recognized all over the world as well as by our government, and it agrees with the creation of an Islamic Council and proposed Sheik Abubacar Hagy Mussá Ismael to coordinate the work of the Council.

152

APPENDIX I

Basing ourselves on this [country's] religious freedom, we will take all measures necessary and have the strength to defend the interests of Islam and of Muslims in Mozambique.

Signed—the Coordinating Commission

Source: DNAR, unclassified folder

APPENDIX II
LETTER FROM THE MUSLIM WORLD LEAGUE TO PRESIDENT SAMORA MACHEL, 1983

Following the 1981 visit referred to in Appendix I, the South African delegate of the Muslim World League wrote to President Samora Machel to follow up on the decisions taken in 1981 that had not yet been implemented. The original letter is in English—it is presented here verbatim.

Muslim World League to President Samora Machel, 16 August 1983

Dear Mr President,
With regards to the religious problems of the Muslims of Mozambique, a high-powered Saudi Delegation, led by the late Sheik Mohamed Ali Al Harakan, the Secretary General of the Muslim World League with headquarters in Makkah, met Justice Minister Teodato Hunguana and the Governor of the Banco de Mozambique, Colonel Sergio Vieira in June 1980.

In spite of fruitful and constructive discussion, no results were achieved, and the matter was not followed up with my office.

In March 1981 a second delegation, led by Sheik Ebrahim Al Dabassi, came for a day visit and besides their monetary contribution to a Mosque in Maputo, the matter again fell in abeyance.

TOWARDS JIHAD?

It has been observed that for five years, no Muslim citizen of Mozambique has performed Haj.

However, it is appreciated that this is due to the lack of foreign currency at the State Treasury. On behalf of Rabita, I have been authorized and instructed to make contacts with your Government for the opening of religious and cultural links with Saudi Arabia.

It will be appreciated if your office could respond early to my proposal and enable me to visit Mozambique to take up the matter at an official level with the Minister designated by yourself.

Mr President, we are looking forward to an era of mutual cooperation, assistance and understanding with your benevolent Government.

Greeting to you with highest considerations,

Signed—Dr M.I. Monariat, director liaison office, Southern Africa region

Source: DNAR, unclassified folder

APPENDIX III
LAW PROJECT FOR TWO MUSLIM NATIONAL HOLIDAYS, 1996

In 1996, a group of Muslim MPs put to the vote a proposal to adopt a new law to turn the Eid Ul Adha and Eid Ul Fitr religious holidays into national holidays. The proposal was hotly debated in parliament but accepted in March 1996. This created a major controversy that is analysed in detail in Chapter 2. The document below is the text of the law voted on in February 1996. One part presents the rationale of the law's proponents as to why the law should be adopted.

ASSEMBLEIA DA REPÚBLICA

Fourth Session February 1996

Proponents: Group of Parliamentarians

Topic: Law Project about national holidays on the date of Eid Ul Fitr and Eid Ul Adha

Observations: ....
....
....
....

Results: ....
....

TOWARDS JIHAD?

....

....

REASONING

The secular nature of the state, consecrated in the Constitution, does not prevent the activities of religious organizations to be duly valued and protected, so that citizens, in this way, have the liberty to practise any religion.

The Muslim religion has roots in Mozambique that are several centuries old and thus is intimately linked to the history of our people.

Professed by millions of Mozambicans, from the Rovuma [River] to Maputo, Islam is today without doubt one of the faiths with the biggest number of believers in the Republic of Mozambique.

Despite having existed for several centuries and being a religious faith with a large number of adherents, it was marginalized throughout the period of colonial domination and its religious rituals were considered something exotic, for folkloric consumption.

The existence of Islam and its continuous presence are due to the efforts, convictions, and dedication of the Muslim communities who, with their own means, have always maintained alive the teaching and dissemination of Islam.

The inauguration of national independence gave the Mozambican people their identity, Mozambican-ness, and dignity.

The recognition and valorization of religious confessions of great popular tradition, with strong roots among the Mozambican people, as is the case of the Islamic religion, which is an integral and indissoluble part of the national religious and cultural heritage, represent an undeniable contribution to a climate of understanding and tolerance and the reinforcement of national unity.

It is intended, indeed, that the commemorative dates of the Eid Ul Fitr and Eid Ul Adha, respectively marking the end of RAMADAN and the day of SACRIFICE, are dignified by being celebrated by a great majority of our people in a balanced

158

APPENDIX III

exercise of justice and respect for one of the largest faiths in the country.

It is also intended that a majority of our people, from the Rovuma to Maputo, takes part in the ceremonies that mark these dates, and this is why these dates should be made into national holidays.

Law Project N __ / 95

Considering that it is important to confer dignity to the days commemorating the end of Ramadan and the day of Sacrifice, and at the same time allowing a great majority of people of Mozambique to take part in the religious ceremonies related to the same, the Assembly of the Republic determines, by the competence conferred to it by No. 1 of Article 135 of the Constitution:

ARTICLE 1
1—The dates referring to the Eid Ul Fitr and Eid Ul Adha are considered national holidays.
2—On these days, it is mandatory that work is interrupted for the whole day, with the exception of services that are considered indispensable.

ARTICLE 2
Competence is delegated to the Council of Ministers to determine, in a timely fashion and after hearing the Council of Islamic Theologians, the days that, according to the Gregorian calendar, correspond to the celebrations mentioned in Article No. 1.

Approved by the Assembly of the Republic.
The President of the Assembly of the Republic, Eduardo Joaquim Muluémbué
Promulgated on __ of 1995
To be published
The President of the Republic, Joaquim Alberto Chissano

Source: Biblioteca da Assembleia da República, Maputo, Mozambique

APPENDIX IV
FINAL COMMUNIQUÉ OF THE FIRST NATIONAL ISLAMIC CONFERENCE, 2003

After the proposal for the official Muslim holidays was defeated, Muslims leaders in Mozambique decided to regroup, rethink, and re-organize. In 2003, they held the First National Islamic Conference to reflect and establish a strategy. Sufi, pro-Sufi, and Wahhabi Muslims from all provinces of the country attended. The document below is the final communiqué of the event, with a summary of what was discussed and decided upon.

Final Communiqué

The First Islamic Conference of national scope took place on the twenty-first and twenty-second of September 2003 in the city of Beira, Sofala province. Its main objectives were the reinforcement of Islamic unity, humanitarian action, and the education of Muslims.

The participants of this great meeting, made up of muftis, sheiks, alims, mawlanas, hafiz, communities, associations, humanitarian organizations, brotherhoods, and leagues at national, provincial, district, and town level took part in a warm debate over two days in search of important solutions that regulate and give direction to the life of Mozambican Muslims.

TOWARDS JIHAD?

To improve cohesion and unity between us, Muslims from the Rovuma [River] to Maputo discussed and approved [resolutions on] various topics that preoccupy us on a daily basis.

Based on this effort, the participants of this First Islamic Conference deliberated over the following resolutions:

Resolution 1: Methodology and functioning of the conference
Resolution 2: Conference agenda
Resolution 3: History of Islam
Resolution 4: Education
Resolution 5: Creation of a database
Resolution 6: Kurbani, Humanitarian Action, and Zakat
Resolution 7: Economic questions and international relations
Resolution 8: Forming a legal affairs commission
Resolution 9: Halal products
Resolution 10: The periodicity of the conference and creating an executive committee
Resolution 11: Visualizing the Ramadan moon and Eid Ul Fitr
Resolution 12: Health

The First National Islamic Conference congratulates the organizers for the warm, efficient, and very professional way in which they prepared this conference. Special thanks go to Mr Zaid Aly and his wife Nacima Aly for their untiring and generous support with accommodation, the installations, and food so that this noble conference could take place with success.

The conference congratulates and thanks the participation of all Muslims from the Rovuma to Maputo who provided time, funds, and other means so that we could be together in the search for a harmonious and Islamic solution.

The Islamic Conference salutes the efforts made by Dr América Assane, President of the Direction of the Muslim Association of Sofala, as well as Mr Rassul Khan, Vice President of the Directorate, [and] Sheik Swaleh Mbwera, *amir* from Beira and President of this great conference.

[The conference] also greets the members of the Direction of the Muslim Sport League of Sofala, businessmen, youngsters, women, and all the men of goodwill who contributed with their

162

APPENDIX IV

efforts and dedication so that it [the conference] took place successfully.

[The conference] acknowledges the consensual and united way in which a solution was reached for the proclamation of the month of Ramadan and the Eid Ul Fitr, through the visualization of the moon at the level of the Mozambican national territory.

The conference proclaims that the achievements reached are proof of the great will of Muslims to unite and develop jointly actions to find consensual solutions.

The conference proclaims that the Second National Islamic Conference will take place next year in the city of Beira, province of Sofala.

The conference proclaims that all resolutions constitute a victory for Islam, they deserved a high consensus, with no losers and no winners.

We are all great winners.

Beira, 21 September 2003

The Conference's Emir

[handwritten signature]

Sheik Swaleh Mbwera

Source: Copy in the possession of the author

APPENDIX V

TRANSCRIPT OF JIHADI INSURGENTS' VIDEO MESSAGES, 2018, 2020, AND 2022

There are only a few instances when speeches by the insurgents have been recorded. One was in January 2018 and a second in March 2020. There are other video clips that circulated in 2020, but these are not considered here because they were poetic in nature rather than a statement of position. The most recent video clip we will consider here appeared in 2022 on ISIS media—the first time this has happened. The three video clips considered are transcribed below, the first two from Portuguese, the third from Arabic. They show both continuity and change in the insurgents' objectives and in how they use language and visuals.

First video clip, January 2018

This video clip is fifty-four seconds long and was circulated on WhatsApp in January 2018, three months after the beginning of the insurgency. Researchers who prefer to remain anonymous confirmed through their research the authenticity of the clip and most of the people depicted in it. A year later, a newspaper revealed the identity of the speaker as Assumane Nvita, also known as Vipodozi ('cosmetic'), a native of Palma who grew up in Mocímboa da Praia and who, before joining the insurgency, worked at the local market as a trader in cosmetics.[1]

TOWARDS JIHAD?

The video begins abruptly, halfway through a sentence. We see five young men, in their twenties or thirties, standing in a row next to each other, under some trees and with leaves lying on the ground. Each is wearing a turban/cloth wrapped over the face and is holding an AK-47. A sixth man, standing behind them, holds a machete, which he brandishes during the recording. Unseen is the individual who is filming the scene (presumably with a phone), moving from right to left. The men are all dressed in civilian clothes, often mismatched, wearing shoes or boots, and a jacket or coat. The man on the far right speaks the following in Portuguese:

> ... that we have, mostly in our Mocímboa da Praia, which is the beginning [where the insurgency began], we have started like this, little by little.
>
> But *Inch Allah*, we believe Allah will give us help, because Allah, as he says 'In Tanssuru Allah Yansurukum' [Support Allah's cause, then He will support you], Allah will give us help, will give us help.
>
> Yeah ... We do not need help from anyone because we are not capable [sic]. But since we have started like this, *Inch Allah*, we trust in Him, Allah will always look at [after?] us.
>
> My brothers, my brother Mozambicans, come, we are together in the fight against *junah* [sin], the fight against *shirk* [idolatry/polytheism], the fight against *taghut* [false gods], the fight against ... Ssss ... Sa ... Satan [the speaker stutters; the others echo what he says], the fight against *shaytân* [Satan], my brothers.
>
> We are here, *Al-ḥamdu lil-lāh* [praise be to God], since we have begun, *Al-ḥamdu lil-lāh*, we are already seeing the fruits from these, from this ... ehh ... from this decision that we have taken, because it is an order from *Allah Subhanahu Wa Ta'ala* [Allah the Most Glorified, the Most High], my brothers. *Allah wakbar* [repeated by all]; *Allah wakbar* [repeated by all].
>
> My brother Mozambicans, come, let us be together to fight *taghut*. *Taghut* is already trying to end the laws of *Allah Subhanahu Wa Ta'ala*.
>
> There is a risk that our generation does not know who Allah is, who Allah is, and not know who Rassul is.

166

APPENDIX V

Because the Quran which is the one which Allah gave, which Rassul, as his messenger, indicated, instructed us, taught us, is already like a simple newspaper, my brothers.

In the meantime, the al-Quran as law, religion as a government of *Allah Subhanahu Wa Ta'ala* and we, like soldiers of *Allah Subhanahu Wa Ta'ala*, and we like hezz … as he said, as *hezbollah*, in a *hezbollah* … [a second man intervenes to finish the sentence]: *hezbollah* the victor [literally 'Party of Allah'].

For now, my brothers, come to be together, *Al-ḥamdu lil-lāh*, all together we will see how we decide to do like this.

It is not because we have more force, not because we are, we are … I don't know, because we are capable. But overall we hope for the help of *Allah Subhanahu Wa Ta'ala* [the groups echoes Allah. The video stops abruptly].

The video was broadcast by the national television channel Televisão de Moçambique on 30 May 2018, five months after it initially circulated, and presented by the broadcaster as a claim for an attack that took place a few days earlier. The video was subsequently presented as being 'doubtful' and possibly even 'false' when only its relation to this May attack was erroneous.[2]

Second video clip, March 2020

This video clip circulated on WhatsApp in March 2020. It is one minute and twenty-three seconds long and was recorded after the insurgents had captured the town of Quissanga on 25 March 2020. Two insurgents stand in front of the town's police station, one is filming from below, presumably with a mobile phone. Both men are dressed in military garb, with a *shemagh* scarf wrapped around their heads, hiding their faces. The speaker wears leather shoes while the other man wears flip flops. The speaker holds a machine gun, with a round of ammunition around his neck, and an ISIS flag. He speaks in Portuguese. The clip starts abruptly—one hears the last two words of a sentence in Kimwani spoken by another person in the background before the speaker begins.

167

TOWARDS JIHAD?

'As-salāmu 'alaykum [Peace be upon you]

My brothers, we are here in Quissanga. You who are watching from afar, we are always calling you to come here to fight under this banner of the Word of God [ISIS flag]. We don't want the Frelimo banner; we want the banner of 'There is no deity but God and Muhammad is his messenger.' Also [we want] to use the law which is in the Quran, as Allah spoke. *Allahu Akbar. Allahu Akbar. Allahu Akbar.* [Allah is the greatest]. [Gunshots in the background].

You have to see this banner which we are using. My brothers, I cannot be deceived. My brothers cannot be deceived. We are not fighting for appearances ... for wealth of this world. We only want ultimate heaven.

As Allah says, well, when you want to be Muslim in truth, first you have to die while fighting for Allah.

Allahu Akbar. Allahu Akbar. Allahu Akbar.

Third video clip, August 2022

This video clip was circulated by the ISIS Amaq News Agency on 9 August 2022. The clip is one minute and fourteen seconds long (including an eight-second jingle). It was filmed in Nangade district a few days earlier. The video shows six men standing in military garb, with a *shemagh* scarf wrapped around their heads, so that only their eyes are visible. Three men wear gloves (possibly to hide their skin colour; the main speaker appears not to be a black African), and two men hold an ISIS flag. Twenty seconds into the video, a seventh man runs into the picture, without scarf or gloves, and kneels in front of the speaker. The speaker is dressed in grey, but with a military waistcoat. He speaks in Arabic—he seems to be a native speaker—rather than in Portuguese or Swahili as in previous video clips.[3] Behind the men are some bushes that separate them from houses that are burning in the immediate background. One hears the sounds of the raging flames.

This is our message to the *tawāghīt* [idolators] of Mozambique and [President] Nyusi.

168

APPENDIX V

We tell you that we'll continue the fight against the army and Christians until the application of sharia law in Mozambique.

The jihad in Mozambique is a continuation of the Islamic State jihad all over the world.

If you dream that we will stop or lay down our weapons, we prefer death to that.

Between us and the Christians, there is an unfinished difficult history and ancient vengeance.

The truth is in what you see rather than what you hear.

Praise be to Allah, Lord of the Worlds.

pp. [4–8]

NOTES

INTRODUCTION

1. Abdullahi Ahmed An-Na'im, 'Islam and Secularism', in Linell E. Cady and Elizabeth Shakman Hurd (eds), *Comparative Secularisms in a Global Age*, New York: Palgrave Macmillan, 2010, pp. 217–28; and Ahmet T. Kuru, 'Passive and Assertive Secularism: Historical Conditions, Ideological Struggles, and State Policies toward Religion', *World Politics*, 59(4), 2007, pp. 568–94.
2. Christian Coulon, 'Introduction: Les nouvelles voies de l'*umma* africaine', *L'Afrique Politique* (Paris), 2002, pp. 19–29.
3. Fernand Braudel, 'Histoire et sciences sociales: La longue durée', *Annales: Economies, sociétés, civilisations*, 13(4), 1958, pp. 725–53.
4. August H. Nimtz, *Islam and Politics in East Africa: The Sufi Order in Tanzania*, Minneapolis: University of Minnesota Press, 1980, p. 3; Bradford G. Martin, *Muslim Brotherhoods in Nineteenth-Century Africa*, Cambridge: Cambridge University Press, 1976; William G. Clarence-Smith, 'Indian Business Communities in the Western Indian Ocean in the Nineteenth Century', *Indian Ocean Review*, 2(4), 1989, pp. 18–21; and Michael N. Pearson, 'The Indian Ocean and the Red Sea', in N. Levtzion and R. Pouwell (eds), *The History of Islam in Africa*, Athens: Ohio University Press, 1999, pp. 37–59.
5. Nancy Hafkin, 'Trade, Society and Politics in Northern Mozambique, *c.*1753–1913', PhD diss., Boston University, 1973; Edward A. Alpers, *Ivory and Slaves in East Central Africa*, London: Heinemann, 1975; Hilário Madiquida, *The Iron-Using Communities of the Cape Delgado Coast from AD 1000*, Uppsala: Uppsala University, 2007; Edward Pollard, Ricardo Duarte, and Yolanda Teixeira Duarte, 'Settlement and Trade

171

pp. [8–10]

NOTES

from AD 500 to 1800 at Angoche, Mozambique', *African Archaeological Review*, 35, 2018, pp. 443–71; and Eugeniusz Rzewuski, 'Origins of the Tungi Sultanate (Northern Mozambique) in the Light of Local Tradition', *Orientalia Varsoviensia* (Warsaw), 2, 1991, pp. 193–213.

6. Hafkin, 'Trade, Society and Politics', Chapter 1, and Edward A. Alpers, 'East Central Africa', in Levtzion and Pouwell, *History of Islam in Africa*, pp. 302–25.

7. Alpers, *Ivory and Slaves*; Alpers, 'East Central Africa'; and Randall L. Pouwels, *Horn and Crescent: Cultural Change and Traditional Islam on the East African Coast, 800–1900*, Cambridge: Cambridge University Press, 1987, Chapters 6–8.

8. Eduardo da Conceição Medeiros, *História de Cabo Delgado e do Niassa (c.1836–1929)*, Maputo: n.p., 1997, pp. 86–7; and Edward A. Alpers, 'Towards a History of the Expansion of Islam in East Africa: The Matrilineal People of the Southern Interior', in Terence Ranger and Isaria Kimambo (eds), *The Historical Study of African Religion*, Berkeley: University of California Press, 1972, pp. 172–201.

9. René Pélissier, *Naissance du Mozambique*, 2 vols, Orgeval: Author's edition, 1984 (for northern Mozambique, see Chapters 3–4); and Eric Axelson, *Portugal and the Scramble for Africa 1875–1891*, Johannesburg: Witwatersrand University Press, 1967, Chapter 5.

10. Barry Neil-Tomlinson, 'The Nyassa Chartered Company: 1891–1929', *Journal of African History*, 18(1), 1977, pp. 109–28; and W. Basil Worsfold, *Portuguese Nyassaland: An Account of the Discovery, Native Population, Agricultural and Mineral Resources, and Present Administration of the Territory of the Nyassa Company, with a Review of the Portuguese Rule on the East Coast of Africa*, New York: Negro Universities Press, 1969.

11. Medeiros, *História de Cabo Delgado e do Niassa*, p. 59.

12. Benedito Brito João, *Abdul Kamal e a história de Chiúre nos séculos XIX–XX*, Maputo: Arquivo histórico de Moçambique, 2000, Chapter 3; Liazzat Bonate, 'Traditions and Transitions: Islam and Chiefship in Northern Mozambique, ca. 1850–1974', PhD diss., University of Cape Town, 2007, Chapter 3; and Bonate, 'Governance of Islam in Colonial Mozambique', in Veit Bader, Annelies Moors, and Marcel Maussen (eds), *Colonial and Post-colonial Governance of Islam: Continuities and Ruptures*, Amsterdam: Amsterdam University Press, 2011, pp. 29–48.

13. Michel Cahen, 'L'État nouveau et la diversification religieuse au Mozambique, 1930–1974: I. Le résistible essor de la portugalisation catholique (1930–1961)', *Cahiers d'Études Africaines*, 158, 2000, pp. 309–50; Eric Morier-Genoud, *Catholicism and the Making of*

NOTES

Politics in Central Mozambique, 1940–1980, Rochester: Rochester University Press, 2019, Chapter 1; and Morier-Genoud, 'Concordat, Concordat …: Church–State Relations in the Portuguese Empire, 1940–74', in Jairzinho Lopes Pereira (ed.), *Church–State Relations in Africa in the Nineteenth and Twentieth Centuries: Mission, Empire, and the Holy See*, London: Palgrave Macmillan, 2022, pp. 111–34.

14. Mário Machaqueiro, 'Foes or Allies? Portuguese Colonial Policies towards Islam in Mozambique and Guinea', *Journal of Imperial and Commonwealth History*, 41(5), 2013, pp. 843–69; Michel Cahen, 'L'État nouveau et la diversification religieuse au Mozambique, 1930–1974: I. Le résistible essor de la portugalisation catholique (1930–1961)', *Cahiers d'Études Africaines*, 158, 2000, pp. 309–50; and João, *Abdul Kamal*.

15. Bonate, 'Traditions and Transitions', Chapter 2; and Gerhard Liesgang, 'The Muridiyya Tariqa in Modern Niassa Province of Mozambique ca. 1880–1935 (A confraria Muridiyya na provincial do Niassa cerca 1880–1935)', draft text, 2nd edn, July 2016.

16. Bonate, 'Traditions and Transitions', pp. 121–3. This happened after this elite 'converted' to Shafi'i Islam; see Pouwels, *Horn and Crescent*, pp. 116–20.

17. Bonate, 'Traditions and Transitions', Chapter 6, and 'Muslims of Northern Mozambique and Liberation Movements', *Social Dynamics*, 35(2), 2009, pp. 280–94.

18. Saskia Siefert, *Muslime in Mosambik: Versuch einer Bestandsaufnahme*, Bielefeld: University of Bielefeld (Forschungsprogamm Entwicklungspolitik: Handlungsbedingungen und Handlungsspielräume für Entwicklungspolitik 36), 1994; Lorenzo Macagno, *Outros muçulmanos: Islão e narrativas coloniais*, Lisbon: Imprensa de Ciências Sociais, 2006, Chapter 8; and Chapter 1 of the present book.

19. Liazzat Bonate, 'Dispute over Islamic Funeral Rites in Mozambique: "A demolidora dos prazeres" by Sheik Aminuddin Mohamad', *LFM Social Sciences and Missions* (Lausanne), 17(1), 2005, pp. 41–59; Bonate, 'Roots of Diversity in Mozambican Islam', *Lusotopie* (Paris), 14, 2007, pp. 129–49; Macagno, *Outros muçulmanos*, Chapter 8; Lorenzo Macagno, 'Les nouveaux Oulémas: La recomposition des autorités musulmanes au nord du Mozambique', *Lusotopie* (Paris), 14, 2007, pp. 151–77; Christian Laheij, 'A Country of Trial: Islamic Reformism, Pluralism and Dispute Management in Peri-urban Northern Mozambique', PhD diss., London School of Economics and Political Science, 2015; and Chapter 1 of the present book.

20. Joseph Hanlon, 'Mozambique's Insurgency: A New Boko Haram or Youth Demanding an End to Marginalisation?', Blog LSE, 19 June 2018,

NOTES

https://blogs.lse.ac.uk/africaatlse/2018/06/19/mozambiques-insurgency-a-new-boko-haram-or-youth-demanding-an-end-to-marginalisation/, accessed 19 June 2018; and Neuton Langa, 'Professor Yussuf Adam fala do terrorismo em Cabo Delgado: "Os terroristas querem a divisão do poder e dos benefícios económicos"', *Canal de Moçambique* (Maputo), 5 October 2022, pp. 5, 14–15.

21. The main works, though not the only ones, are: Saide Habibe, Salvador Forquilha, and João Pereira, *Radicalização islâmica no norte de Moçambique: O caso de Mocímboa da Praia*, Maputo: IESE, 2019; João Feijó, 'Social Asymmetries: Clues to Understand the Spread of Islamist Jihadism in Cabo Delgado', *Observador Rural*, 93, 2020; Feijó, 'The Role of Women in Conflict in Cabo Delgado: Understanding Vicious Cycles of Violence', *Observador Rural*, 114, 2021; and Geraldo Luís Macalane and Jafar Silvestre Jafar (eds), *Ataques terroristas em Cabo Delgado (2017–2020): As causas do fenómeno pela boca da população de Mocímboa da Praia*, Pemba: Universidade Rovuma, 2021.

22. David M. Matsinhe and Estácio Valoi, 'The Genesis of Insurgency in Northern Mozambique', ISS Southern Africa Report, 27, 2019.

23. Francesca Declich, 'Transmission of Muslim Practices and Women's Agency in Ibo Island and Pemba (Mozambique)', *Journal of Eastern African Studies*, 7(4), 2013, pp. 588–606; Daria Trentini, '"Muslims of the Spirits"—"Muslims of the Mosque": Performing Contested Ideas of Being Muslim in Northern Mozambique', *Journal for Islamic Studies*, 35, 2016, pp. 70–106; and Trentini, *At Ansha's: Life in the Spirit Mosque of a Healer in Mozambique*, New Brunswick: Rutgers University Press, 2021.

24. James A. Beckford, *Social Theory and Religion*, Cambridge: Cambridge University Press, 2003, pp. 94–7.

25. Among the large literature about the church–sect typology, see Michael Hill, *A Sociology of Religion*, London: Heinemann, 1973, Chapter 3; and Johnson Benton, 'A Critical Appraisal of the Church–Sect Typology', *American Sociological Review*, 22(1), 1957, pp. 88–92.

26. Among others, see Eric Morier-Genoud, 'Why Islamist Attack Demands a Careful Response from Mozambique', The Conversation, 20 October 2017, https://theconversation.com/why-islamist-attack-demands-a-careful-response-from-mozambique-85504, accessed 26 November 2022; and Morier-Genoud, 'Le Mozambique face à son "Boko Haram"', *Le Monde Afrique*, 14 June 2019, https://www.lemonde.fr/afrique/article/2018/06/14/le-mozambique-face-a-son-boko-haram_5314910_3212.html, accessed 26 November 2019.

pp. [14–21]

NOTES

27. Karl Marx, *Le 18 Brumaire de Louis Bonaparte*, Paris: Les Éditions sociales, 1969, p. 85.

28. Roman Loimeier, *Islamic Reform in Twentieth-Century Africa*, Edinburgh: Edinburgh University Press, 2016, p. 20; and Loimeier, 'What Is "Reform"? Approaches to a Problematic Term in African Muslim Contexts', *Journal for Islamic Studies*, 32(1), 2012, pp. 7–23.

29. Bassam Tibi, *Islamism and Islam*, New Haven: Yale University Press, 2012; and Shiraz Maher, *Salafi-Jihadism: The History of an Idea*, London: Penguin Books, 2016. See also Bruno Etienne, *L'Islam Radical*, Paris: Hachette, 1987; and Olivier Roy, *Généalogie de l'Islamisme*, Paris: Hachette, 1995. For a short and didactic introduction to these terms, see Willow J. Berridge, *Islamism in the Modern World: A Historical Approach*, London: Bloomsbury Academic, 2019, pp. 2–8.

30. Etienne, *L'Islam Radical*, Chapter 2; and Gilles Kepel, *Fitna: Guerre au coeur de l'Islam*, Paris: Gallimard, 2004.

1. THE 'RISE' OF ISLAM AFTER INDEPENDENCE, 1974–94

1. The Portuguese census of 1960 found that about 1.2 million Mozambicans (18 per cent of the population) were Muslim; see 'III Recenseamento general da população (1960)', 1995. For a discussion of the number of Muslims in Mozambique, see François Constantin, David S. Bone, and Ephraim C. Mandivenga, *Les communautés musulmanes d'Afrique orientale*, Pau: Centre de recherche et d'études sur les pays d'Afrique orientale, Université de Pau et des Pays de l'Adour, 1983, pp. 87–8; and Chapter 4 in the present book.

2. For a thorough analysis of the expansion of Sufism in Mozambique, see Bonate, 'Traditions and Transitions', Chapter 2.

3. M. J. Correia de Lemos, 'Reviver a Ilha, na Mafalala', *Arquivo* (Maputo), 4, 1988, pp. 49–58. Information about the sanctuary is derived from the author's interview with Amilcar Hussein Abdurremane, 8 November 2001, Beira; and Arcénio Sebastião, 'Moçambique: Um santuário especial em Búzi,' Deutsche Welle, 25 May 2021, https://www.dw.com/pt-002/mo%C3%A7ambique-um-santu%C3%A1rio-especial-em-b%C3%BAzi/video-57660679, accessed 25 April 2023.

4. I estimate the number of Muslims belonging to the Asian-Mozambican community at no fewer than 20,000 in 1960. This estimate is based on the official figures of the time that list 17,241 'Indians' and 31,455 *mestiços*, half of whom might have been Muslim. The Ismaili community

175

p. [22]

NOTES

(locally known as Nizari) represented 2,250 individuals in 1968. See Instituto Nacional de Estatística, 'Annuário Estatístico 1972', Lourenço Marques: Instituto Nacional de Estatística, Delegação de Moçambique, Direcção Provincial dos Serviços de Estatísticas, 1974, p. 31. About the Ismaeli, see D. Rebelo, 'Breves apontamentos sobre um grupo de indianos em Moçambique (A comunidade ismaília maometana)', *Boletim da Sociedade de Estudos da Colónia de Moçambique*, 128, 1961, pp. 83–9; and Rebelo, 'Inauguração do edifício S.A. Real Aga Khan da Comunidade Xi'ia-Muçulmano-Ismaelita', Lourenço Marques, 30 November 1968. For the Nizari, see Chapter 4.

5. Chapane Mutiua, 'Ajami Literacy, "Class" and Portuguese Pre-colonial Administration in Northern Mozambique', MA thesis, University of Cape Town, 2014; Mutiua, 'Islão e o processo de literacia no norte de Moçambique entre os finais do século XIX e princípios do século XX', in Teresa Cruz e Silva and Isabel Maria Casimiro (eds), *A ciência ao serviço do desenvolvimento?*, Dakar: CODESRIA, 2015, pp. 205–19; and Mutiua, 'O norte de Moçambique entre os séculos XIX e XX: Um contexto histórico', in Teresa Cruz e Silva, Manuel G. Mendes de Araújo, and Amélia Neves de Souto (eds), *Comunidades Costeiras: Perspectivas e realidades*, Maputo: Centro de Estudos Sociais Aquino de Bragança, 2015, pp. 233–55.

6. Instituto Nacional dos Arquivos Nacionais da Torre de Tombo (hereafter IAN/TT), Serviço de Centralização e Coordenação da Informação de Moçambique (hereafter SCCIM), Box 47, 'Relatório das conversações havidas em Porto Amélia, de segunda-feira 01jun64 a 07jun64, entre um dos adjuntos dos SCCI e Yussuf Arabe'; IAN/ TT, SCCIM, Box 71, 'Elementos recebidos da região militar a título particular em Setembro 67'; and Frederico J. Peirone, *A tribo Ajaua do Alto Niassa (Moçambique) e alguns aspectos da sua problemática neo-islâmica*, Lisbon: Junta da Investigação de Ultramar, Centro de Estudos Missionários, 1967, pp. 123–5.

7. Álvaro de Carvalho, 'Notas para a história das confrarias islâmica na Ilha de Moçambique', *Arquivo* (Maputo), 4, 1998, pp. 59–66; Eduardo Medeiros, 'Irmandades muçulmanas do Norte de Moçambique', in Matteo Angius and Mario Zamponi (eds), *Ilha de Moçambique: convergência de povos e culturas*, San Marino: AIEP Editore, 1999, pp. 70–85; and Liazzat Bonate, 'Muslim Personal Law among the Koti of Northern Mozambique', paper presented at the conference 'Islamic Law in Africa', 21–3 July 2000, Dar-es-Salaam.

8. Malyn D.D. Newitt, 'The Early History of the Sultanate of Angoche', *Journal of African History*, 13(3), 1972, pp. 397–406; Liazzat Bonate,

176

NOTES

'The Ascendance of Angoche: The Politics of Kinship and Territory in Nineteenth Century Northern Mozambique', *Lusotopie* (Paris), 10, 2003, pp. 115–40; and Regiane Augusto de Mattos, *As dimensões da resistência em Angoche: Da expansão política do sultanato à política colonialista Portuguesa no norte de Moçambique, 1842–1910*, Lisbon: Alameda, 2018. For other sultanates, see Hafkin, 'Trade, Society and Politics'; Mutiua, 'Ajami Literacy'; Mutiua, 'O norte de Moçambique'; and Rzewuski, 'Origins of the Tungi Sultanate', pp. 193–213.

9. After the invasion of Goa in 1961, the Indians who were not expelled from Mozambique by the Portuguese left the Comunidade Mahometana and created the Associação Mahometana. The latter was dissolved at independence, and the mostly Gujarati Indian Muslims re-joined the Comunidade Mahometana.

10. The full name of the Anuaril is Associação de Soccorros Mútuos Anjuman Anuaril Isslamo. For elements of the history of the organization and the Bezme brotherhood, see Liacat H. Dulá, *Vida e Obra do Professor Ahmade Dulá (Muālimo)*, Matola: Ciedima, 2018; *A Voz da Anuaril* (Maputo), no. 1, 21 September 1995, p. 1; and Isack Aly Amade, 'Amade Dulá: Obreiro de mão-cheia', *Crescente* (Maputo), 10 March 1995, p. 11.

11. For Islam in southern Mozambique, see Correia de Lemos, 'Reviver a Ilha, na Mafalala'; Raúl Honwana, *The Life History of Raúl Honwana: An Inside View of Mozambique from Colonialism to Independence, 1905–1975*, Boulder: Lynne Rienner, 1988, passim; and Valdemir Zamparoni, 'Monhés, Baneanes, Chinas e Afro-Maometanos: Colonialismo e racismo em Lourenço Marques, Moçambique, 1890–1940', *Lusotopie* (Paris), 7, 2000, pp. 191–222.

12. Cahen, 'L'État nouveau et la diversification religieuse au Mozambique, 1930–1974: I', p. 317.

13. João, *Abdul Kamal*; and Morier-Genoud, 'Concordat, Concordat ...', pp. 111–34.

14. Fernando Amaro Monteiro, *O Islão, o poder e a guerra (Moçambique 1964–1974)*, Porto: Universidade Portucalense, 1993; Edward A. Alpers, 'Islam in the Service of Colonialism? Portuguese Strategy during the Armed Liberation Struggle in Mozambique', *Lusotopie* (Paris), 6, 1998, pp. 165–84; Michel Cahen, 'L'État nouveau et la diversification religieuse au Mozambique, 1930–1974; II. La portugalisation désespérée (1959–1974)', *Cahiers d'Études Africaines*, 159, 2000, pp. 551–92; Mário Machaqueiro, 'The Islamic Policy of Portuguese Colonial Mozambique, 1960–1973', *Historical Journal*, 55(4), 2012, pp. 1097–116; and Machaqueiro, 'Foes or Allies?', pp. 843–69.

p. [24]

NOTES

15. Monteiro and Alpers both refer to Frelimo's socialist orientation to explain the movement's lack of interest in Islam. See Monteiro, *O Islão, o poder e a guerra*; and Alpers, 'Islam in the Service of Colonialism?'. I believe there is an additional factor in the sociology of Frelimo's leadership: for one, it contained few Muslims; for another, these few were either Ismaili or secularized Muslims, both singular groups within Islam. Also, Frelimo rapidly became dominated by Makonde, Nyanja, Chewa, and southerners, who were Christian or animist, leading to ethno-religious misunderstandings, if not tensions, with Muslims in northern Mozambique (Yao, Makua, and Mwani). A further line of explanation worth exploring would be that of international relations.

16. Among others, Frelimo arrested several evangelical pastors whom it suspected of collaborating with the Central Intelligence Agency to further the imperialism of the United States: all were Americans, and one of their leaders had been close to the Portuguese colonial state. Frelimo also deported Jehovah's Witnesses because they refused to recognize the new state authorities and had been manipulated by the Portuguese military to counter the liberation war. (The Portuguese colonial state had settled some Jehovah Witness refugees who had been persecuted in Malawi in select areas to create a buffer between the colonial state and the areas where the liberation war was being fought.) On the Jehovah's Witnesses, see Pedro Pinto, 'Jehovah's Witnesses in Colonial Mozambique', *LFM Social Sciences and Missions* (Lausanne), 17, 2005, pp. 61–123.

17. Among other organizations, Frelimo banned the Associação Indo-Portuguesa, the Mútuo Auxílio da Associação de Indianos, the Associação Mahometana da Lourenço Marques, and the Associação Muçulmana Portuguesa da Zambézia. See Anabela M.S. Carvalho, 'O empresariado islâmico em Moçambique no período pós-colonial: 1974–1994', PhD diss., Universidade Técnica de Lisboa, 1999, p. 314. For a short period, it also banned the Associação Afro-Mahometana; Yussuf Adam, personal communication, 1 September 2000, Maputo; and author interview, Sheik Issufo Bin Hagy, 30 August 2000, Maputo.

18. See President Samora Machel's address during the proclamation of independence at the Machava stadium, in *Notícias* (Lourenço Marques), 25 June 1975. For more details on the period, see Eric Morier-Genoud, 'Of God and Caesar: The Relation between Christian Churches and the State in Postcolonial Mozambique, 1974–1981', *Le Fait Missionnaire* (Lausanne), 3, 1996, pp. 1–80.

178

pp. [24–26]

NOTES

19. *Notícias* (Lourenço Marques), 18 August 1974; and Yussuf Adam, personal communication, 1 September 2000, Maputo.
20. Carvalho, 'O empresariado islâmico', pp. 235–48.
21. Author interview, Sheik Abdurrahman Amuri bin Jimba, 21 August 2000, Ilha de Moçambique.
22. Achille Mbembe, *Afriques indociles: Christianisme, pouvoir et état en société postcoloniale*, Paris: Karthala, 1988, Chapter 6.
23. F. Constantin and C. Coulon, 'Minorités musulmanes et pouvoir politique en Afrique orientale', *Annuaire des Pays de l'Océan Indien*, 6, 1979, p. 32. For more details on this period, see Morier-Genoud, 'Of God and Caesar', Chapter 4.
24. Ministério da Justiça (hereafter MJ), Direcção Nacional dos Assuntos Religiosos (hereafter DNAR), 'Síntese da reunião de analise da implementação das recomendacções traçadas após a reunião de 6 de Dezembro de 1978 com o Episcopado Católico Moçambicano em 30 de Dezembro de 1978', 3 January 1979; and MJ, DNAR, 'Proposta sobre a participação de elementos do ministério do Interior ao seminário nacional sobre questões religiosas', 28 November 1979. (The archive of the Ministry of Justice is not catalogued; references are therefore to each specific document.)
25. MJ, DNAR, Ministério do Interior, *Circular*, 25 August 1979. For the radio programmes, see *Échos d'Outre-Mer* (Lausanne), 4, 1977, p. 8; and MJ, DNAR, director DAR to minister of justice, note 8/DAR/MJ/86, 31 January 1986.
26. About the pilgrimage to Mecca, see Constantin, Bone, and Mandivenga, *Les communautés musulmanes d'Afrique orientale*, p. 92; and MJ, DNAR, 'Actas das conversações tidas com o SG da Liga mundial islâmica', 11 May 1984. For the rest, see the section 'errors committed' in MJ, DNAR, 'Síntese do I seminário nacional sobre questões religiosas', 28 June 1980. For the recommencement of pilgrimages, see Appendix II.
27. MJ, DNAR, SAAR-Inhambane, 'Relatório', 6 October 1980; MJ, DNAR, SAAR-Niassa, 'Relatório', 17 June 1980; and MJ, DNAR, SAAR-Niassa to national director, note 10/SPAAR/18–4/83.
28. MJ, DNAR, Síntese do I seminário nacional sobre questões religiosas, 4 July 1980; and MJ, DNAR, SAAR-Niassa, 'Relatório', 17 June 1980.
29. *Tempo* (Maputo), 13 April 1980, pp. 14–15; and MJ, DNAR, SAAR-Tete to SAAR-National, note 6/SAART/80, 21 April 1980.
30. On the whole affair and how it is remembered, see Macagno, *Outros muçulmanos*, Chapter 8.
31. For example, in the early 1980s a pigsty was set up in a Muslim

179

pp. [26–27]

NOTES

neighbourhood in the town of Maxixe, Inhambane province. In January 1979, President Samora Machel gave a speech in the town of Angoche where he accused all Muslims present of being hypocrites because they all ate pork in secret, not least when they were drunk, hence Islam was no excuse, he declared, to stop 'development'. See notes about the address in *Noticias* (Maputo), 16 January 1979 (reproduced in *Intercambio* [Breda], 19, March 1979, p. 17). About soldiers being forced to eat pork, see J. Ramalho, 'Frelimo Grinds Down on Muslims', *To the Point* (Belgium), 23 March 1979, p. 44. See also Muhammad Ali Marques da Silva, *Escritos Islâmicos*, Lisbon: Al Furquán, 1991, pp. 70–3.

32. MJ, DNAR, 'Acta da audiência concedida a uma representação do Congresso islâmico encabeçada pelos Senhores Cassamo Suleman e Hassan Makdá', August 1983.

33. MJ, DNAR, Serviço de actividades associativas e religiosas (SAAR), Serviço de Cabo Delgado, note 6/SPAAR/CD/80, 5 August 1980.

34. Ramalho, 'Frelimo Grinds Down on Muslims', p. 44. By 2022, Issufo Moamed had adopted the name Ossufo Momade and had become Renamo's president. Author interview, Ossufo Momade, 23 September 2004, Maputo; and author interview, Raimundo Samuge, 22 August 2002, Maputo.

35. Alpers, 'East Central Africa', p. 319.

36. João M. Cabrita, *Mozambique: The Tortuous Road to Democracy*, London: Palgrave, p. 152; B.T. Muianga, 'Respondendo à Albino Magaia', *Savana* (Maputo), 29 December 1995, p. 6; and author interview, José Augusto (director of Renamo's Department of Foreign Affairs, Section Europe and United States), 13 May 1994, Maputo.

37. Christian Geffray and Mögens Pedersen, 'Nampula en guerre', *Politique Africaine*, 29, pp. 28–40; Gervase Clarence-Smith, 'The Roots of the Mozambican Counter-Revolution', *Southern African Review of Books*, April–May 1989, p. 10; Alex Vines, *Renamo: Terrorism in Mozambique*, London: James Currey, 1991, pp. 110–11; and Ken B. Wilson, 'Cults of Violence and Counter-Violence in Mozambique', *Journal of Southern African Studies*, 18(3), p. 540.

38. Paulo Oliveira, 'Os donos da Renamo', unpublished manuscript, Maputo, 1989, p. 57; Vines, *Renamo*, pp. 67–8; William Finnegan, *A Complicated War: The Harrowing of Mozambique*, Berkeley: University of California Press, 1992, pp. 33–4; Cabrita, *Mozambique*, p. 152; and *Jeune Afrique* (Paris), 1355–6, 24 December 1986, p. 44. There were also rumours of support from Yemen and Iraq (the latter soon after the start of its war with Iran, a country to which Frelimo was aligned).

pp. [28–30]

NOTES

39. For a discussion of the terms used, see the introduction.
40. Alan Thorold, 'Metamorphoses of the Yao Muslims', in Louis Brenner (ed.), *Muslim Identity and Social Change in Sub-Saharan Africa*, London: Hurst, 1993, pp. 79–90; Alpers, 'East Central Africa', pp. 313–14; and Bonate, 'Dispute over Islamic Funeral Rites', pp. 43–4.
41. IAN/TT, SCCIM, Box 395, Administração do Concelho de Lourenço Marques, 'Respostas ao questionário a que se refere a nota 164 de 24/2/66 do extinto Gabinete de Zona do Serviço de Acção Psicossocial de Lourenço Marques'. About Deobandism, see Barbara D. Metcalf, *Islamic Revival in British India, 1860–1960*, Princeton: Princeton University Press, 1982; and Massimo Introvigne, 'Tra fondamentalismo e conservatorismo islâmico: Nota sui Deobandi', Centre for Studies on New Religions, 2001, https://www.cesnur. org/2001/mi_dic04.htm, accessed 6 December 2001.
42. MJ, DNAR, Letter by Nuro Amade Dulá to Cassamo Tayob, 25 March 1957. This and all subsequent translations have been done by the author. About Amade Dulá, see his biography by Dulá, *Vida e Obra do Professor Ahmade Dulá*.
43. IAN/TT, SCCIM, Box 221, various documents; and IAN/TT, SCCIM, Box 395, various documents.
44. Fernando Amaro Monteiro, 'Sobre a actuação da corrente "wahhabitta" no Islão moçambicano: Algumas notas relativas ao período 1964–1974', *Africana Studia* (Porto), 12, 1993, pp. 85–107.
45. Abdulkader Tayob, *Islamic Resurgence in South Africa: The Muslim Youth Movement*, Cape Town: University of Cape Town Press, 1995, p. 66. One member of the Miya family lived in the Mozambican capital, where he owned a shop called Bazar Mayet.
46. See also IAN/TT, Policia Internacional e de Defesa do Estado (hereafter PIDE)/Direcção Geral de Segurança (hereafter DGS), Processo 6037–CI(2) 'Unitários ou Wahhabitas'; Monteiro, 'Sobre a actuação da corrente "wahhabitta"', p. 92.
47. Monteiro, 'Sobre a actuação da corrente "wahhabitta"', p. 411.
48. Author interview, Idrisse Sharfuddin, 15 August 2001, Beira. Carvalho refers to differences of caste between reformists and the Indo-Mozambicans from the Muslim associations, the former being Surdi and the latter Memam; Carvalho, 'O empresariado islâmico em Moçambique', pp. 317–18.
49. Regarding nationalism, it should be noted that, under colonial rule, (1) some Sufi leaders were repressed for their support of the liberation struggle and some were even killed in Cabo Delgado; (2) part of the clandestine Frelimo network in southern Mozambique (its fourth

181

pp. [30–33]

NOTES

region) relied on reformist Muslims; and (3) Mawlana Cassamo Tayob defended a young nationalist Muslim in court and managed to have him freed before the latter fled abroad and joined Frelimo. Author interview, Sheik Issufo Bin Hagy, 30 August 2000, Maputo; Teresa Cruz e Silva, 'A rede clandestina da Frelimo em Lourenço Marques (1960–1974)', BA honours thesis, Eduardo Mondlane University, 1986, pp. 91–2; and IAN/TT, SCCIM, Box 47, Oficio no. 2023, Chefe interino SCCIM (Ivens-Ferraz) ào Governador do Distrito de Lourenço Marques, 24 June 1963, confidencial.

50. MJ, DNAR, petition to the government dated 13 April 1979, signed by ten individuals.

51. The faction opposed to the reformists taking control of the Anuaril mosque had to retreat to the Afro-Mahometana mosque and organization; see M. Arrune, personal communication, 27 August 2000, Maputo.

52. MJ, DNAR, Conselho islâmico (em formação), Folha Informativa, 1, n.d. (reproduced in Appendix I). CISLAMO was formally launched only in March 1983; see Notícias (Maputo), 24 February 1983.

53. For the minutes of the meeting, see Frelimo, '"Consolidemos aquilo que nos une": Reunião da Direcção do Partido e do Estado com os representantes das confissões religiosas, 14 à 17 de Dezembro 1982', Maputo: Instituto Nacional do Livro e do Disco, 1983.

54. MJ, DNAR, C. Sulemane, 'Breve histórial do Congresso Islâmico de Moçambique (SUNNI)', 30 April 1984, 5pp.

55. MJ, DNAR, 'Balanço das actividades do DAR desde a sua criação', 4 April 1984.

56. MJ, DNAR, DAR director to the minister of justice, letter no. 41/DAR/MJ/89, 24 April 1989; MJ, DNAR, C. Sulemane, 'Breve histórial do Congresso'; and MJ/DNAR, DAR, 'Síntese do encontro havido entre Sua Excia o Ministro da Justiça e elementos do Congresso islâmico de Moçambique', 9 September 1984.

57. MJ, DNAR, Informação 08/2ª·S/DAR/MJ/84, 13 September 1984.

58. MJ, DNAR, Conselho islâmico, 'Folha Informativa', 3 December 1983.

59. Respectively: MJ, DNAR, Conselho islâmico de Moçambique, Circular 2/1983, August 1984; MJ, DNAR, DAR director to the general secretary of the African Muslim Committee, note 565/DAR/MJ/84, 13 July 1984; and MJ, DNAR, DAR director to minister of justice, note 27/DAR/MJ/84, 11 August 1984.

60. MJ, DNAR, DAR director to general secretary of AMA, note 565/DAR/KJ/84, 13 July 1984; MJ, DNAR, director of DAR to minister

pp. [33–35]

NOTES

of justice, note 27/DAR/MJ/84, 11 August 1984; and MJ, DNAR, DAR, 'Actas das conversações tidas com o SG da Liga Mundial Islâmica', 11 May 1984.

61. MJ, DNAR, director of DAR to minister of justice, note 107/DAR/MJ/88, n.d.

62. MJ, DNAR, 'Relatório das actividades de 1985', 3 December 1985, p. 4.

63. MJ, DNAR, 'Situação no seio da comunidade muçulmana', note 4/DAR/MJ/89, 24 April 1989.

64. According to the DAR, in 1988 Mozambique received aid worth only US$2 million from all Muslim countries combined; see MJ, DNAR, 'Situação no seio da Comunidade Muçulmana' (DAR director to minister of justice), note 4/DAR/MJ/89, 24 April 1989.

65. MJ, DNAR, 'Balanço das actividades do DAR desde a sua criação', 4 July 1984; and MJ, DNAR, 'Situação no seio da Comunidade Muçulmana'.

66. Among others, see Joseph Hanlon, *Mozambique:The Revolution under Fire*, London: Zed Books, 1984; and Michel Cahen, *La révolution implosée: Études sur 12 ans d'indépendance (1975–1987)*, Paris: Karthala, 1987.

67. Margaret Hall and Tom Young, *Confronting the Leviathan: Mozambique since Independence*, London: Hurst, 1997, pp. 199–205.

68. Roger Finke, 'Religious Deregulation: Origins and Consequences', *Journal of Church and State*, 32, 1990, pp. 609–26; Roland Robertson, 'The Economization of Religion? Reflections on the Promise and Limitations of the Economic Approach', *Social Compass*, 39(1), 1992, pp. 147–57; and Laurence R. Iannaccone, 'Introduction to the Economics of Religion', *Journal of Economic Literature*, 36, 1998, pp. 1465–96.

69. MJ, DNAR, 'Requisitos necessários para o registo das instituições religiosas', n.d, 3 pp.

70. *Notícias* (Maputo), 28 July 1990; and *InformÁfrica* (Lisbon), 17, 28 July 1990, p. 2. For the donation of sacrificial meat, see Organisation of Islamic Cooperation (OIC), 'Distribution of Sacrificial Meat in Hajj Seasons during the Period from 1403H to 1419H', http://www.oic-oci.org, accessed 1 July 2000.

71. *Notícias*, 2 July 1992; *Crescente* (Maputo), 17 March 1995, p. 12; author interview, Ibrahimo Nordine, 20 September 2004, Maputo; and author interview, Job Chambal, 14 August 2002, Maputo.

72. Xinhua News Agency, 15 December 1994; and *Muslim World League Journal*, 15(2), June 1997, p. 16.

183

NOTES

73. Thus, whereas Mozambique only received US$2 million from all Muslim countries combined in 1988, in mid-1999 the Islamic Development Bank promised US$80 million to Mozambique for the next three years and in December of the same year signed a credit protocol for US$10 million. See, respectively, Charles Mangwiro, 'Mozambique: Islamic Bank Pledges US $80 Million to Mozambique', African Eye News Service, 7 July 1999, https://allafrica.com/stories/199907070158.html; 'Comunicados de imprensa do Conselho de Ministros', *Masoko* (Maputo), 6 December 1999, http://www.mozambique.mz/governo/masoko/communi11.htm, accessed 7 December 1999 (link no longer active); and MJ, DNAR, 'Situação no seio da Comunidade Muçulmana'.

74. For a more detailed discussion, see Chapter 2.

75. The most recent statistics, from 1997, do not indicate a significant rise in the percentage of Muslims in the country, with Muslims listed as forming 17.8 per cent of the total population. Some Muslim leaders contest the statistics. For a fuller and more recent discussion on the subject, see Chapter 4.

76. *Indian Ocean Newsletter* (Paris), 695, 25 October 1995, p. 3.

77. Some of these clashes took place in the district of Memba in Nampula province; see *Notícias* (Maputo), 21 October 1993.

78. See, for example, *Notícias* (Maputo), 10 March 1995. For post-socialist Indo-Pakistani entrepreneurs, see M. Anne Pitcher, *Transforming Mozambique: The Politics of Privatization, 1975–2000*, Cambridge: Cambridge University Press, 2002, passim.

79. Cédric Mayrargue, 'Pluralisation et compétition religieuses en Afrique subsaharienne: Pour une étude comparée des logiques sociales et politiques du christianisme et de l'Islam', *Revue internationale de politique comparée*, 16(1), 2009, pp. 83–98.

80. See, for example, the debates and accusation in *mediaFAX* (Maputo), 568, 10 August 1994, p. 3; and in *Savana* (Maputo), 6 January 1995, pp. 1–4. For the official recognition of the Eid holiday as a national holiday in 1996, see Chapter 2.

81. Eric Morier-Genoud, 'The Politics of Church and Religion in the First Multi-party Elections of Mozambique', *Internet Journal of African Studies*, 1, April 1996, http://www.bradford.ac.uk/research/ijas/ijasnol.htm, accessed April 1996. See also Chapter 2.

82. Carvalho, 'O empresariado islâmico em Moçambique'; and Joana Pereira Leite, 'A guerra do caju e as relações Moçambique–Índia na época pós-colonial', *Lusotopie* (Paris), 7, 2000, pp. 295–332.

83. Michel Cahen, *Mozambique: Analyse politique de conjoncture*, Paris:

pp. [37–39]

NOTES

Indigo Publications, 1990, p. 40; and *Mozambiquefile*, 158, September 1989, p. 18.

84. *Notmoc* (Maputo), 37, 8 March 1995; and *Notmoc* (Maputo), 75, 31 March 1996.

85. In view of the government's lack of reaction, several analysts believe that Frelimo played a role in the creation of the party and that it used it to weaken Renamo's social base. PIMO's leader is a nephew of Renamo's leader and a former government soldier. On PIMO, see Raul Braga Pires, 'A formação do Partido Independente de Moçambique (PIMO)', *Africana Studia*, 12, 2009, pp. 91–109.

86. Secretariado técnico de administração eleitoral (STAE), 'Definitive Electoral List of Candidates for Parliament', 22 September 1994; see also Assembleia da República and AWEPA, *Quem é quem na Assembleia da República de Moçambique*, Maputo: Assembleia da República and AWEPA, 1996. For a fuller analysis, see Chapter 3.

87. See also the declaration of the Renamo president, Alfonso Dhlakama, in *Marchés Tropicaux* (Paris), 1118, 31 May 1996.

88. The election results triggered a profound crisis in the party, which led to divisions, then a split. By the early 2020s, the party continued to exist, but only the bombastic or purposefully controversial declarations of its president kept it in the news.

89. José Abudo is from the reigning Koti family of Angoche. He lived and worked in Beira for several years, where he developed connections to pro-Sufi elements. See his official biography in Bureau de Informação Pública, *Quem é quem no Governo de Moçambique 2000*, Maputo: Bureau de Informação Pública, 2000, pp. 7–8; and Isabelle Verdier, *Mozambique: 100 Men in Power*, Paris: Indigo, 1996, p. 24.

90. See Chapter 2. The law was neither cancelled nor redrafted. It was suspended and the discussion about it postponed indefinitely.

91. 'Nova lei da família não deve discriminar a mulher', *Diário de Notícias* (Lisbon), 13 April 2000.

92. Among others, see Marcelo Mosse, 'Nova lei de matrimónio: A charia para Moçambique?', *Público* (Lisbon), 9 May 2000.

93. For an overview of the law and its adoption, see Maria José Arthur, Teresa Cruz e Silva, Yolanda Sitoe, and Edson Mussa, 'Lei da Família (1): Antecedentes e contextos da sua aprovação', *OutrasVozes* (Maputo), 35–6, 2011, pp. 15–25.

94. The AMA claims that it gave its name to mosques not because of an 'imperialist' drive but to get around the never-ending conflict between CISLAMO and the Islamic Congress, as both wanted to appropriate and give their names to the new mosques. See MJ,

NOTES

DNAR, ref. AMA/120/0488, transcript of a letter from the general secretary to its delegate in Mozambique, 19 April 1988.

95. 'American Christian Missionaries Invade Maputo Mosque', Panafrican News Agency (Dakar), 8 January 2000; and 'Christian Missionaries Invade Maputo Mosque', Islam Voice, February 2000 (via the discussion list dunia-islam@egroups.com).

96. See *Savana* (Maputo), 7 April 2000; and *Domingo* (Maputo), 18 June 2000, 23 and 30 July 2000, 13 and 20 August 2000, 3, 10, and 17 September 2000, and 1, 8, 15, and 22 October 2000. The debate went beyond the print media when reformists tried to discover which pro-Sufi elements were writing newspaper reports under pseudonyms. About Sheik Aminuddin, see Bonate, 'Dispute over Islamic Funeral Rites', pp. 41–59.

97. Author interview, Sheik Issufo Amada Sualé, 23 August 2000, Ilha de Moçambique; and author interview, A. Zaina, 23 August 2000, Ilha de Moçambique. M. Zaina, a former deputy at the National Assembly, showed me several documents regarding this matter.

98. Siefert, *Muslime in Mosambik*.

99. In 2004, the Supreme Court ruled that its former facilities, which the state had transferred to CISLAMO, were to be returned to its original owners, the Dulá family. But this legal decision was never implemented. In 2022, the mosque and its facilities were still in the hands of CISLAMO. See *Domingo* (Maputo), 24 October 2004, p. 18.

100. *Notícias* (Maputo), 21 September 1992 and *mediaFAX* (Maputo), no. 568, 10 August 1994.

101. *Notmoc* (Maputo), 27, 24 July 2000; *Notícias* (Maputo), 31 October 1996; author interview, Sheik Issufo Bin Hagy, 30 August 2000, Maputo; M. Arrune, personal communication, 27 August 2000, Maputo; and author interview, Sheik Abdul Rashid Ismail, 11 September 2001, Beira. For more recent developments in the CFI, see Chapter 4.

102. Bonate, 'Muslim Personal Law', pp. 19–20. An organization with a very similar name (Ansaru Sunna) was launched earlier in Cabo Delgado and was officially recognized in 1997, a year before the Nampula organization (see Chapter 4).

103. Such a co-optation does of course not mean that believers necessarily followed their leaders; but it was a start. Author interview, Sheik Abdurrahman Amuri bin Jimba, 21 August 2000, Ilha de Moçambique; and author interview, Sheik M. Anifo, 24 August 2000, Ilha de Moçambique.

104. Curiously, the alleged perpetrator did not know the sheik's name.

186

pp. [41–48]

NOTES

Still, the sheik was arrested together with the criminal. The latter was quickly released, while the sheik was released with the imposition of certain conditions and was soon rearrested. It would take until 2000 for the sheik's name to be cleared by the Supreme Court.

105. For the main articles, see *Metical* (Maputo), 5 March 1999, 30 April 1999, 3 May 1999; and *Savana* (Maputo), 5 March 1999, 23 and 30 April 1999.

106. Throughout 2000, Renamo contested the election results, with demonstrations in November that were violently repressed by the government. It seems that Renamo was at least partly right in its protest: a number of diplomats and journalists recognized that there had been fraud and that this might have erroneously put Joaquim Chissano (though not Frelimo) into power. See Michel Cahen, 'Mozambique: L'instabilité comme gouvernance?', *Politique Africaine*, 80, 2000, pp. 111–35.

107. *Savana* (Maputo), 1 September 2000.

108. See the articles and debate in *Metical*, October and November 2001.

109. *Domingo* (Maputo), 7 October 2001; *Metical* (Maputo), 3 October 2001; and *Savana* (Maputo), 9 November 2001.

2. THE 1996 'MUSLIM HOLIDAYS' AFFAIR

1. See the *Mail and Guardian* (Johannesburg), 5–11 July 1996, p. 16; *Africa Confidential* (London), 37(15), 19 July 1996, pp. 6–7; Catholic World News (Rome), 30 April 1996; and *Marchés Tropicaux* (Paris), 14 June 1996, pp. 1222–3.

2. S. Huntington, *The Clash of Civilizations and the Remaking of World Order*, New York: Touchstone, 1996. For a critique, see S. Chan, 'Too Neat and Under-Thought a World Order: Huntington and Civilisations', *Millennium*, 26(1), 1997, pp. 137–40; and S. Brower, P. Gifford, and S. Rose, *Exporting the American Gospel: Global Christian Fundamentalism*, London: Routledge, 1996, p. 9.

3. On Protestant aggression, see Brower et al., *Exporting the American Gospel*; for Southern Africa more specifically, P. Gifford, *The New Crusaders: Christianity and the New Right in Southern Africa*, London: Pluto Press, 1988; on the renewed militancy of the Catholic Church, see Andrea Riccardi, 'Le primat de l'évangélisation', in Gilles Kepel (ed.), *Les politiques de Dieu*, Paris: Seuil, 1993, pp. 99–117.

4. This defect is found in much if not most of the literature on Islam and more particularly on Islamic fundamentalism. See, for example,

pp. [49–51]

NOTES

J.S. Trimingham, *The Influence of Islam upon Africa*, 2nd edn, London: Longman, 1980, Chapter 6; J.L. Esposito, *The Islamic Threat: Myth or Reality?*, Oxford: Oxford University Press, 1992; and L. Davidson, *Islamic Fundamentalism*, Westport: Greenwood Press, 1998.

5. Among others, see G. Kepel, *The Revenge of God: The Resurgence of Islam, Christianity and Judaism in the Modern World*, University Park: Pennsylvania State University Press, 1994; and Richard Antoun and Mary E. Hegland (eds), *Religious Resurgence: Contemporary Cases in Islam, Christianity, and Judaism*, Syracuse: Syracuse University Press, 1987.

6. L. Iannaccone, 'Religious Markets and the Economics of Religion', *Social Compass*, 39(1), 1992, pp. 123–31; Mark Chaves, Peter J. Schraeder, and Mario Sprindys, 'State Regulation of Religion and Muslim Vitality in the Industrialized West', *Journal of Politics*, 56(4), 1994, pp. 1087–97; and Malika Zeghal, 'Etat et marché des biens religieux: Les voies égyptienne et tunisienne', *Critique Internationale*, 5, 1999, pp. 75–95. For a critique of this approach, see Roland Robertson, 'The Economization of Religion? Reflections on the Promise and Limitations of the Economic Approach', *Social Compass*, 39(1), 1992, pp. 147–57. It should be said here that this literature draws from insights made by Peter Berger more than twenty years ago; Peter Berger, *The Sacred Canopy: Elements of a Sociological Theory of Religion*, New York: Doubleday Anchor Book, 1969. Although a Marxist, Berger did not mention or consider religious tension and conflict either.

7. On the history of Family Day, see *mediaFAX* (Maputo), 971, 15 March 1996, pp. 3–4; and *mediaFAX*, 978, 26 March 1996, p. 1.

8. The Holy Friday law project was to be discussed in the following parliamentary session but never was. See *Notícias* (Maputo), 5 March 1996 and 21 May 1996.

9. See the judges' decision and argumentation in *mediaFAX*, 1172, 30 December 1996, pp. 5–6.

10. See *mediaFAX*, 1659, 9 December 1998; and *Metical* (Maputo), 369, 9 December 1998.

11. Copies of the letters in possession of the author. The Episcopal Conference's letter is reproduced in *Rumo Novo* (Beira), 16 August 1996, while various Catholic declarations can be found in *Notícias*, 6 and 7 March 1996.

12. *Imparcial* (Maputo), 10 April 1996.

13. Among others, see Cardinal dos Santos' declarations in *Notícias*

188

pp. [51–55]

NOTES

(Maputo), 6 March 1996, p. 56; and the editorial of *Vida Nova* (Nampula), 4, April 1996, p. 2.

14. See the CCM secretary general's declarations in *Savana* (Maputo), 8 March 1996, pp. 2–3; and *mediaFAX*, 968, 12 March 1996, p. 1.

15. Copies in possession of the author.

16. Two Muslim voices opposed the law. One came from the Association Anuaril Isslamo. There is good reason to believe that its position had more to do with politics within the Muslim community than with opposition to the law per se. The other voice came from PIMO, a political party that claims to represent Muslims (see below) and argued that the law was not enough. For Anuaril, see *A Voz da Anuaril* (Maputo), 12, 29 March 1996; for PIMO, see *Savana*, 8 March 1996, pp. 14–15.

17. Hindu and Zionist statements can be found in *mediaFAX*, 970, 14 March 1996, p. 3; *mediaFAX*, 976, 22 March 1996, p. 1; and *Savana*, 8 March 1996, p. 3.

18. Author interview, José Chicuara Massinga (deputy for the União Democrática and president of the PANADE party), 10 November 1994, Maputo.

19. See, for example, the declarations made in *Notícias*, 5 March 1996.

20. In 1991, the National Directorate of Statistics estimated that 24.1 per cent of the population was Muslim, 21.5 per cent Catholic, and 19.7 per cent Protestant. For a critique of these estimates, see *Africa Confidential* (London), 37(15), 19 July 1996, p. 7; and Chapter 4.

21. Some of the census results are simply not credible. For example, 'animism' would have almost disappeared, dropping from 50 per cent in 1975 to 2.1 per cent in 2022. Similarly, people 'without religion' would now number 23.1 per cent. The methodology used seems at best disputable. The question used was vague ('what is your religion or belief?') and was addressed to anyone down to five-year-old children. See further discussion in Chapter 4.

22. *Imparcial*, 489, 8 May 1996, pp. 1–2; and *Demos* (Maputo), 27 March 1996, pp. 8–9.

23. Quoted in *mediaFAX*, 963, 5 March 1996, p. 1.

24. See details in Chapter 1.

25. See, for example, *Notícias*, 29 August 1996, p. 7.

26. See *Bilal* (Maputo), 29 March 1996, p. 11; and *mediaFAX*, 976, 22 March 1996, p. 2.

27. Dhlakama's most explicit statement on this issue can be found in *Marchés Tropicaux*, 31 May 1996, p. 1119.

pp. [55–59]

NOTES

28. A. Meldrum, 'Mozambique Fears Growth of Islam', *Mail and Guardian* (Johannesburg), 5–11 July 1996, p. 16.

29. Yussuf Adam, personal communication; *Notmoc* (Maputo), 37, 8 March 1995; and *Notmoc* (Maputo), 75, 31 March 1996. See also Chapter 1, p. 23.

30. Morier-Genoud, 'Politics of Church and Religion'.

31. *Africa Confidential* (London), 37(15), 19 July 1996, p. 7; and *Imparcial* (Maputo), 8 May 1996, pp. 1–2.

32. Yves Léonard, *Salazarisme et Fascisme*, Paris: Editions Chandeigne, 1996.

33. Manuel da Braga Cruz, 'O Estado Novo e a Igreja Católica', in Fernando Rosas (ed.), *Portugal e o Estado Novo*, Lisbon: Editorial Presença, 1992, pp. 201–21; and Morier-Genoud, 'Concordat, Concordat …', pp. 111–34.

34. Helgesson, *Church, State and People in Mozambique*; and Teresa Cruz e Silva, 'Igrejas protestantes no Sul de Moçambique e nacionalismo: o caso da "Missão Suíça" (1940–1974)', *Estudos Moçambicanos* (Maputo), 10 (1992), pp. 19–39.

35. This policy could not, however, prevent the existence of some Muslim centres in central and southern Mozambique and a few Evangelical missions in the centre of the country. On the latter, see Phyllis Thompson, *Life Out of Death: A Miracle of Church Growth in the Face of Opposition*, London: Hodder and Stoughton, 1989; and Lorraine Schultz, *Moçambique Milestones*, Kansas City: Nazarene Publishing House, 1982, Chapter 6.

36. See Cahen, 'Le colonialisme tardif et la diversification religieuse'; and Alpers, 'Islam in the Service of Colonialism?'

37. On Frelimo's postcolonial religious policy, see Morier-Genoud, 'Of God and Caesar'. On the civil war, see, among others Hall and Young, *Confronting the Leviathan*, Chapters 5 and 7; and Eric Morier-Genoud, Domingos do Rosario, and Michel Cahen (eds), *The War Within: New Perspectives on the Civil War in Mozambique, 1976–1992*, Oxford: James Currey, 2018.

38. See the examples of the Nazarene and Presbyterian Churches in, respectively, Frank Howie, *The Mozambique Story*, Kansas City: Nazarene Publishing House, 1993, Chapter 3; and Charles Biber, *Cent ans au Mozambique: Le parcours d'une minorité; Reportage sur l'histoire de l'église presbytérienne du Mozambique*, 2nd edn, Lausanne: Edition du Soc, 1992.

39. For the Lutheran Church, see E. Theodore Bachmann and Mercia B. Bachmann, *Lutheran Churches in the World: A Handbook*, Minneapolis:

p. [59]

NOTES

Augsburg Fortress, 1989, pp. 76–7. For the AMA, see *Crescente* (Maputo), 14 April 1995, p. 7; and MJ, DNAR, director of DAR to director of the Africa and Middle East section of the Ministry of Foreign Affairs, note 65/DAR/MJ/85, 26 January 1985.

40. Evangelical institutions are often accused of practising 'rice bowl Christianity', that is, conditioning their aid on conversion. In Mozambique, two different mainline Protestant pastors told us about their encounters in the late 1980s with evangelicals (including World Vision) who preached while giving humanitarian aid. For similar accusations in the Latin America context and a balanced discussion of the World Vision case, see David Stoll, *Is Latin America Turning Protestant? The Politics of Evangelical Growth*, Berkeley: University of California Press, 1990, Chapter 9.

41. The Baptist Convention Church (Convenção Baptista, linked to the American Southern and First Baptists) was quite explicit in this strategy. It called it 'refugee ministries'. Most bluntly, a 1992 issue of the American Southern Baptists' magazine stated the following about Mozambique: 'The Brocks [a missionary couple] stress they do not need war and suffering to evangelise. But the country may never again see such a concentration of people searching for answers.' Mr Brock himself declared that 'when the war is over, our opportunity is over'. *The Commission* (Richmond, VA), December 1992, p. 40.

42. Steve Askin, 'Mission to Renamo: The Militarisation of the Religious Right', *Journal of Theology for Southern Africa*, 69, December 1989, pp. 106–16; and Askin, 'Mission to Renamo: The Militarization of the Religious Right', *Issue*, 18(2), 1990, pp. 29–38 (the two papers are different despite carrying similar titles). Note that Askin's argument that these churches or individuals were simply manipulated by politicians is contradicted by the fact that some of these institutions worked on both the government's and Renamo's side and by the fact that some of them were still working in Mozambique in the 2000s. In other words, if there was manipulation, then it worked both ways. A case in point is the organization called Open Doors; see Sarel Jordan (Open Doors International), personal communication by e-mail, 17 June 1999.

43. *Muslim World League Journal*, 25(2), June 1997, p. 15; *Domingo* (Maputo), 9 July 1995; and *Notícias* (Maputo), 24 September 1987.

44. Considering the number of Christian churches in Mozambique and the scattered nature of data, it is impossible to give a global figure for Mozambican Christians studying abroad. But most churches sent at least one pastor or priest to a regional seminary (for example, in

191

p. [60]

NOTES

Kenya for the Nazarenes and in South Africa for Open Doors) or to the religious university of the respective church's home country (for example, Italy for Catholics and the United States or Brazil for Methodists).

45. The university is known as the Catholic University of Mozambique. For some background, see *Rumo Novo* (Beira), 15, April 1996, pp. 4–14 and the university's internet homepage, http://www.ucm. ac.mz, accessed 30 January 2023.

46. Among the new organizations or movements are Campus Crusade for Christ, Good News Ministries International, Jesus Alive!, Korean Evangelical Mission Fellowship, OMS International, Friends Reaching Out Ministries, and Operation Mobilisation.

47. Catholic statistics indicate a restoration to the 1978 levels of personnel and population percentage (though not yet to those of the pre-independence era). Individual Protestant churches all talk of tremendous increases in membership—the Baptists claim to have tripled the number of their believers between 1989 and 1998, the Presbyterians to now have more believers in the north than in their historical base in the south, and the Nazarene to have grown by 40 per cent in 1995 alone. Although there are no figures for Islam, it is generally believed that the faith has expanded in the south, even if the national figures from the 1997 census do not indicate any significant overall increase (see Introduction and Chapter 4). For Catholic figures, see Felician A. Foy (ed.), *Catholic Almanac 1978*, Huntington: Our Sunday Visitor Publishing Division, 1977, p. 433; and Foy, *Catholic Almanac 1998*, Huntington: Our Sunday Visitor Publishing Division, 1997, p. 354. For Protestant figures: *Together: A Newsletter for Nazarene in Higher Education*, 4(4), November 1996, p. 2; Baptist statistics reported by Sandra Higgins, personal communication via e-mail (International Mission Board), 3 March 1999; and author interview, Simião Chamangu (president of the Presbyterian Synod Council), 10 May 1996, Maputo.

48. For a case of controversy (attacks and counter-attacks) over fundamentalism, see *Savana*, 6 January 1995, pp. 1–4; for some accusations of false teaching in Islam, see *Notícias* (Maputo), 25 April 1991; and for accusations against neo-Pentecostals, see the controversy around the Universal Church of the Kingdom of God.

49. P. Gifford, 'Some Recent Developments in African Christianity', *African Affairs*, 93(373), October 1994, pp. 513–34.

50. Although the US government does not officially support churches, in Mozambique USAID works with, and finances, American evangelical

192

pp. [61–62]

NOTES

NGOs such as World Vision and the Adventist Development and Relief Agency. See 'USAID Congressional Presentation FY 1997', https://web.archive.org/web/20010211031845/http://www.usaid.gov/pubs/cp97/countries/mz.htm, accessed 30 January 2023.

51. *Notícias* (Maputo), 25 April 1991, 15 May 1991, and 21 October 1993.

52. Consultant of the Christian Council of Mozambique, personal communication, December 1997, Lisbon; author interview, Pierre Jeannet (Département Missionnaire des Églises de la Suisse Romande), 10 November 1993, Lausanne; and author interview, Elias Nacaca and Silvino Jossene (Igreja Evangélica de Cristo de Moçambique), 5 March 1994, Cuamba.

53. *Indian Ocean Newsletter* (Paris), 695, 25 November 1995, p. 3. On the collaboration between Muslims and the Catholic Church more generally, see João de Deus Damião, 'O Islamismo em Moçambique à Luz do Sínodo Africano (Experiências Pastorais)', *Rumo Novo*, 9 April 1994, pp. 36–51.

54. On fundamentalism, see *Savana* (Maputo), 6 January 1995, pp. 1–4. On the Universal Church of the Kingdom of God, see *Savana* (Maputo), 7 October 1994; and *mediaFAX* (Maputo), 721, 23 March 1995. For an academic take on the church, see Linda Van de Kamp, *Violent Conversion: Brazilian Pentecostalism and Urban Women in Mozambique*, Woodbridge: James Currey, 2016.

55. Secularism has a Christian origin, and it is therefore usually biased against non-Christian faiths and believers. Constitutionally, this was the case in Mozambique after independence. In practice, however, Frelimo favoured accommodation. This was notably the case with family law, a classic and crucial bone of contention between Muslims and the secular state in Africa. For a discussion at the level of the continent, see Lamin Sanneh, *The Crown and the Turban: Muslim and West Africa Pluralism*, Boulder: Westview Press, 1997, part 4. For Mozambique, see Signe Arnfred, 'Reflection on Family Forms and Gender Policy in Mozambique', unpublished paper, 1990; and B. Isaacman and J. Stephen, 'Mozambique: Women, the Law and Agrarian Reform', Addis Ababa: United Nations Economic Commission for Africa, 1989, Chapter 4.

56. For an overview of the period, see Morier-Genoud, 'Of God and Caesar', Chapter 4.

57. See, for example, Alex Vines and Ken Wilson, 'Churches and the Peace Process in Mozambique', in Paul Gifford (ed.), *The Christian Churches and the Democratisation of Africa*, Leiden: Brill, 1995, p. 133;

193

NOTES

and Helgesson, *Church, State and People in Mozambique*, Chapter 1. An exception is J. Luiza, 'A Igreja das Palhotas: Génese da Igreja em Moçambique, entre o colonialismo e a independência', *Cadernos de Estudos Africanos* (Lisbon), 4, September 1989, p. 71.

58. See the minutes of the meeting in Frelimo, '"Consolidemos aquilo que nos une": Reunião da Direcção do Partido e do Estado com os representantes das confissões religiosas, 14 à 17 de Dezembro 1982', Maputo: Instituto Nacional do Livro e do Disco, 1983, 100pp.

59. Alexandrino José, 'Samora e as confissões religiosas: Um diálogo inacabado', in António Sopa (ed.), *Samora: Homem do Povo*, Maputo: Maguezo Editores, 2001, pp. 157–8; and Cristiane Nascimento da Silva, '"Viver a Fé em Moçambique": As Relações entre a Frelimo e as Confissões Religiosas (1962–1982)', PhD diss., Federal Fluminense University, 2017, pp. 167, 265.

60. MJ, DNAR, 'Possibilidade de restituição dos imoveis de certas seitas religiosas ocupadas ou encerradas sem nenhuma base legal' (director of DAR to governor of Gaza), note 41/DAR/MJ/84, 27 January 1984; and MJ, DNAR, 'Balanço das actividades do DAR desde a sua criação', 4 July 1984.

61. MJ, DNAR, 'Relatório das actividades do DAR no ano de 1984', 15 January 1985; and MJ, DNAR, 'Relatório das actividades de 1985', 3 December 1985.

62. After 1975, there existed a Service of Religious and Associational Affairs (SAAR), on the basis of which the DAR was developed. But the SAAR existed little more than on paper, with no full-time employees and no offices in the provinces. MJ, DNAR, 006/SAAR/MJ/1983, 'Relatório restrito dos serviços' (SAAR to minister of justice), 6 January 1983; MJ, DNAR, director of DAR to government, note 200/DAR/MJ/84, 20 March 1984; and author interview, Manuel Alferes (former SAAR director), 24 June 1996, Maputo.

63. On Frelimo's gradual change of policy, see E. Morier-Genoud, 'Y a-t-il un spécificité protestante au Mozambique? Discours du pouvoir postcolonial et histoire des églises chrétiennes', *Lusotopie* (Paris), 7, esp. pp. 416–17.

64. *Notícias* (Maputo), 9 November 1988.

65. On Frelimo's Fifth Congress, see Hall and Young, *Confronting the Leviathan*, pp. 201–3.

66. Hall and Young, *Confronting the Leviathan*, p. 200, note 42; and author interview, Isaias Funzamo (former head of the Presbyterian Church

pp. [63–64]

NOTES

and former president of the Christian Council of Mozambique), 31 March 1994, Maputo.

67. There were at least two drafts of the law, one or the other of which was discussed with each major organized faith in the country. See MJ, DNAR, director of DAR to minister of justice, note 54/DAR/ MJ/88, 4 June 1988; and MJ, DNAR, director of DAR to minister of justice, note 59/DAR/MJ/89, 16 May 1989. I consulted the 1989 draft of the law at the Eduardo Mondlane University (hereafter UEM), Centro de Estudos Africanos (hereafter CEA), folder 357.

68. *Boletim da República* (Maputo), Series 1, Second Supplement, 1 June 1990 (Decreto 11/90); and *Boletim da República*, Series 1, Second Supplement, 31 December 1991 (Lei 26/91).

69. Between 1990 and 1995, DAR registered 150 new religious institutions, in effect doubling the number of (legal) churches in the country. MJ, DNAR, list of registered religious institutions, 5 June 1991; and *Nova Vida* (Beira), 6, June 1995, p. 11. At the provincial level, numbers also exploded, even in such a remote province as Niassa. Author interview, Jean-Barnabé Manuel Tabou (director of DAR-Niassa), 5 May 1994, Cuamba.

70. On the 'religious market', see Roger Finke, 'Religious Deregulation: Origins and Consequences', *Journal of Church and State*, 32 (1990), pp. 609–26; and Berger, *Sacred Canopy*, Chapter 6.

71. UEM/CEA, folder 357, 'Ausência de legislação em certos sectores da vida social das populações' (director of DAR to the president of the Commission of Social Affairs of the Assembly of the Republic), note 172/DAR/MJ/1992, 28 April 1992, p. 1.

72. UEM/CEA, folder 357, 'Ausência de legislação', p. 2.

73. The governor of Nampula could do little more than offer mediation when physical fights broke out between different Muslim organizations in Nampula in 1993; see above. Similarly, the state could do nothing when, in 1999, some American fundamentalist Protestants in Maputo went to evangelize inside a mosque during Ramadan. See Panafrican News Agency, 8 January 2000; and US embassy official, personal communication by e-mail, January 2000.

74. For a broader and longer-term analysis of patronage in Mozambique, see José Magode, *Pouvoir et réseaux sociaux au Mozambique:Appartenances, interactivité du social et du politique (1933–1994)*, Paris: Connaissances et Savoirs, 2005.

195

pp. [64–73]

NOTES

75. For a good overview of the activities of the Universal Church of the Kingdom of God in Mozambique, see *Savana* (Maputo), 7 October 1994, pp. 16–17; *mediaFAX* (Maputo), 721, 23 March 1995; and *Imparcial* (Maputo), 492, 13 May 1996.

76. See details about the party in Chapter 1.

77. See P. Oliveira, 'Le président et le transcendant', *Politique Africaine*, 52, December 1993, pp. 150–1; and *Savana* (Maputo), 4 February 1994, 18 February 1994, 18 March 1994, and 20 May 1994.

78. *Monthly Review Bulletin* (London), 16, 11 November 1997, p. 3; and *Indian Ocean Newsletter* (Paris), 17 July 1993, p. 2.

79. For Muslim accusations, see *mediaFAX* (Maputo), 568 (10 August 1994), p. 3; and *Savana* (Maputo), 6 January 1995, pp. 1–4. For Christian accusations, see the discussion of the Eid affair in Chapter 2.

80. On transcendental meditation, see endnote 87, and the sect's electronic magazine Enlightenment, March 1999, http://www.enlightenment-magazine.org (now accessible via the Internet Archive at https://web.archive.org/). On the television channel of the Universal Church of the Kingdom of God, see *Domingo* (Maputo), 25 May 1997, p. 33; and *mediaFAX* (Maputo), 28 December 1998, p. 2.

81. See the DAR director's statements in *Domingo* (Maputo), 17 March 1996, p. 9.

3. A PROSPECT OF SECULARIZATION? MUSLIMS AND POLITICAL POWER, 1994–2004

1. Ministry of Justice (hereafter MJ), Direcção Nacional dos Assuntos Religiosos (hereafter DNAR), director of DAR to minister of justice, note 54/DAR/MJ/88, 4 June 1988; and MJ, DNAR, director of DAR to minister of justice, note 59/DAR/MJ/89, 16 May 1989. I consulted the 1989 draft of the law in the library of the Centre of African Studies at Eduardo Mondlane University, folder 357.

2. These were Decree 11/90 for education and Law 26/91 for healthcare.

3. Marcello Mosse, 'Discriminação implicita?', *Metical* (Maputo), 645, 12 January 2000.

4. MJ, DNAR, 'Relatório das actividades de 1985', p. 3.

5. MJ, DNAR, 'Situação no seio da comunidade muçulmana' (DAR director to minister of justice), note 4/DAR/M, 24 April 1989.

6. *Notícias* (Maputo), 3 and 12 September 1987.

pp. [73–78]

NOTES

7. Respectively, *Notícias* (Maputo), 12 September 1987; *Fact and Report* (Amsterdam), 21 (PQ), 23 August 1991; *InformÁfrica* (Lisbon), 28 July 1990, p. 2; and 'Islamic Summit Communiqué', Xinhua News Agency (China), 15 December 1994.

8. *Notícias* (Maputo), 11 November 1992; *Boletim da República* (Maputo), 3rd series, 6, 10 February 1993, p. 85; and *Notícias* (Maputo), 31 October 1996.

9. Editorial, *Metical* (Maputo), 649, 18 January 2000; and Salomão Moyana, 'Novo executivo visto pelo Savana', *Savana* (Maputo), 315, 21 January 2000.

10. About the PIMO party, see Chapter 1.

11. See articles in *Domingo* (Maputo) on 18 and 25 April 1999. See also *Metical* (Maputo) on 30 April and 3 May. After many developments, the Indian mawlana was cleared by the Supreme Court in 2000; see *Metical* (Maputo), 20 February 2000.

12. The details of this alliance remain secret to the time of writing. The chief Muslim negotiator, Mawlana Nazir Lunat, admitted that there had been negotiations and an agreement with the president, but he refused to say who (apart from himself) had been involved, which parliamentarians were thus elected, and what the Muslims had promised in exchange. Author interview, Nazir Lunat, 23 October 2004, Maputo; and author interview, Sheik Cassimo David Dafine, 21 October 2004, Maputo.

13. Among others, see 'Nova lei da família não deve discriminar a mulher', *Diário de Notícias* (Lisbon), 13 April 2000; 'Nova lei de matrimónio: A Charia para Moçambique?', *Público* (Lisbon), 9 May 2000; 'Lei da família divide religiosos', *Demos* (Maputo), 1 September 2004, p. 13; and 'Moçambique já tem nova lei da família', *Domingo* (Maputo), 29 August 2004, p. 4. For the context of the law and the situation on the ground, see Bonate, 'Muslim Personal Law among the Koti'.

14. Bernhard Weimer, 'Abstaining from the 1998 Local Government Elections in Mozambique: Some Hypotheses', *L'Afrique Politique* (Paris), 1999, pp. 125–45.

15. República de Moçambique and AWEPA, *As primeiras 33 autarquias em Moçambique: Realidade, conquistas, constrangimentos, perspectivas*, Maputo: República de Moçambique and AWEPA, 2003, pp. 202–3.

16. República de Moçambique and AWEPA, *As primeiras 33 autarquias em Moçambique*; and *Mozambique Peace Process Bulletin*, 21, 21 July 1998, 21 pp.

17. Adriano Nuvunga, *Cartography of Local Government, 2003 to 2008*, Maputo: AWEPA, 2004.

pp. [78–83]

NOTES

18. 'Final Results of 2003 Local Elections', *Mozambique Political Process Bulletin*, 29, December 2003, pp. 22–32.

19. In fact, small parties and citizens' groups participating in 1998 had benefitted from the opposition's boycott. The number of votes they obtained dropped drastically in 2003.

20. Library of the Centro de Estudos Africanos, Universidade Eduardo Mondlane, Folder 357, 'Ausência de legislação em certos sectores da vida social das populações', DNAR director to president of the Commission of Social Affairs of the Assembly of the Republic, 28 April 1992.

21. I witnessed two ceremonies in the offices of the DNAR at which churches were officially recognized. Both were simple. At each, the four or five representatives of the respective church were seated around a table, and the DNAR director gave a fifteen-minute speech in which he dwelt on the rights and duties of religious institutions and on the authority of the DNAR and the state.

22. MJ, DNAR, 'Lista das confissões religiosas registadas', lists for 1991, 1995, and 2004.

23. MJ, Direcção Provincial dos Assuntos Religiosos de Nampula (hereafter DPAR-Nampula), 'Lista nominal das confissões religiosas à nivel provincial', lists for 2000 and 2004.

24. Pitcher, *Transforming Mozambique*, Chapter 3.

25. Joana Pereira Leite, 'A guerra do caju e as relações Moçambique–Índia na época pós-colonial', *Lusotopie* (Paris), 2000, pp. 295–332; and Carvalho, 'O empresariado islâmico em Moçambique', Chapter 4.

26. See for example *Notícias* (Maputo), 23 October 1996, p. 1.

27. Sheik Abdurazzaque Jamú would subsequently take credit for initiating the legislation. See *Bilal* (Maputo), 29 March 1996, p. 11.

28. Michel Cahen, 'Mozambique: L'instabilité comme gouvernance?', *Politique Africaine*, 80, December 2000, p. 115.

29. In 2002, the Americans even opened an 'American corner' in Mussa Bin Bique University of Nampula, where interested individuals could find literature about the United States. See US Bureau of Democracy, Human Rights and Labor, 'International Religious Freedom Report 2004', 15 September 2004, http://www.state.gov/g/drl/rls/irf/2004/35373. htm, accessed 25 April 2005 (now accessible at https://2009-2017. state.gov/j/drl/rls/irf/2004/index.htm).

30. As a result, five municipalities were created in Nampula in 1998 and a pilot programme of decentralized planning and finances was established. See Francisco Ussene Mucanheia, 'Participação no processo de tomada de decisões em Nampula', http://www.iid.org.

198

pp. [83–87]

NOTES

mz/Participacao_no_processo_de_tomada_de_decisoes_Nampula_
final.pdf, accessed 1 April 2005 (now accessible at https://web.
archive.org/web/20081203005253/http://www.iid.org.mz/
Participacao_no_processo_de_tomada_de_decisoes_Nampula_
final.pdf).

31. Pascale David, 'Entretien avec Francisco Ussene Mucanheia, dirigeant du Front de Libération du Mozambique', *Témoignages* (La Réunion), 6 July 2004; and Osvaldo Tembe, 'Após garantir vitória de Guebuza', *Zambeze* (Maputo), 17 February 2005, p. 14.

32. Tembe, 'Após garantir vitória de Guebuza', p. 14. For the denunciations, see 'Moslem Clerics Accused of Mobilising for Renamo' and 'Moslem Leader Denies Frelimo Claim', Agência de Informação de Moçambique (Maputo), 11 November 2003.

33. See the *Mozambique Political Process Bulletin*, 31, December 2004; *Mozambique Political Process Bulletin*, 33, 3 January 2005; and *Mozambique Political Process Bulletin*, 36 (special e-mail election issue), 27 January 2005. I personally witnessed organized violent incidents in Ilha de Moçambique during the pre-election campaign.

34. Donal Cruise O'Brien, *Symbolic Confrontations: Muslims Imagining the State in Africa*, London: Hurst, 2003, p. 8.

35. Christian Coulon discusses the 'institutionalization of Islam' as distinguished from the 'islamization of the state'. See 'Introduction: Les nouvelles voies de l'umma africaine', *L'Afrique Politique* (Paris), 2002, pp. 19–29.

36. Author interview, Nazir Lunat, 23 October 2004, Maputo.

37. Author interview, Sheik Cassimo David Dafine, 21 October 2004, Maputo; see also author interview, Sheik Abdul Carimo Nordine Sau, 21 September 2004, Maputo.

38. Author interview, Sheik Ali Adam Ali, 7 November 2004, Nacala; and author interview, Rachid Kacimi, 7 November 2004, Nacala. Both men were at the time administrators of the AMA.

39. For a biography of Aminuddine Muhammad and an analysis of his writings, see Bonate, 'Dispute over Islamic Funeral Rites', pp. 41–59.

40. 'União muçulmana de Moçambique', *Comunicado*, 4 July 2002 (copy in possession of the author); author interview, Imam Idrissa Imede, 7 November 2004, Nacala; and author interview, Sheik Ali Adam Ali, 7 November 2004, Nacala.

41. Primeira Conferência Islâmica Nacional, 'Comunicado final' and 'Resoluções', 21 September 2003. See Appendix IV for the English version of the final communiqué (documents in possession of the author).

199

NOTES

42. Primeira Conferência Islâmica Nacional, 'Resoluções', 21 September 2003.
43. Primeira Conferência Islâmica Nacional, 'Comunicado final', 21 September 2003. See Appendix IV for the document in English.
44. *Zambeze* (Maputo), 7 November 2002, p. 21; and *Domingo* (Maputo), 9 February 2003, p. 30. The problem was only resolved momentarily, however: the issue of the sighting of the moon returned rapidly and was still live and causing problems in 2023.
45. At Ilha de Moçambique, a group of radical reformists opened a prayer room in the building next to the main mosque. They refused to join the rest of the community for Friday prayers despite the community and the main reformist leaders of the country pleading with and even ordering them to do so. Author interview, Momade Gulamo Issufo, 5 November 2004, Ilha de Moçambique; and author interview, leaders of the Qadiriyya Sadat, 4 November 2004, Ilha de Moçambique.

4. GROWTH AND RADICALIZATION? ISLAM AND POLITICS AFTER 2004

1. See Chapter 1.
2. See Chapter 2.
3. Bonate, 'Muslim Personal Law among the Koti', p. 6.
4. Eric Morier-Genoud, 'Renouveau religieux et politique au Mozambique: Entre permanence, rupture et historicité', *Politique Africaine*, 134, 2014, pp. 155–77.
5. Pew Research Center, Forum on Religion and Public Life, 'Tolerance and Tension: Islam and Christianity in Sub-Saharan Africa', Washington: Pew Research Center, 2010, p. 64.
6. See Chapters 1 and 2.
7. On AMA/Direct Aid, see Mara A. Leichtman, 'Da'wa as Development: Kuwaiti Islamic Charity in East and West Africa', *Muslim World*, 112(1), 2022, pp. 100–29.
8. See Chapters 1 and 2.
9. See, for example, https://africamuslimsagency.co.za/masjid/, accessed 7 April 2022.
10. See Alex P. Schmidt, 'Radicalisation, De-radicalisation, Counter-radicalisation: A Conceptual Discussion and Literature Review', ICCT Research Paper, The Hague: International Centre for Counter-Terrorism, March 2013. For Africa, see Kate Meagher and Abdul Raufu Mustapha, 'Introduction: Faith, Society and Boko Haram', in Abdul Raufu Mustapha and Kate Meagher (eds), *Overcoming Boko*

pp. [103–108]

NOTES

Haram: Faith, Society and Islamic Radicalisation in Northern Nigeria, Woodbridge: James Currey, 2020, pp. 1–29.

11. 'Mozambique: Moslem Groups Make Threats over Burqas', Agência de Informação de Moçambique (Maputo), 27 June 2011, https://wwrn.org/articles/35639/, accessed 24 June 2022.

12. Tiago Valoi, 'Governo não pode tolerar uso de símbolos religiosos nas escolas', *O País* (Maputo), 14 June 2011.

13. 'Uso de véu nas escolas: Governo cedeu mas muçulmanos querem mais', *Canal de Moçambique* (Maputo), 22 August 2012, p. 20.

14. 'Uso de véu nas escolas'.

15. 'Autorizado uso do lenço nas escolas', *Notícias* (Maputo), 24 August 2012, http://jornalnoticias.co.mz/pls/mptimz2/getxml/pt/contes/1492831, accessed 24 August 2012.

16. For the incident at the Pemba hospital, see 'Proibido uso de burka no hospital de Pemba', *Notícias* (Maputo), 16 August 2014; for the debate around the identity card, see US Department of State, Bureau of Democracy, Human Rights, and Labor, 'Mozambique 2014 International Religious Freedom Report', p. 3, https://2009-2017.state.gov/documents/organization/238454.pdf, accessed 16 May 2015.

17. For a broader, more nuanced, and non-political discussion of the veil in Africa, see Elisha P. Renne (ed.), *Veiling in Africa*, Bloomington: Indiana University Press, 2013.

18. See Chapter 1.

19. Laheij, 'Country of Trial'.

20. Pew Research Forum, 'Tolerance and Tensions'.

21. Pew Research Forum, 'Tolerance and Tensions', p. 17.

22. Pew Research Forum, 'Tolerance and Tensions', p. 196.

23. Pew Research Forum, 'Tolerance and Tensions', p. 55.

24. Pew Research Forum, 'Tolerance and Tensions', p. 289.

25. Pew Research Forum, 'Tolerance and Tensions', p. 285.

26. See Chapter 3.

27. Marcelo Mosse, 'Nova lei de matrimónio: A Charia para Moçambique?', *Público* (Lisbon), 9 May 2000.

28. Pew Research Forum, 'Tolerance and Tensions', pp. 291–3.

29. Pew Research Forum, 'Tolerance and Tensions', pp. 184–5.

30. Pew Research Forum, 'Tolerance and Tensions', p. 183.

31. Pew Research Forum, 'Tolerance and Tensions', p. 47.

32. Pew Research Forum, 'Tolerance and Tensions', p. 279

33. Pew Research Forum, 'Tolerance and Tensions', p. 90.

34. Pew Research Forum, 'The World's Muslims: Religion, Politics and

201

NOTES

Society', Washington: Pew Research Center, 30 April 2013, p. 63—this report used the data from the 'Tolerance and Tensions' report.

35. Pew Research Forum, 'Tolerance and Tensions', p. 44.
36. Pew Research Forum, 'Tolerance and Tensions', p. 277.
37. Pew Research Forum, 'Tolerance and Tensions', p. 278.
38. Pew Research Forum, 'Tolerance and Tensions', p. 278.
39. See Chapter 1.
40. Independent Party of Mozambique, 'Proposta para debate: Fenómeno Fundamentalismo', 2003, 2 pp. (in possession of the author).
41. Ahmad Jamal, 'Fundamentalism', *Al Calam* (Matola), 1, 15 November 2003, pp. 29–32.
42. Aminuddin Muhammad, 'O terrorismo e a "media"' (transcript), IslamHouse.com, 17 December 2016, https://islamhouse.com/read/pt/o-terrorismo-e-a-media-2788712, accessed 30 July 2022.
43. Zahir Kazmi, 'Radical Islam in the Western Academy', *Review of International Studies*, 1(23), 2021, pp. 1–23.
44. See Chapter 5.
45. *Sautul Isslam* (Maputo), 14, 1998, p. 46.
46. Kadara Swaleh, 'Islamic Proselytising between Lamu and Mozambique: The Case of Kizingitini Village', *Social Dynamics*, 38(3), 2012, pp. 398–418.
47. *Boletim da República* (Maputo), 3(13), 26 March 1997, p. 211.
48. Liazzat Bonate, 'Roots of Diversity in Mozambican Islam', *Lusotopie* (Paris), 14, 2007, pp. 146; and Bonate, 'Muslim Personal Law among the Koti', pp. 19–20. Bonate did research in Pemba in 2007 and 2008 but wrongly concluded that Nampula (where she had begun her research) was where the organization was founded and from where it expanded into Cabo Delgado; see Liazzat Bonate, 'Transformations de l'Islam à Pemba au Mozambique', *Afrique Contemporaine*, 231(3), 2009, p. 71.
49. See Chapter 1.
50. Pedro Soares claims CIMO is a Barelwi organization, but the founder and president of CIMO vehemently contests this. See Pedro Soares, 'Sustaining the Periphery: Transnational Articulations of Portuguese Barelwi Muslims', in Paul Anderson and Julian Hargreaves (eds), *Muslims in the UK and Europe V*, Cambridge: Centre of Islamic Studies, University of Cambridge, 2019, p. 34; and Sheik Abdul Rashid Ismail, personal communication, 1 February 2022.
51. See the organization's website: https://www.cimo.org.mz/; Comunidade Islâmica de Moçambique (CIMO), 'Objectivos, Actividades e Projectos', Beira, n.d.; and Sheik Abdul Rashid Ismail, personal communication, 16 June 2022.

pp. [112–114]

NOTES

52. Among others, see 'Para responder às exigências do Governo: Universidade Mussa Bin Bique nomeia novo reitor', *CanalMoz* (Maputo), 476, 13 June 2011, p. 8; Argunaldo Nhampossa, 'Ambiente de cortar à faca na Mussa Bin Bique', *Savana* (Maputo), 25 May 2012, p. 4; and Alvarito de Carvalho, 'José Abudo medito no barulho da Mussa Bin Bique', *Zambeze* (Maputo), 24 May 2012, p. 2.

53. Confraria muculmana Qadiryya Bagdad, https://www.facebook.com/Confraria-muculmana-Qadiryya-Bagdad-640561199324162/ (see the section 'About'), accessed 26 July 2022.

54. Author interview, Mohamed Omargy, 9 September 2021, Beira; and Sheik Idrisse Sharfuddin (Muslim Association of Sofala), 15 August and 5 September 2001, Beira.

55. See Chapter 1.

56. US Department of the Treasury, 'Treasury Sanctions Entities Owned by Drug Kingpin Mohamed Bachir Suleman: Treasury Action Targets Narcotics Trafficking Network in Mozambique, Builds on President Obama's Drug Kinpin Identification', 1 June 2010, ref. TG-729, https://home.treasury.gov/news/press-releases/tg729, accessed 2 June 2010; and Fernando Veloso, 'MBS em maus lençóis na Comunidade Mahometana', *Canal de Moçambique* (Maputo), 7 June 2010.

57. A good summary can be found in 'Comunidade Mahometana de Maputo em polvorosa: Eleições no meio de graves alegações contra o incumbente, Saleem Karim', *Carta de Moçambique* (Maputo), 13 May 2022, https://www.cartamz.com/~cartamzc/index.php/politica/item/10634-comunidade-mahometana-de-maputo-em-polvorosa-eleicoes-no-meio-de-graves-alegacoes-contra-o-incumbente-saleem-karim, accessed 17 August 2022.

58. Joseph Hanlon, 'The Uberization of Mozambique's Heroin Trade', Working Papers Series, 18–190, London: School of Economics and Political Science (LSE), Department of International Development, 2018; and Simone Haysom, Peter Gastrow and Mark Shaw, 'The Heroin Coast: A Political Economy along the Eastern African Seaboard', ENACT Research Paper, 2, 2018, Pretoria: ISS-Enhancing Africa's Response to Transnational Organised Crime (ENACT).

59. See Chapter 1 and Nicole Khouri and Joana Pereira Leite, 'The Ismailis of Mozambique: History of a Twofold Migration (Late 19th Century–1975)', in Eric Morier-Genoud and Michel Cahen (eds), *Imperial Migrations: Colonial Communities and Diaspora in the Portuguese World*, London: Palgrave Macmillan, 2013, pp. 168–89.

60. Among others, see 'Aga Khan em Moçambique', *Notícias* (Maputo),

203

pp. [114–115]

NOTES

20 November 2007; and 'Os grandes desafios de Moçambique na actualidade segundo Aga Khan: Erradicar Pobreza, doenças endémicas e o analfabetismo', *mediaFAX* (Maputo), 22 November 2007.

61. Federation of the Khoja Shia Ithna Asheri Jamaats of Africa, 'Africa Federation Visit to Mozambique: Charting Out a Road Map for the Future of our Community Members', Ref: AK/PR/45/2011, 30 November 2011, https://www.yumpu.com/en/document/view/35262056/view-full-report-the-world-federation-of-ksimc, accessed 17 June 2022; and MJ, DPAR-Nampula, letter from the president of the community to the DPAR-Nampula, 30 June 2001.

62. Federation of the Khoja Shia Ithna Asheri Jamaats of Africa, 'Africa Federation Visit to Mozambique', p. 2.

63. See the section on radio stations owned by religious organizations in Tavares Cebola, 'Music Media in Mozambique', Music in Africa, 11 August 2021, https://www.musicinafrica.net/magazine/music-media-mozambique, accessed 17 June 2022.

64. See the Al Haq radio website, https://radiohaqeditor.wixsite.com/radiohaqweb_1/about-us, accessed 17 July 2022; and Radio Frequencies and Transmitter Maps worldwide, https://fmscan.org/net.php?r=f&m=s&itu=MOZ&pxf=R%E1dio+HAQ, accessed 17 June 2022.

65. See, for example, Rádio a Voz do Islam, https://openradio.app/station/radio-a-voz-do-islam-oluacklf, accessed 7 September 2022.

66. CISLAMO, https://www.facebook.com/cislamo, accessed 26 July 2022; CIMO, https://www.facebook.com/cimomoz, accessed 26 July 2022; and Confraria muculmana Qadiryya Bagdad, https://www.facebook.com/Confraria-muculmana-Qadiryya-Bagdad-640561199324162/, accessed 26 July 2022.

67. Among others, see 'CEDIM—Centro de Divulgação do Islam de Moçambique', https://www.facebook.com/mozcedim/, accessed 17 July 2022; and the discussion group 'Dawah Islam em Moçambique', https://www.facebook.com/groups/156756266287615/, accessed 17 July 2022.

68. Boletim Minarete, https://boletimminarete.blogspot.com, accessed 17 June 2022; and Boletim Minarete, https://www.facebook.com/boletimminarete/, accessed 17 June 2022.

69. See Chapter 1.

70. 'Médio Oriente: Um gigante por explorar', *Notícias* (Maputo), 15 November 2010.

71. *Notícias* (Maputo), 11 June 2015, p. 6.

pp. [118–120]

NOTES

5. 2017: THE BIRTH OF A JIHADI INSURGENCY

1. Hanlon, 'Mozambique's Insurgency'. João Mosca sees the insurgency as part of a 'resource curse'; 'João Mosca: Cabo Delgado já vive "maldição dos recursos naturais"', Deutsche Welle, 3 January 2020, https://www.dw.com/pt-002/jo%C3%A3o-mosca-cabodelgado-j%C3%A1-vive-maldi%C3%A7%C3%A3o-dos-recursosnaturais/a-51711555, accessed 3 January 2020.

2. Habibe, Forquilha, and Pereira, Radicalização Islâmica no Norte de Moçambique, pp. 11–12.

3. Francisco Almeida dos Santos, 'War in Resource-Rich Northern Mozambique: Six Scenarios', CMI Insight, 2, 2020, pp. 11–12; and Liazzat Bonate, 'Why the Mozambican Government's Alliance with the Islamic Council of Mozambique Might Not End the Insurgency in Cabo Delgado', Zitamar (Maputo), 14 June 2019, https://www.zitamar.com/mozambican-governments-alliance-islamic-councilmozambique-might-not-end-insurgency-cabo-delgado/, accessed 14 June 2019.

4. International Crisis Group, 'Al-Shabaab Five Years after Westgate: Still a Menace in East Africa', Africa Report, 265, 21 September 2018. See also Sunguta West, 'Ansar al-Sunna: A New Militant Islamist Group Emerges in Mozambique', Terrorism Monitor (Jamestown Foundation), 14 June 2018, pp. 5–7; and Eleanor Beevor, 'Who Are Mozambique's Jihadists?', International Institute for Strategic Studies blog 'Analysis', 25 March 2020, https://www.iiss.org/blogs/analysis/2020/03/csdp-mozambique-jihadists, accessed 3 February 2020.

5. David M. Matsinhe and Estácio Valoi, 'The Genesis of Insurgency in Northern Mozambique', ISS Southern Africa Report, 27, 2019, p. 9; and Habibe, Forquilha, and Pereira, Radicalização Islâmica. See also Gregory Pirio, Robert Pittelli, and Yussuf Adam, 'The Emergence of Violent Extremism in Northern Mozambique', Spotlight Africa, Centre for Strategic Studies (US), https://africacenter.org/spotlight/the-emergence-of-violent-extremism-in-northernmozambique/, accessed 26 March 2018.

6. Abdul Raufu Mustapha, Sects and Social Disorder: Muslim Identities and Conflict in Northern Nigeria, Oxford: James Currey, 2017, p. 3.

7. Ngala Chome, 'From Islamic Reform to Muslim Activism: The Evolution of an Islamist Ideology in Kenya', African Affairs, 118(472), 2019, pp. 531–52.

8. Raquel Loureiro and António Cascais, 'Ataque em Mocímboa da Praia

205

pp. [120–121]

NOTES

terá sido "caso isolado"', Deutsche Welle, 16 October 2017, https://www.dw.com/pt-002/ataque-em-moc%C3%ADmboa-da-praia-ter%C3%A1-sido-caso-isolado/a-40977442, accessed 16 October 2017.

9. Agência Lusa, 'Grupo que atacou polícia no norte de Moçambique visava provocar desordem', Deutsche Welle, 6 October 2017, https://www.dw.com/pt-002/grupo-que-atacoupol%C3%ADcia-no-norte-de-mo%C3%A7ambique-visava-provocar-desordem/a-40849000, accessed 8 October 2017.

10. Francisco Mandlate, 'Jovens radicais sonham com califado em Mocímboa da Praia', *O País* (Maputo), 9 October 2017, http://opais.sapo.mz/jovens-radicais-sonham-com-califado-emmocimboa-da-praia-, accessed 9 October 2017 (now accessible at https://macua.blogs.com/moambique_para_todos/2017/10/jovens-radicais-sonham-com-califado-em-mocímboa-da-praia.html).

11. Habibe, Forquilha, and Pereira, *Radicalização Islâmica*, p. 11.

12. Habibe, Forquilha, and Pereira, *Radicalização Islâmica*, p. 11. Some authors mistakenly use the term Ansar al-Sunna, which is the name of a youth branch of the Islamic Council of Mozambique. Ansar al-Sunna has nothing to do with the insurgency; in Cabo Delgado, there was a youth organization registered as Ansaru-Sunna, which is also tied to CISLAMO and also has nothing to do with the insurgency; see footnote 102 of Chapter 1.

13. For this reason, I have chosen to use 'al-Shabaab' in my analysis. In contrast, the administration of the United States seems to have made a tactical choice to use the term 'Ahl al-Sunnah wal-Jamaah' to avoid politicians in Washington conflating the Mozambican movement with the Somali organization. See, for example, US Embassy in Mozambique, 'Mozambique 2018 International Religious Freedom Report', United States Department of State, Bureau of Democracy, Human Rights, and Labor, 2018, https://mz.usembassy.gov/mozambique-2018-international-religiousfreedom-report, accessed 7 October 2019.

14. Cited by Agência Lusa, 'Grupo que atacou polícia'.

15. Mandlate, 'Jovens radicais sonham'.

16. Lusa, 'Mocímboa culpa migrações e recrutamento no estrangeiro pelos ataques em Moçambique', *Diário de Notícias* (Lisbon), 15 October 2017, https://www.dn.pt/lusa/reportagemmocimboa-culpa-migracoes-e-recrutamento-no-estrangeiro-pelos-ataques-emmocambique-8844248.html, accessed 7 October 2019.

17. Mandlate, 'Jovens radicais sonham'; the quote is from Geraldo Luís

206

NOTES

Macalane and Jafar Silvestre (eds), *Ataques Terroristas em Cabo Delgado (2017–2020): As causas do fenómeno pela boca da população de Mocímboa da Praia*, Pemba: Universidade Rovuma, 2021, p. 54.

18. 'Interview by journalist' (in possession of the author), April 2019.
19. Cited by Nádia Issufo, 'Ataques em Moçambique: "Está tudo sob controlo em Palma"', Deutsche Welle, 2 May 2018, https://www.dw.com/pt-002/ataques-em-mo%C3%A7ambique-est%C3%A1-tudo-sob-controlo-em-palma/a-43600360, accessed 2 May 2018.
20. *Monhés* is a pejorative term in Mozambique meaning 'Asian Muslims'.
21. Cited by Mandlate, 'Jovens radicais sonham'.
22. Cited by Loureiro and Cascais, 'Ataque em Mocímboa da Praia'.
23. Quranists pray three times a day; they do not recognize the hadiths that specify five prayers per day. Quranists derive their name from the fact that they only recognize the Quran as a legitimate source of religious law and guidance. For the quote, 'interview by Salvador Forquilha', Sheik Adam Bonoumar, 8 December 2020, Lichinga.
24. 'Interview by journalist' (in possession of the author), Sheik M., 2018, Mocímboa da Praia.
25. Kaarsholm claims the secularism practised in Mozambique was 'radical'. See Preben Kaarsholm, 'Islam, Secularist Government, and State–Civil Society Interaction in Mozambique and South Africa since 1994', *Journal of Eastern African Studies*, 9(3), 2015, pp. 468–87. For another viewpoint, see Chapters 3 and 4.
26. Tibi, *Islamism and Islam*. Olivier Roy made the same point more than twenty years ago, calling it 'le grand malentendu' (the great misunderstanding); see Olivier Roy, *Généalogie de l'Islamisme*, Paris: Hachette, 1995.
27. Among the large literature on 'sects', see Johnson Benton, 'A Critical Appraisal of the Church–Sect Typology', *American Sociological Review*, 22(1), 1957, pp. 88–92.
28. *Relatório da Conferência islâmica, Nampula 10–13 de Novembro de 2016*, pp. 13–14. There are only a few Shia in Cabo Delgado, and the presenter talking about this province boasted that they had managed to expel them from the town of Mocímboa da Praia.
29. Author interview, Sheik X., 2019, Pemba.
30. Author interview, Sheik X., 2019, Pemba.
31. Mustapha makes the same point in relation to Boko Haram in Nigeria; see Mustapha, *Sects and Social Disorder*, Chapter 3.
32. Copy of the application in possession of the author.
33. Interview by research assistant, official head of Nhacole, 2019, Balama.

pp. [126–131]

NOTES

34. Copies of the minutes of the meeting in possession of the author; interview by research assistant, CISLAMO sheik, 2019, Balama.
35. There is another version of the story whereby the state expelled Sualehe in 2009 and he returned in 2010, only to be expelled again in 2011.
36. For details of the establishment of the sect in Mocímboa da Praia, see Habibe, Forquilha, and Pereira, *Radicalização Islâmica*.
37. Interview by research assistant, A. and B., 2019, Chiure.
38. Sheik Abdulcarimo Fadile, 'O Problema do Muçulmano ser um Funcionário Público', *Al-Hujomu* (Pemba), 40, 13 December 2015.
39. Interview by research assistant, C., 2019, Chiure.
40. Interview by research assistant, C., A. and B., and D., 2019, Chiure.
41. *Relatório da Conferência islâmica*, Nampula 10–13 de Novembro de 2016, p. 13.
42. Salvador Forquilha and João Pereira, 'Afinal, não é só Cabo Delgado! Dinâmica da Insurgência em Nampula e Niassa', *IDeIAS* (Maputo), 138, 9 March 2021.
43. Habibe, Forquilha, and Pereira, *Radicalização Islâmica*, p. 13.
44. Author interview, Sheik X., 2019, Pemba; and Habibe, Forquilha, and Pereira, *Radicalização Islâmica*, pp. 13–15.
45. Habibe, Forquilha, and Pereira, *Radicalização Islâmica*, p. 10.
46. Author interview, Y., 2018, Pemba; and author interview, W., 2018, Pemba.
47. Author interview, D., 2019, Pemba.
48. Habibe, Forquilha, and Pereira, *Radicalização Islâmica*, p. 13; and author interview, F., 2019, Pemba.
49. 'Tumultos em Pangane provocam morte e feridos', *Domingo* (Maputo), 9 November 2015, https://www.jornaldomingo.co.mz/reportagem/tumultos-em-pangane-provocam-morte-e-feridos/, accessed 3 February 2018.
50. Author interview, Y., 2018, Pemba; and author interview, W., 2018, Pemba.
51. Sérgio Chichava, 'Os primeiros sinais do "Al Shabaab" em Cabo Delgado: algumas histórias de Macomia e Ancuabe', *IDeIAS*, 129, 2020, pp. 1–2.
52. Adelina Pinto, 'Detidos três membros de grupo muçulmano que promove desinformação em Cabo Delgado', *Magazine Independente* (Maputo), 21 June 2017, http://www.magazineindependente.com/www2/detidos-tres-membros-grupo-muculmano-promovedesinformacao-cabo-delgado, accessed 27 April 2020. Rádio Moçambique published the item the day before, but it has disappeared from its website; most of the quote was also reproduced in Voice of

pp. [131–132]

NOTES

America, 'Polícia de Moçambique prende três membros do grupo Al-Shabab', 20 June 2017, https://www.voaportugues.com/a/policia-mocambique-prende-membros-al-shabab/3907828.html, accessed 23 June 2023.

53. Tibi, *Islamism and Islam*, p. 135. The term 'jihadi' is problematic since it has two meanings, the less known one referring to the self-discipline that is necessary to become a good religious person. Bonelli and Carrié offer as an alternative the cumbersome expression 'political violence making reference to Islam'. I use the term 'armed jihadi' or 'violent jihadi'. See Laurent Bonelli and Fabien Carrié, *La fabrique de la radicalité: Une sociologie des jeunes djihadistes français*, Paris: Éditions du Seuil, 2018, p. 15.

54. For a constructivist reading of ethnicity in Mozambique, see Sérgio Chichava, 'Por uma leitura sócio-histórica da etnicidade em Moçambique', IESE Discussion Paper, 1, 2008.

55. Feijó, 'Social Asymmetries: Clues to Understand the Spread of Islamist Jihadism in Cabo Delgado', *Observador Rural*, 93, 2020.

56. Ana Sousa Santos, 'History, Memory and Violence: Changing Patterns of Group Relationship in Mocímboa da Praia, Mozambique', PhD diss., University of Oxford, 2011, Chapter 8; and Macalane and Silvestre, *Ataques Terroristas em Cabo Delgado*, pp. 42–4.

57. Simone Haysom, 'Where Crime Compounds Conflict: Understanding Northern Mozambique's Vulnerabilities', Geneva: Global Initiative against Transnational Organized Crime, 2018.

58. Bonate, 'Transformations de l'Islam à Pemba', pp. 61–76; Francesca Declich, 'Transmission of Muslim Practices and Women's Agency in Ibo Island and Pemba (Mozambique)', *Journal of Eastern African Studies*, 7(4), 2013, pp. 588–606; Lorenzo Macagno, 'Les nouveaux Oulémas: La recomposition des autorités musulmanes au nord du Mozambique', *Lusotopie* (Paris), 14, 2007, pp. 151–77; and Chapter 1 of the present book.

59. See Chapter 2 of the present book. For Cabo Delgado specifically, see, for example, the Joshua project, https://joshuaproject.net/people_groups/13902/MZ, accessed 4 November 2019.

60. Jacinto Veloso, 'O cenário mais provável', *Savana* (Maputo), 5 June 2020. Veloso is a very influential Mozambican politician who has held many high positions, including minister of security and minister in the presidency.

61. Among others, see the (controversial) writings on Facebook of Julião João Cumbane, CEO of Empresa Nacional de Parques de Ciências e Tecnologias (Maputo).

209

pp. [132–133]

NOTES

62. The opposition and some Frelimo officials are very keen on this idea. See, for example, the declaration of the late head of the opposition in André Baptista, 'Dhlakama fala de "cunho politico" nos ataques de Mocímboa da Praia', Voice of America, 17 October 2017, https://www.voaportugues.com/a/dhlakama-fala-de-cunho-politico-nos-ataques-de-mocimboa/4074861.html, accessed 17 October 2017.

63. Dom Luiz Fernando Lisboa, bishop of Pemba, has argued repeatedly that the insurgents have 'no face', and Mozambique's president has said the same on several occasions. Among others, see the bishop's 'Comunicado do Bispo de Pemba aos cristãos e às pessoas de boa vontade', Pemba, 10 June 2018; and President Nyusi, cited in Ramos Miguel, 'Nyusi reconhece ser difícil conhecer motivações dos ataques em Cabo Delgado', VOA Português, 6 June 2019, https://www.voaportugues.com/a/nyusi-reconhece-ser-dif%C3%ADcil-conhecer-motiva%C3%A7%C3%B5es-dos-ataques-em-cabo-delgado/4948100.html, accessed 14 October 2019.

64. For a good critique of the 'jihadi international' as a prism to understand jihadi wars in Africa, see Marc-Antoine Pérouse de Montclos, L'Afrique, nouvelle frontière du djihad?, Paris: La Découverte, 2018, Chapter 4.

65. US Department of State, 'State Department Terrorist Designations of ISIS Affiliates and Leaders in the Democratic Republic of the Congo and Mozambique', 10 March 2021, https://www.state.gov/state-department-terrorist-designations-of-isis-affiliates-and-leaders-in-the-democratic-republic-of-the-congo-and-mozambique, accessed 10 March 2021.

66. For Amisse Mucuthaya, see 'Os tentáculos do terrorismo em Cabo Delgado (I), por Omardine Omar', Carta de Moçambique, 7 December 2021, https://cartamz.com/index.php/politica/item/9455-os-tentaculos-do-terrorismo-em-cabo-delgado-i-por-omardine-omar, accessed 7 December 2022. For the others, see 'Mozambique Aware of Tanzanian Islamists in Cabo Delgado since 2012, Nyusi Says', Zitamar News, 17 December 2020, https://zitamar.com/mozambique-aware-of-tanzanian-islamists-in-cabo-delgado-since-2012-nyusi-says, accessed 17 December 2020.

67. For Sualehe Rafayel, see earlier discussion. For a biography of Likongo, see 'Abdala Likongo ou fantasma da Selva', Centro de Jornalismo Investigativo, 30 September 2022, https://cjimoz.org/news/abdala-likongo-ou-fantasma-da-selva/, accessed 30 September 2022. I have uncovered many of the same details through interviews, including with Likongo's wife.

210

NOTES

68. Habibe, Forquilha, and Pereira, *Radicalização Islâmica*, pp. 12, 15, 17–18, 28.

69. For the imprisoned Congolese, see Darren Taylor, 'Jihadists in Mozambique Far from a Spent Force: Intelligence Report', The Epoch Times (New York), 26 September 2022 (updated 29 September 2022), https://www.theepochtimes.com/jihadists-in-mozambique-far-from-a-spent-force-says-new-intelligence-report_4756309.html, accessed 29 September 2022. For the woman married to a Congolese insurgent, see Laurent Delhomme and Guillaume Lhotellier, 'Mozambique: Le Mirage Africain', Yemaya Productions (Paris, France), 2022, https://vimeo.com/722957457, accessed 16 October 2023 (interview with Adia at 30 minutes and 45 seconds).

70. United Nations Security Council's Groupe d'experts sur la République démocratique du Congo, 'Rapport final du Groupe d'experts sur la République démocratique du Congo', 13 June 2023, http://www.undocs.org/fr/S/2023/431, accessed 21 June 2023. See Annex 15 in particular.

71. Ibid.; and International Crisis Group, 'Stemming the Insurrection in Mozambique's Cabo Delgado', Crisis Group Africa Report, 303, 11 June 2021, pp. 21–2.

72. Among others, see Nicaise Kibel'bel Oka, *L'État islamique en Afrique centrale: De l'ADF/MTM en RDC à Al Sunnah au Mozambique*, Brussels: Editions Scribe, 2022, pp. 40–3; Jason Warner with Ryan O'Farrell, Héni Nsaibia, and Ryan Cummings, *The Islamic State in Africa: The Emergence, Evolution, and Future of the Next Jihadist Battlefront*, London: Hurst, 2021, pp. 261–2; and Sérgio Chichava, 'Ugandeses e Tanzanianos do Al-Shabaab: Um olhar à dimensão internacional do conflito em Cabo Delgado', in Salvador Forquilha (ed.), *Desafios para Moçambique 2020*, Maputo: IESE, 2020, pp. 429–39.

73. 'Alleged Cabo Delgado Insurgent Leader Ran Rebel Mosque in Uganda', *Zitamar* (Maputo), 29 January 2019, https://zitamar.com/alleged-cabo-delgado-insurgent-leader-ran-rebel-mosque-uganda, accessed 29 January 2019.

74. 'Three Ugandans Held in Mozambique over Terrorism', *The Monitor* (Kampala), 17 May 2018, https://www.monitor.co.ug/uganda/news/national/three-ugandans-held-in-mozambique-over-terrorism-1756752, accessed 30 January 2019; and 'Uganda, Mozambique Agree to Cooperate in the Areas of Defence, Trade, Tourism and Diplomacy', *Newz Post* (Uganda), 17 May 2018, https://

newz.ug/uganda-mozambique-agree-to-cooperate-in-the-areas-of-defence-trade-tourism-diplomacy, accessed 31 January 2019.

75. Baker Batte Lule, 'Was Usafi Mosque a Terrorist Hide-Out, or Security Front?', *Observer* (Kampala), 9 May 2018, https://observer.ug/news/headlines/57642-was-usafi-mosque-a-terrorist-hide-out-or-security-front.html, accessed 29 January 2019.

76. 'Three Ugandans Held'.

77. 'Three Ugandans Held'.

78. Wassim Nasr, '#RDC #EI dans son discours, en appelant au combat et au jihad, du 22 août 2018 #Baghdadi avait bien mentionné l'Afrique centrale dans une phrase qui se termine avec "Asie de l'Est [sud-est], le Caucase et les autres wilayas"', Twitter post, 10.54 am, 19 April 2019, https://twitter.com/SimNasr/status/1119161605650915328, accessed 19 April 2019.

79. JihadoScope, 'Au lendemain de témoignages faisant état de la décapitation de 10 personnes au #Mozambique par des militants islamistes, des sympathisants de l'#EI sur Telegram partagent des photos de supposés militants dans le pays, et promettent une prochaine allégeance à Abou Bakr al-Baghdadi', Twitter post, 9.50 am, 31 May 2018, https://twitter.com/JihadoScope/status/1002094878359261184, accessed 31 May 2018.

80. Wassim Nasr, 'L'#EI revendique officiellement sa première opération au #Mozambique dans la région Mocimboa "une attaque de l'armée repoussée" // photo qui a circulé en mai 2018 de jihadistes de l'EI dans le pays', Twitter post, 6.40 pm, 4 June 2019, https://twitter.com/SimNasr/status/1135949357193322497, accessed 4 June 2019.

81. Nuno Rogeiro, *O Cabo do Medo*, p. 163 (and p. 204 for the commanders).

82. Joseph Hanlon, 'Mozambique Palma Attack: Why IS Involvement Is Exaggerated', 17 April 2021, https://www.bbc.co.uk/news/world-africa-56773012, accessed 17 April 2021.

83. Rivka Azoulay, 'Islamic State Franchising: Tribes, Transnational Jihadi Networks and Generational Shifts', The Hague: Netherlands Institute of International Relations Clingendael, April 2015, https://www.clingendael.org/sites/default/files/pdfs/Rivka-Azoulay_Islamic_State_expansion_CRU_April2015.pdf, accessed 1 August 2022; and Vincent Foucher, 'The Islamic State Franchises in Africa: Lessons from Lake Chad', International Crisis Group Commentary, 29 October 2020, https://www.crisisgroup.org/africa/west-africa/nigeria/islamic-state-franchises-africa-lessons-lake-chad, accessed 4 February 2021.

NOTES

84. Warner et al., *Islamic State in Africa*, p. 6.
85. 'IS Designates Mozambique as Its Own Province following Battle in Quiterajo', *Zitamar*, 13 May 2022, https://zitamar.com/is-designates-mozambique-as-its-own-province-following-battle-in-quiterajo/, accessed 13 May 2022.
86. For example, see TV Miramar (Maputo), 'Terrorismo em Cabo Delgado', 13 August 2020, https://www.youtube.com/watch?v=QvfSX51MZko, accessed 14 August 2020.
87. For the insurgents' videos in Swahili, see Pinnacle News, [no title], 29 May 2020, https://www.facebook.com/pinnaclenews79/videos/661998864382015, accessed 29 May 2020.
88. Vincent Foucher, 'Nigeria: divisions au sein du groupe jihadiste Boko Haram', Radio France Internationale, 25 February 2017, https://www.rfi.fr/fr/afrique/20170225-nigeria-boko-haram-divisions-al-barnawi-shekau-vincent-foucher-icg, accessed 3 January 2020; International Crisis Group, 'Facing the Challenge of the Islamic State in West Africa Province', ICG Report, 273, 16 May 2019, https://www.crisisgroup.org/africa/west-africa/nigeria/273-facing-challenge-islamic-state-west-africa-province, accessed 3 January 2020; and Jacob Zenn, 'Boko Haram's Conquest for the Caliphate: How Al Qaeda Helped Islamic State Acquire Territory', *Studies in Conflict and Terrorism*, 43(2), 2020, pp. 89–122.
89. The al-Qaeda claim was made by the Thabat Agency on 22 May 2020. See Caleb Weiss, 'This is quite interesting. Al Qaeda's Al Thabat news agency is reporting an attack inside the Mocimboa region of #Mozambique's Cabo Delgado Province earlier this month.' Twitter post, 6.36 pm, 22 May 2020, https://twitter.com/Weissenberg7/status/1263961890599899136, accessed 22 May 2020.

CONCLUSION

1. See the law at the Ministry of Justice's website, http://www.mjcr.gov.mz/wp-content/uploads/2020/04/30.01.2020-PROPOSTA-DE-LEI-DE-LIBERDADE-RELIGIOSA.pdf, accessed 17 October 2022.
2. Among others, Agência de Informação de Moçambique, 'Governo procura colocar ordem no mundo religioso', 30 May 2019, https://www.portaldogoverno.gov.mz/por/Imprensa/Noticias/Governo-procura-colocar-ordem-no-mundo-religioso, accessed 31 May 2019; and Inalcídio Uamusse, 'Governo quer combater proliferação de igrejas ilegais no país', *O País* (Maputo), 22 April 2022, https://opais.

NOTES

co.mz/governo-quer-combater-proliferacao-de-igrejas-ilegais-no-pais/, accessed 22 April 2022.

3. Cited in Yuran Roque, 'O Estado não pode ficar indiferente ao que se passa nas igrejas', *O País* (Maputo), 29 October 2017, https://opais.co.mz/o-estado-nao-pode-ficar-indiferente-ao-que-se-passa-nas-igrejas/, accessed 29 October 2017. Ngoenha went on to publish an academic article on the subject under the title 'O desafio moçambicano da laicidade' in Carlos Nuno Castel-Branco, Rosimina Ali, Sérgio Chichava, Salvador Forquilha, and Carlos Muiangaal (eds), *Desafios Para Mocambique 2022*, Maputo: IESE, 2022, pp. 70–81.

4. Agência de Informação de Moçambique, 'Religious Freedom Law under Discussion', *Mozambique File* (London), 157, August 1989, p. 25.

5. Marta Afonso, 'Igrejas contestam projecto-lei que as obriga a pagar imposto ao Estado', *Carta de Moçambique* (Maputo), 27 May 2022, https://cartamz.com/index.php/sociedade/item/10789-igrejas-contestam-projecto-lei-que-as-obriga-a-pagar-imposto-ao-estado, accessed 27 May 2022.

APPENDIX I

1. About Abubacar's relation with the colonial authorities, see Fernando Amaro Monteiro, 'Sobre a actuação da corrente "wahhabitta" no Islão moçambicano: Algumas notas relativas ao período 1964–1974', *Africana Studia* (Porto), 12, pp. 85–107.

APPENDIX V

1. 'Conheça Assumane Vipodozi, um "insurgente" de Mocímboa da Praia', *Carta de Moçambique* (Maputo), 30 October 2019, https://www.cartamz.com/index.php/politica/item/3475-conheca-assumane-vipodozi-um-insurgente-de-mocimboa-da-praia, accessed 30 October 2019.

2. Club of Mozambique, 'Watch: TVM Revives Video of Doubtful Authenticity—AIM Report', 2 June 2018, https://clubofmozambique.com/news/watch-tvm-revives-video-of-doubtful-authenticity-aim-report/, accessed 2 June 2018.

3. Two native Arabic speakers helped with this translation.

BIBLIOGRAPHY

Primary sources

Arquivos Históricos de Moçambique: Administração civil, Maputo, Mozambique (AHM)
Biblioteca da Assembleia da República, Maputo, Mozambique (BAR)
Instituto Nacional dos Arquivos Nacionais da Torre de Tombo, Lisbon, Portugal (IAN/TT), Serviço de Centralização e Coordenação da Informação de Moçambique (SCCIM)
Instituto Nacional dos Arquivos Nacionais da Torre de Tombo, Lisbon, Portugal (IAN/TT), Polícia Internacional e de Defesa do Estado/Direcção Geral de Segurança (PIDE/DGS)
Ministério da Justiça, Direcção Nacional dos Assuntos Religiosos, Maputo, Mozambique (MJ, DNAR) [Before the 1990s, the directorate was a department—Departamento dos Assuntos Religiosos (DAR)]
Ministério da Justiça, Direcção Provincial dos Assuntos Religiosos de Nampula, Mozambique (MJ, DPAR-Nampula)
Universidade Eduardo Mondlane, Centro de Estudos Africanos (UEM/CEA)

Newspapers, magazine, newsletters

Africa Confidential (London)
Agência de Informação de Moçambique (Maputo)
Al Calam (Matola)
A Mensagem (Maputo)
A Voz da Anuaril (Maputo)
Bilal (Maputo)

BIBLIOGRAPHY

Boletim da República (Maputo)
Canal de Moçambique (Maputo)
CanalMoz (Maputo)
Carta de Moçambique (Maputo)
Catholic World News (Rome)
Commission (Richmond, VA)
Crescente (Maputo)
Demos (Maputo)
Diário de Notícias (Lisbon)
Domingo (Maputo)
Echos d'Outre-Mer (Lausanne, Switzerland)
Fact & Report (Amsterdam)
Imparcial (Maputo)
Indian Ocean Newsletter (Paris)
InformÁfrica (Lisbon)
Intercambio (Breda, Netherlands)
Jeune Afrique (Paris)
Magazine Independente (Maputo)
Mail and Guardian (Johannesburg)
Marchés Tropicaux (Paris)
mediaFAX (Maputo)
Metical (Maputo)
Monthly Review Bulletin (London)
Mozambique File (London)
Mozambique Political Process Bulletin (Milton Keynes)
Muslim World League Journal (Makka)
Notícias (Lourenço Marques/Maputo)
Notmoc (Maputo)
Panafrican News Agency (Dakar)
Público (Lisbon)
Rumo Novo (Beira)
Sautul Isslam (Maputo)
Savana (Maputo)
Témoignages (La Réunion)
Vida Nova (Nampula)
Xinhua News Agency (Beijing)
Zambeze (Maputo)
Zitamar (Maputo)

216

BIBLIOGRAPHY

Interviews

Abdurremane, Amilcar Hussein, 8 November 2001, Beira.

Abubakar, Ossumane (imam of Cumbana Mosque), 17 September 2006, Cumbana (Inhambane).

Alferes, Manuel (former SAAR director), 24 June 1996, Maputo.

Ali, Sheik Ali Adam (Africa Muslims Agency), 7 October 2004, Nacala.

Amade, Habibo and Omar Salimo Ioncubo, 29 September 2004, Nampula.

Amuri bin Jimba, Sheik Abdurrahman (leader of the *tariqa* Shadhiliyya Liaxuruti), 21 August 2000 and 6 October 2004, Ilha de Moçambique.

Anifo, Sheik Momade (imam of the central mosque, Ilha de Moçambique), 24 August 2000, Ilha de Moçambique.

Augusto, José (director of Renamo's department of foreign affairs, section Europe and United States), 13 May 1994, Maputo.

Bin Hagy, Sheik Issufo (*tariqa* Shadhiliyya Itifaque), 30 August 2000, Maputo.

Bonoumar, Sheik Adam, interview by Salvador Forquilha, 8 December 2020, Lichinga.

Cassamo, Suleimane (Núcleo Islâmico de Matola), 25 October 2004, Matola.

Chamangu, Simião (president of the Presbyterian Synod Council), 10 May 1996, Maputo.

Chambal, Job (director of the DAR/DNAR, Ministry of Justice), 14 August 2002, Maputo.

David Dafine, Sheik Cassimo (Islamic Council of Mozambique), 21 October 2004, Maputo.

Funzamo, Isaias (former head of the Presbyterian Church in Mozambique and former president of the Christian Council of Mozambique), 31 March 1994, Maputo.

Gulamo Issufo, Sheik Momade (leader of the Muslim Association of Ilha de Moçambique), 5 October 2004, Ilha de Moçambique.

Imede, Imam Idrissa (União Muçulmana de Moçambique), 7 October 2004, Nacala.

Ismail, Sheik Abdul Rashid (Islamic Congress delegate in central Mozambique), 11 September 2001, Beira.

Issufo, Sheik Amahd Amadha (leader of the *tariqa* Qadririya Machereba), 4 October 2004, Ilha de Moçambique.

Jamal, Sheik Nazir Zaide (imam of Inhambane central mosque), 16 September 2006, Inhambane.

Jamú, Hafiz Abdurazaque (leader of the *tariqa* Bagdad), 4 October 2004, Ilha de Moçambique.

217

BIBLIOGRAPHY

Jeannet, Pierre (Département Missionnaire des Églises de la Suisse Romande), 10 November 1993, Lausanne, Switzerland.

Kacimi, Sheik Rachid (Africa Muslims Agency), 7 October 2004, Nacala.

Lopes, Father António Maria (Catholic priest), 5 October 2004, Ilha de Moçambique.

Lunat, Mawlana Nazir (imam of the Taqwa mosque), 23 October 2004, Maputo.

Mahomed, Valy, 24 October 2004, Maputo.

Massinga, José Chicuara (deputy for the União Democrática and president of the PANADE party), 10 November 1994, Maputo.

Momade, Ossufo (Renamo parliamentarian and former head of religious affairs), 23 September 2004, Maputo.

Nacaca, Elias and Jossene, Silvino (Igreja Evangélica de Cristo de Moçambique), 5 March 1994, Cuamba.

Nordine, Ibrahimo, 20 September 2004, Maputo.

Omargy, Mohamed, 9 September 2021, Beira.

Qadiriyya Sadat, group interview with leaders, 4 November 2004, Ilha de Moçambique.

Samuge, Raimundo (Renamo head of mobilization), 22 August 2002, Maputo.

Satar, Abdulhamid Abdul (Muslim Association of Nampula), 28 September 2004, Nampula.

Sau, Sheik Abdul Carimo Nordine (Islamic Council of Mozambique), 21 September 2004, Maputo.

Sharfuddin, Sheik Idrisse (Muslim Association of Sofala), 15 August and 5 September 2001, Beira.

Sualé, Sheik Issufo Amada (no. 2 of the *tariqa* Qadiriyya Sadat), 23 August 2000, Ilha de Moçambique.

Tabou, Jean-Barnabé Manuel (director of DAR-Niassa), 5 May 1994, Cuamba.

Umargy, Mahomed (Muslim Association of Sofala), 9 and 14 August 2001, Beira.

Zaina, A., 23 August 2000, Ilha de Moçambique.

Dozens of interviews were also conducted in Cabo Delgado, but the interviewees need to remain anonymous in view of the unfolding armed conflict.

BIBLIOGRAPHY

Secondary sources

Ahmet, T. Kuru, 'Passive and Assertive Secularism: Historical Conditions, Ideological Struggles, and State Policies toward Religion', *World Politics*, 59(4), 2007, pp. 568–94.

Alpers, Edward A., 'East Central Africa', in N. Levtzion and R. Pouwell (eds), *History of Islam in Africa*, Athens: Ohio University Press, 1999, pp. 303–25.

———— 'Islam in the Service of Colonialism? Portuguese Strategy during the Armed Liberation Struggle in Mozambique', *Lusotopie* (Paris), 6, 1999, pp. 165–84.

———— *Ivory and Slaves in East Central Africa*, London: Heinemann, 1975.

———— 'Towards a History of the Expansion of Islam in East Africa: The Matrilineal People of the Southern Interior', in Terence Ranger and Isaria Kimambo (eds), *The Historical Study of African Religion*, Berkeley: University of California Press, 1972, pp. 172–201.

An-Na'im, Abdullahi Ahmed, 'Islam and Secularism', in Linell E. Cady and Elizabeth Shakman Hurd (eds), *Comparative Secularisms in a Global Age*, New York: Palgrave Macmillan, 2010, pp. 217–28.

Antoun, Richard T. and Mary Elaine Hegland (eds), *Religious Resurgence: Contemporary Cases in Islam, Christianity, and Judaism*, Syracuse: Syracuse University Press, 1987.

Arnfred, Signe, *Family Forms and Gender Policy in Revolutionary Mozambique (1975–1985)*, Bordeaux: CEAN, 2001.

———— 'Reflection on Family Forms and Gender Policy in Mozambique', unpublished paper, 1990.

Arthur, Maria José, Teresa Cruz e Silva, Yolanda Sitoe, and Edson Mussa, 'Lei da Família (1): Antecedentes e contextos da sua aprovação', *Outras Vozes* (Maputo), 35–6, 2011, pp. 15–25.

Askin, Steve, 'Mission to Renamo: The Militarisation of the Religious Right', *Journal of Theology for Southern Africa*, 69, 1989, pp. 106–16.

————, 'Mission to Renamo: The Militarization of the Religious Right', *Issue*, 18(2), 1990, pp. 29–38.

Assembleia da República and AWEPA, *Quem é quem na Assembleia da República de Moçambique*, Maputo: Assembleia da República and AWEPA, 1996.

Axelson, Eric, *Portugal and the Scramble for Africa 1875–1891*, Johannesburg: Witwatersrand University Press, 1967.

Azoulay, Rivka, *Islamic State Franchising: Tribes, Transnational Jihadi Networks and Generational Shifts*, The Hague: Netherlands Institute of International Relations Clingendael, April 2015.

BIBLIOGRAPHY

Bachmann, E. Theodore and Mercia Brenne Bachmann, *Lutheran Churches in the World: A Handbook*, Minneapolis: Augsburg Fortress, 1989.

Beckford, James A., *Social Theory and Religion*, Cambridge: Cambridge University Press, 2003.

Berger, Peter, *The Sacred Canopy: Elements of a Sociological Theory of Religion*, New York: Doubleday Anchor Book, 1969.

Berridge, Willow J., *Islamism in the Modern World: A Historical Approach*, London: Bloomsbury Academic, 2019.

Biber, Charles, *Cent ans au Mozambique: Le parcours d'une minorité; Reportage sur l'histoire de l'église presbytérienne du Mozambique*, 2nd edn, Lausanne: Edition du Soc, 1992.

Bonate, Liazzat J.K., 'Governance of Islam in Colonial Mozambique', in Veit Bader, Annelies Moors, and Marcel Maussen (eds), *Colonial and Post-colonial Governance of Islam: Continuities and Ruptures*, Amsterdam: Amsterdam University Press, 2011, pp. 29–48.

————— 'Muslims of Northern Mozambique and Liberation Movements', *Social Dynamics*, 35(2), 2009, pp. 280–94.

————— 'Transformations de l'Islam à Pemba au Mozambique', *Afrique Contemporaine*, 231, 2009, pp. 61–76.

————— 'Dispute over Islamic Funeral Rites in Mozambique: "A demolidora dos prazeres" by Shaykh Aminuddin Mohamad', *LFM Social Sciences and Missions* (Lausanne), 17(1), 2005, pp. 41–59.

————— 'The Ascendance of Angoche: The Politics of Kinship and Territory in Nineteenth Century Northern Mozambique', *Lusotopie* (Paris), 10, 2003, pp. 115–40.

————— 'Muslim Personal Law among the Koti of Northern Mozambique', paper presented at the conference 'Islamic Law in Africa', 21–23 July 2000, Dar-es-Salaam.

Bonelli, Laurent and Fabien Carrié, *La fabrique de la radicalité: Une sociologie des jeunes djihadistes français*, Paris: Éditions du Seuil, 2018.

Braga Cruz, Manuel, 'O Estado Novo e a Igreja Católica', in F. Rosas (ed.), *Portugal e o Estado Novo*, Lisbon: Editorial Presença, 1992, pp. 201–21.

Braudel, Fernand, 'Histoire et sciences sociales: La longue durée', *Annales: Economies, sociétés, civilisations*, 13(4), 1958, pp. 725–53.

Brito, Luís de, *Cartografia eleitoral de Moçambique: 1994*, Maputo: Livraria Universitária, 2000.

————— 'O comportamento eleitoral nas primeiras eleições multipartidárias em Moçambique', in Brazão Mazula (ed.), *Eleições, Democracia e Desenvolvimento*, Maputo: n.p., 1995, pp. 473–99.

Brower, Steve, Paul Gifford, and Susan Rose, *Exporting the American Gospel: Global Christian Fundamentalism*, London: Routledge, 1996.

BIBLIOGRAPHY

Bureau de Informação Pública, *Quem é quem no Governo de Moçambique 2000*, Maputo: Bureau de Informação Pública, 2000.

Cabrita, João M., *Mozambique: The Tortuous Road to Democracy*, London: Palgrave, 2000.

Cahen, Michel, 'Mozambique: L'instabilité comme gouvernance?', *Politique Africaine*, 80, 2000, pp. 111–35.

——— 'L'État nouveau et la diversification religieuse au Mozambique, 1930–1974: I. Le résistible essor de la portugalisation catholique (1930–1961)', *Cahiers d'Études Africaines*, 158, 2000, pp. 309–50.

——— 'L'État nouveau et la diversification religieuse au Mozambique, 1930–1974: II. La portugalisation désespérée (1959–1974)', *Cahiers d'Études Africaines*, 159, 2000, pp. 551–92.

——— 'Le colonialisme tardif et la diversification religieuse au Mozambique (1959–1974)', *Lusotopie* (Paris), 5, 1998, pp. 377–95.

——— *Mozambique: Analyse politique de conjoncture*, Paris: Indigo Publications, 1990.

——— *La Révolution implosée: Études sur 12 ans d'indépendance (1975–1987)*, Paris: Karthala, 1987.

Carvalho, Álvaro Pinto de, 'Notas para a história das confrarias islâmica na Ilha de Moçambique', *Arquivo* (Maputo), 4, 1998, pp. 59–66.

Carvalho, Álvaro Pinto de, 'O empresariado islâmico em Moçambique no período pós-colonial: 1974–1994', PhD dissertation, Universidade Técnica de Lisboa, 1999.

Chan, Stephen, 'Too Neat and Under-Thought a World Order: Huntington and Civilisations', *Millennium*, 26(1), 1997, pp. 137–40.

Chaves, Mark, Peter J. Schraeder, and Mario Sprindys, 'State Regulation of Religion and Muslim Vitality in the Industrialized West', *Journal of Politics*, 56(4), 1994, pp. 1087–97.

Chichava, Sérgio, 'Os primeiros sinais do "Al Shabaab" em Cabo Delgado: Algumas histórias de Macomia e Ancuabe', *IDeIAS*, 129, 2020, pp. 1–2.

——— 'Ugandeses e Tanzanianos do Al-Shabaab: Um olhar à dimensão internacional do conflito em Cabo Delgado', in Salvador Forquilha (ed.), *Desafios para Moçambique 2020*, Maputo: IESE, 2020, pp. 429–39.

——— 'Por uma leitura sócio-histórica da etnicidade em Moçambique', Instituto de Estudos Sociais e Económicos, Discussion Paper 1, 2008.

Chilundo, Arlindo Gonçalo, *Os camponeses e os caminhos de ferro e estradas em Nampula (1900–1961)*, Maputo: Promédia, 2001.

Chome, Ngala, 'From Islamic Reform to Muslim Activism: The Evolution of an Islamist Ideology in Kenya', *African Affairs*, 118(472), 2019, pp. 531–52.

BIBLIOGRAPHY

Clarence-Smith, William G., 'Indian Business Communities in the Western Indian Ocean in the Nineteenth Century', *Indian Ocean Review*, 2(4), 1989, pp. 18–21.

———— 'The Roots of the Mozambican Counter-Revolution', *Southern African Review of Books*, April–May 1989.

Constantin, François, David S. Bone, and Ephraim C. Mandivenga, *Les communautés musulmanes d'Afrique orientale*, Pau: Centre de recherche et d'études sur les pays d'Afrique orientale, Université de Pau et des Pays de l'Adour, 1983.

Constantin, François and Christian Coulon, 'Minorités musulmanes et pouvoir politique en Afrique orientale', *Annuaire des Pays de l'Océan Indien*, 6, 1979, pp. 19–47.

Correia de Lemos, M.J., 'Reviver a Ilha, na Mafalala', *Arquivo* (Maputo), 4, 1988, pp. 49–58.

Coulon, Christian, 'Introduction: Les nouvelles voies de l'*umma* africaine', *L'Afrique Politique* (Paris), 2002, pp. 19–29.

Cruise O'Brien, Donal, *Symbolic Confrontations: Muslims Imagining the State in Africa*, London: Hurst, 2003.

Cruz e Silva, Teresa, 'Igrejas protestantes no Sul de Moçambique e nacionalismo: O caso da "Missão Suíça" (1940–1974)', *Estudos Moçambicanos* (Maputo), 10, 1992, pp. 19–39.

———— 'A rede clandestina da Frelimo em Lourenço Marques (1960–1974)', BA honours thesis, Eduardo Mondlane University, 1986.

Damião, João de Deus, 'O Islamismo em Moçambique à Luz do Sínodo Africano (Experiências Pastorais)', *Rumo Novo*, 9, 1994, pp. 36–51.

Davidson, Lawrence, *Islamic Fundamentalism*, Westport: Greenwood Press, 1998.

Declich, Francesca, 'Transmission of Muslim Practices and Women's Agency in Ibo Island and Pemba (Mozambique)', *Journal of Eastern African Studies*, 7(4), 2013, pp. 588–606.

Duffy, James, *Portuguese Africa*, Cambridge, MA: Harvard University Press, 1959.

Dulá, Liacat H., *Vida e Obra do Professor Ahmade Dulá (Muãlimo)*, Matola: Ciedima, 2018.

Esposito, John L., *The Islamic Threat: Myth or Reality?*, Oxford: Oxford University Press, 1992.

Etienne, Bruno, *L'Islam Radical*, Paris: Hachette, 1987.

Feijó, João, 'The Role of Women in Conflict in Cabo Delgado: Understanding Vicious Cycles of Violence', *Observador Rural*, 114, 2021.

———— 'Social Asymmetries: Clues to Understand the Spread of Islamist Jihadism in Cabo Delgado', *Observador Rural*, 93, 2020.

BIBLIOGRAPHY

Finke, Roger, 'Religious Deregulation: Origins and Consequences', *Journal of Church and State*, 32, 1990, pp. 609–26.

Finnegan, William, *A Complicated War: The Harrowing of Mozambique*, Berkeley: University of California Press, 1992.

Forquilha, Salvador and João Pereira, 'Afinal, não é só Cabo Delgado! Dinâmica da Insurgência em Nampula e Niassa', *IDeIAS* (Maputo), 138, 9 March 2021.

Foucher, Vincent, 'The Islamic State Franchises in Africa: Lessons from Lake Chad', International Crisis Group Commentary, 29 October 2020, https://www.crisisgroup.org/africa/west-africa/nigeria/islamic-state-franchises-africa-lessons-lake-chad, accessed 4 February 2021.

Foy, Felician A. (ed.), *Catholic Almanac 1998*, Huntington: Our Sunday Visitor Publishing Division, 1997.

———— *Catholic Almanac 1978*, Huntington: Our Sunday Visitor Publishing Division, 1977.

Frelimo, *'Consolidemos aquilo que nos une': Reunião da Direcção do Partido e do Estado com os representantes das confissões religiosas, 14 à 17 de Dezembro 1982*, Maputo: Instituto Nacional do Livro e do Disco, 1983, 100pp.

Geffray, Christian and Mögens Pedersen, 'Nampula en guerre', *Politique Africaine*, 29, 1988, pp. 28–40.

Gifford, Paul (ed.), *The Christian Churches and the Democratisation of Africa*, Leiden: Brill, 1995.

———— 'Some Recent Developments in African Christianity', *African Affairs*, 93(373), 1994, pp. 513–34.

———— *The New Crusaders: Christianity and the New Right in Southern Africa*, London: Pluto Press, 1988.

Habibe, Saide, Salvador Forquilha, and João Pereira, *Radicalização Islâmica no Norte de Moçambique: O Caso de Mocímboa da Praia*, Maputo: IESE, 2019.

Hafkin, Nancy, 'Trade, Society and Politics in Northern Mozambique, c.1753–1913', PhD dissertation, Boston University, 1973.

Hall, Margaret and Tom Young, *Confronting the Leviathan: Mozambique since Independence*, London: Hurst, 1997.

Hanlon, Joseph, 'The Uberization of Mozambique's Heroin Trade', Working Papers Series, no. 18–190, London: School of Economics and Political Science (LSE), Department of International Development, 2018.

———— *Mozambique: The Revolution under Fire*, London: Zed Books, 1984.

Harries, Patrick, 'Christianity in Black and White: The Establishment of Protestant Churches in Southern Mozambique', *Lusotopie* (Paris), 1998, pp. 317–33.

BIBLIOGRAPHY

Haysom, Simone, 'Where Crime Compounds Conflict: Understanding Northern Mozambique's Vulnerabilities', Geneva: Global Initiative Against Transnational Organized Crime, 2018.

Haysom, Simone, Peter Gastrow and Mark Shaw, 'The Heroin Coast: A Political Economy along the Eastern African Seaboard', ENACT Research Paper, 2, 2018, Pretoria: ISS-Enhancing Africa's Response to Transnational Organised Crime (ENACT).

Helgesson, Alf, *Church, State and People in Mozambique: A Historical Study with Special Emphasis on Methodist Developments in the Inhambane Region*, Uppsala: Swedish Institute of Missionary Research, 1994.

Henriksen, Thomas, *Mozambique: A History*, London: Rex Collings, 1978.

Hill, Michael, *A Sociology of Religion*, London: Heinemann, 1973.

Honwana, Raul, *The Life History of Raúl Honwana: An Inside View of Mozambique from Colonialism to Independence, 1905–1975*, Boulder: Lynne Rienner, 1988.

Howie, Frank, *The Mozambique Story*, Kansas City: Nazarene Publishing House, 1993.

Huntington, Samuel, *The Clash of Civilizations and the Remaking of World Order*, New York: Touchstone, 1996.

Iannaccone, Laurence, 'Introduction to the Economics of Religion', *Journal of Economic Literature*, 36, 1998, pp. 1465–96.

———'Religious Markets and the Economics of Religion', *Social Compass*, 39(1), 1992, pp. 123–31.

Instituto Nacional de Estatística, 'II Recenseamento Geral da População e Habitação 1997', Maputo: Instituto Nacional de Estatística, 1999.

——— 'Annuário Estatístico 1972', Lourenço Marques: Instituto Nacional de Estatística, Delegação de Moçambique, Direcção Provincial dos Serviços de Estatísticas, 1974.

International Crisis Group, 'Stemming the Insurrection in Mozambique's Cabo Delgado', ICG Report, 303, 11 June 2021.

——— 'Facing the Challenge of the Islamic State in West Africa Province', ICG Report, 273, 16 May 2019.

——— 'Al-Shabaab Five Years after Westgate: Still a Menace in East Africa', ICG Report, 265, 21 September 2018.

Introvigne, Massimo, 'Tra fondamentalismo e conservatorismo islâmico: nota sui Deobandi', Center for Studies on New Religions, 2001, https://www.cesnur.org/2001/mi_dic04.htm, accessed 6 December 2001.

Isaacman, Allen, *Mozambique: From Colonialism to Revolution, 1900–1982*, Boulder: Westview Press, 1983.

BIBLIOGRAPHY

Isaacman, Barbara and June Stephen, 'Mozambique: Women, the Law and Agrarian Reform', Addis Ababa: United Nations Economic Commission for Africa, 1989.

João, Benedito Brito, *Abdul Kamal e a história de Chiúre nos séculos xix–xx*, Maputo: Arquivos históricos de Moçambique, 2000.

———— 'Abdul Kamal-Megama (1892–1966): Pouvoir et religion dans un district du nord-Mozambique', *Islam et Société au Sud du Sahara*, 4, 1990, pp. 137–41.

Johnson, Benton, 'A Critical Appraisal of the Church–Sect Typology', *American Sociological Review*, 22(1), 1957, pp. 88–92.

José, Alexandrino, 'Samora e as confissões religiosas: Um diálogo inacabado', in António Sopa (ed.), *Samora: Homem do Povo*, Maputo: Maguezo Editores, 2001, pp. 149–61.

Kaarsholm, Preben, 'Islam, Secularist Government, and State–Civil Society Interaction in Mozambique and South Africa Since 1994', *Journal of Eastern African Studies*, 9(3), 2015, pp. 468–87.

Kazmi, Zahir, 'Radical Islam in the Western Academy', *Review of International Studies*, 1(23), 2021, pp. 1–23.

Kepel, Gilles, *Fitna: Guerre au Coeur de L'Islam*, Paris: Gallimard, 2004.

———— *The Revenge of God: The Resurgence of Islam, Christianity and Judaism in the Modern World*, University Park: Pennsylvania State University Press, 1994.

Khouri, Nicole and Joana Pereira Leite, 'The Ismailis of Mozambique: History of a Twofold Migration (Late 19th Century–1975)', in Eric Morier-Genoud and Michel Cahen (eds), *Imperial Migrations: Colonial Communities and Diaspora in the Portuguese World*, London: Palgrave Macmillan, 2013, pp. 168–89.

Kibel'bel Oka, Nicaise, *L'État islamique en Afrique centrale: De l'ADF/MTM en RDC à Al Sunnah au Mozambique*, Brussels: Editions Scribe, 2022.

Kuru, Ahmet T., 'Passive and Assertive Secularism: Historical Conditions, Ideological Struggles, and State Policies toward Religion', *World Politics*, 59(4), 2007, pp. 568–94.

Laheij, Christian, 'A Country of Trial: Islamic Reformism, Pluralism and Dispute Management in Peri-Urban Northern Mozambique', PhD dissertation, London School of Economics and Political Science, 2015.

Leichtman, Mara A., 'Da'wa as Development: Kuwaiti Islamic Charity in East and West Africa', *Muslim World*, 112(1), 2022, pp. 100–29.

Léonard, Yves, *Salazarisme et Fascisme*, Paris: Editions Chandeigne, 1996.

Liesegang, Gerhard, 'The Muridiyya Tariqa in modern Niassa Province of Mozambique ca.1880–1935 (A confraria Muridiyya na provincial do Niassa cerca 1880-1935)', draft text, 2nd edn, July 2016.

BIBLIOGRAPHY

Loimeier, Roman, *Islamic Reform in Twentieth-Century Africa*, Edinburgh: Edinburgh University Press, 2016.

———— 'What Is "Reform"? Approaches to a Problematic Term in African Muslim Contexts', *Journal for Islamic Studies* (Cape Town), 32(1), 2012, pp. 7–23.

Luiza, José, 'A Igreja das Palhotas: Génese da Igreja em Moçambique, entre o Colonialismo e a Independência', *Cadernos de Estudos Africanos* (Lisbon), 4, 1989, pp. 9–125.

Macagno, Lorenzo, 'Les nouveaux Oulémas: La recomposition des autorités musulmanes au nord du Mozambique', *Lusotopie* (Paris), 14, 2007, pp. 151–77.

———— *Outros muçulmanos: Islão e narrativas coloniais*, Lisbon: Imprensa de Ciências Sociais, 2006.

Macalane, Geraldo Luís and Jafar Silvestre (eds), *Ataques Terroristas em Cabo Delgado (2017–2020): As causas do fenómeno pela boca da população de Mocímboa da Praia*, Pemba: Universidade Rovuma, 2021.

Machaqueiro, Mário, 'Foes or Allies? Portuguese Colonial Policies towards Islam in Mozambique and Guinea', *Journal of Imperial and Commonwealth History*, 41(5), 2013, pp. 843–69.

———— 'The Islamic Policy of Portuguese Colonial Mozambique, 1960–1973', *Historical Journal*, 55(4), 2012, pp. 1097–116.

Magode, José, *Pouvoir et réseaux sociaux au Mozambique: Appartenances, interactivité du social et du politique (1933–1994)*, Paris: Connaissances et Savoirs, 2005.

Maher, Shiraz, *Salafi-Jihadism: The History of an Idea*, London: Penguin Books, 2016.

Marques da Silva, Muhamed Ali, *Escritos Islâmicos*, Lisbon: Al Furquán, 1991.

Martin, B.G., *Muslim Brotherhoods in XIXth Century Africa*, Cambridge: Cambridge University Press, 1976.

Marx, Karl, *Le 18 Brumaire de Louis Bonaparte*, Paris: Les Éditions sociales, 1969.

Matsinhe, David M. and Estácio Valoi, 'The Genesis of Insurgency in Northern Mozambique', ISS Southern Africa Report, 27, 2019.

Mattos, Regiane Augusto de, *As dimensões da resistência em Angoche: Da expansão política do sultanato à política colonialista Portuguesa no norte de Moçambique, 1842–1910*, Lisbon: Alameda, 2018.

Mayrargue, Cédric, 'Pluralisation et compétition religieuses en Afrique subsaharienne. Pour une étude comparée des logiques sociales et politiques du christianisme et de l'Islam', *Revue internationale de politique comparée*, 16(1), 2009, pp. 83–98.

BIBLIOGRAPHY

Mbembe, Achille, *Afriques indociles: Christianisme, pouvoir et état en société postcoloniale*, Paris: Karthala, 1988.

Meagher, Kate and Abdul Raufu Mustapha, 'Introduction: Faith, Society and Boko Haram', in Abdul Raufu Mustapha and Kate Meagher (eds), *Overcoming Boko Haram: Faith, Society and Islamic Radicalisation in Northern Nigeria*, Woodbridge: James Currey, 2020, pp. 1–29.

Medeiros, Eduardo da Conceição, 'Irmandades muçulmanas do norte de Moçambique', in Matteo Angius and Mario Zamponi (eds), *Ilha de Moçambique: Convergência de povos e culturas*, San Marin: AIEP Editore, 1999, pp. 70–85.

———— *História de Cabo Delgado e do Niassa (c.1836–1929)*, Maputo: n.p., 1997.

Metcalf, Barbara D., *Islamic Revival in British India, 1860–1960*, Princeton: Princeton University Press, 1982.

Monteiro, Fernando Amaro, *O Islão, o poder e a guerra (Moçambique 1964–1974)*, Porto: Universidade Portucalense, 1993.

———— 'Sobre a actuação da corrente "wahhabitta" no Islão moçambicano: Algumas notas relativas ao período 1964–1974', *Africana Studia* (Porto), 12, 1993, pp. 85–107.

Morier-Genoud, Eric, 'Concordat, Concordat …: Church–State Relations in the Portuguese Empire, 1940–74', in Jairzinho Lopes Pereira (ed.), *Church–State Relations in Africa in the Nineteenth and Twentieth Centuries: Mission, Empire, and the Holy See*, London: Palgrave Macmillan, 2022, pp. 111–34.

———— *Catholicism and the Making of Politics in Central Mozambique, 1940–1980*, Rochester: Rochester University Press, 2019.

———— 'Renouveau religieux et politique au Mozambique: Entre permanence, rupture et historicité', *Politique Africaine*, 134, 2014, pp. 155–77.

———— 'Y a-t-il une spécificité protestante au Mozambique? Discours du pouvoir postcolonial et histoire des églises chrétiennes', *Lusotopie* (Paris), 1998, pp. 407–20.

———— 'Of God and Caesar: The Relation between Christian Churches and the State in Postcolonial Mozambique, 1974–1981', *Le Fait Missionnaire* (Lausanne), 3, 1996.

———— 'The Politics of Church and Religion in the First Multi-Party Elections of Mozambique', *Internet Journal of African Studies*, 1, April 1996, www.bradford.ac.uk/research/ijas/ijasnol.htm, accessed 21 April 1996 (link no longer active).

Morier-Genoud, Eric, Domingos do Rosario, and Michel Cahen (eds), *The

BIBLIOGRAPHY

War Within: New Perspectives on the Civil War in Mozambique, 1976–1992, Oxford: James Currey, 2018.

Mustapha, Abdul Raufu (ed.), *Sects and Social Disorder: Muslim Identities and Conflict in Northern Nigeria*, Oxford: James Currey, 2017.

Mutiua, Chapane, 'Islão e o processo de literacia no norte de Moçambique entre os finais do século XIX e princípios do século XX', in Teresa Cruz e Silva and Isabel Maria Casimiro (eds), *A ciência ao serviço do desenvolvimento?*, Dakar: CODESRIA, 2015, pp. 205–19.

———'O norte de Moçambique entre os séculos XIX e XX: Um contexto histórico', in Teresa Cruz e Silva, Manuel G. Mendes de Araújo, and Amélia Neves de Souto (eds), *Comunidades Costeiras: Perspectivas e realidades*, Maputo: Centro de Estudos Sociais Aquino de Bragança, 2015, pp. 233–55.

———'Ajami Literacy, "Class", and Portuguese Pre-colonial Administration in Northern Mozambique', MA thesis, University of Cape Town, 2014.

Nascimento da Silva, Cristiane, '"Viver a Fé em Moçambique": As Relações entre a Frelimo e as Confissões Religiosas (1962–1982)', PhD dissertation, Federal Fluminense University, 2017.

Nasr, Wassim, *État islamique, le fait accompli*, Paris: Plon, 2016.

Neil-Tomlinson, Barry, 'The Nyassa Chartered Company: 1891–1929', *Journal of African History*, 18(1), 1977, pp. 109–28.

Ngoenha, Severino, 'O desafio moçambicano da laicidade', in Carlos Nuno Castel-Branco, Rosimina Ali, Sérgio Chichava, Salvador Forquilha, and Carlos Muiangaal (eds), *Desafios Para Mocambique 2022*, Maputo: IESE, 2022, pp. 70–81.

Nimtz, August H., *Islam and Politics in East Africa: The Sufi Order in Tanzania*, Minneapolis: University of Minnesota Press, 1980.

Newitt, Malyn D.D., *A History of Mozambique*, Johannesburg: Wits University Press, 1995.

———'The Early History of the Sultanate of Angoche', *Journal of African History*, 13(3), 1972, pp. 397–406.

Nuvunga, Adriano, *Cartography of Local Government, 2003 to 2008*, Maputo: AWEPA, 2004.

Oliveira, Paulo, 'Os donos da Renamo', unpublished manuscript, Maputo, 1989.

Oliveira, P., 'Le président et le transcendant', *Politique Africaine*, 52, December 1993, pp. 150–1.

Pearson, M.N., 'The Indian Ocean and the Red Sea', in N. Levtzion and R. Pouwell (eds), *History of Islam in Africa*, Athens: Ohio University Press, 1999, pp. 37–59.

Peirone, Frederico J., *A tribo Ajaua do Alto Niassa (Moçambique) e alguns*

BIBLIOGRAPHY

aspectos da sua problemática neo-islâmica, Lisbon: Junta da Investigação de Ultramar, Centro de Estudos Missionários, 1967.

Pélissier, René, *Naissance du Mozambique*, 2 vols, Orgeval: author's edition, 1984.

Pereira Leite, Joana, 'A guerra do caju e as relações Moçambique-Índia na época pós-colonial', *Lusotopie* (Paris), 2000, pp. 295–332.

Pérouse de Montclos, Marc-Antoine, *L'Afrique, nouvelle frontière du djihad?*, Paris: La Découverte, 2018.

Pew Research Center, Forum on Religion and Public Life, 'The World's Muslims: Religion, Politics and Society', Washington: Pew Research Center, 2013.

———— 'Tolerance and Tension: Islam and Christianity in Sub-Saharan Africa', Washington: Pew Research Center, 2010.

Pínheiro, Cónego Francisco Maria, *Na Entrega do Testemunho 1975*, Torres Novas, Portugal: Acção Missionéria Portuguesa em Moçambique, 1992.

Pinto, Pedro, 'Jehovah's Witnesses in Colonial Mozambique', *LFM Social Sciences and Missions* (Lausanne), 17, 2005, pp. 61–123.

Pires, Raúl Braga, 'A formação do Partido Independente de Moçambique (PIMO)', *Africana Studia*, 12, 2009, pp. 91–109.

Pitcher, M. Anne, *Transforming Mozambique: The Politics of Privatization, 1975–2000*, Cambridge: Cambridge University Press, 2002.

Pollard, Edward, Ricardo Duarte, and Yolanda Teixeira Duarte, 'Settlement and Trade from AD 500 to 1800 at Angoche, Mozambique', *African Archaeological Review*, 35, 2018, pp. 443–71.

Pouwels, Randall L., *Horn and Crescent: Cultural Change and Traditional Islam on the East African Coast, 800–1900*, Cambridge: Cambridge University Press, 1987.

Rebelo, D., 'Inauguração do edifício S. A. Real Aga Khan da Comunidade Xi'ia-Muçulmano-Ismaelita', Lourenço Marques, 30 November 1968.

———— 'Breves apontamentos sobre um grupo de indianos em Moçambique (A comunidade ismaília maometana)', *Boletim da Sociedade de Estudos da Colónia de Moçambique*, 128, 1961, pp. 83–9.

Renne, Elisha P. (ed.), *Veiling in Africa*, Bloomington: Indiana University Press, 2013.

República de Moçambique and AWEPA, *As primeiras 33 autarquias em Moçambique: realidade, conquistas, constrangimentos, perspectivas*, Maputo: República de Moçambique and AWEPA, 2003.

Riccardi, Andrea, 'Le primat de l'évangélisation', in Gilles Kepel (ed.), *Les politiques de Dieu*, Paris: Seuil, 1993, pp. 99–117.

BIBLIOGRAPHY

Robertson, Roland, 'The Economization of Religion? Reflections on the Promise and Limitations of the Economic Approach', *Social Compass*, 39(1), 1992, pp. 147–57.

Rogeiro, Nuno, *O Cabo do Medo: O Daesh em Moçambique*, Lisbon: Dom Quixote, 2020.

Roy, Olivier, *Généalogie de l'Islamisme*, Paris: Hachette, 1995.

Rzewuski, Eugeniusz, 'Origins of the Tungi Sultanate (Northern Mozambique) in the Light of Local Tradition', *Orientalia Varsoviensia* (Warsaw), 2, 1991, pp. 193–213.

Sanneh, Lamin, *The Crown and the Turban: Muslim and West Africa Pluralism*, Boulder: Westview Press, 1997.

Santos, Ana Margarida Sousa, 'History, Memory and Violence: Changing Patterns of Group Relationship in Mocímboa da Praia, Mozambique', PhD dissertation, University of Oxford, 2011.

Santos, Francisco Almeida dos, 'War in Resource-Rich Northern Mozambique: Six Scenarios', *CMI Insight*, 2, 2020.

Schmidt, Alex P., 'Radicalisation, De-radicalisation, Counter-radicalisation: A Conceptual Discussion and Literature Review', ICCT Research Paper, International Centre for Counter-Terrorism, The Hague, March 2013.

Schultz, Lorraine, *Mozambique Milestones*, Kansas City: Nazarene Publishing House, 1982.

Siefert, Saskia, *Muslime in Mosambik: Versuch einer Bestandsaufnahme*, Bielefeld: University of Bielefeld (Forschungsprogramm Entwicklungspolitik: Handlungsbedingungen und Handlungsspielräume für Entwicklungspolitik 36), 1994.

Soares, Pedro, 'Sustaining the Periphery: Transnational Articulations of Portuguese Barelwi Muslims', in Paul Anderson and Julian Hargreaves (eds), *Muslims in the UK and Europe V*, Cambridge: Centre of Islamic Studies, University of Cambridge, 2019.

Stoll, David, *Is Latin America Turning Protestant? The Politics of Evangelical Growth*, Berkeley: University of California Press, 1990.

Swaleh, Kadara, 'Islamic Proselytising between Lamu and Mozambique: The Case of Kizingitini Village', *Social Dynamics*, 38(3), 2012, pp. 398–418.

Tayob, Abdulkader, *Islamic Resurgence in South Africa: The Muslim Youth Movement*, Cape Town: University of Cape Town Press, 1995.

Thompson, Phyllis, *Life Out of Death: A Miracle of Church Growth in the Face of Opposition*, London: Hodder and Stoughton, 1989.

Thorold, A., 'Metamorphoses of the Yao Muslims', in Louis Brenner (ed.), *Muslim Identity and Social Change in Sub-Saharan Africa*, London: Hurst, 1993, pp. 79–90.

BIBLIOGRAPHY

Tibi, Bassam, *Islamism and Islam*, New Haven: Yale University Press, 2012.

Trentini, Daria, *At Ansha's: Life in the Spirit Mosque of a Healer in Mozambique*, New Brunswick: Rutgers University Press, 2021.

———— '"Muslims of the Spirits"—"Muslims of the Mosque": Performing Contested Ideas of Being Muslim in Northern Mozambique', *Journal for Islamic Studies*, 35, 2016, pp. 70–106.

Trimingham, J. Spencer, *The Influence of Islam upon Africa*, 2nd edn, London: Longman, 1980.

United Nations Security Council's Groupe d'experts sur la République démocratique du Congo, 'Rapport final du Groupe d'experts sur la République démocratique du Congo', 13 June 2023, http://www.undocs.org/fr/S/2023/431, accessed 21 June 2023.

US Bureau of Democracy, Human Rights and Labor, 'International Religious Freedom Report 2004', 15 September 2004, https://2009-2017.state.gov/j/drl/rls/irf/2004/index.htm, accessed 23 June 2023.

US Embassy in Mozambique, 'Mozambique 2018 International Religious Freedom Report', Washington: United States Department of State, Bureau of Democracy, Human Rights, and Labor, 2018, https://mz.usembassy.gov/wp-content/uploads/sites/182/MOZAMBIQUE-2018-INTERNATIONAL-RELIGIOUS-FREEDOM-REPORT-002.pdf, accessed 7 October 2019.

Van de Kamp, Linda, *Violent Conversion: Brazilian Pentecostalism and Urban Women in Mozambique*, Woodbridge: James Currey, 2016.

Verdier, Isabelle, *Mozambique: 100 Men in Power*, Paris: Indigo, 1996.

Vines, Alex, *Renamo: Terrorism in Mozambique*, London: James Currey, 1991.

Vines, Alex and Ken Wilson, 'Churches and the Peace Process in Mozambique', in Paul Gifford (ed.), *The Christian Churches and the Democratisation of Africa*, Leiden: Brill, 1995, pp. 130–47.

Warner, Jason with Ryan O'Farrell, Héni Nsaibia, and Ryan Cummings, *The Islamic State in Africa: The Emergence, Evolution, and Future of the Next Jihadist Battlefront*, London: Hurst, 2021.

Weimer, Bernhard, 'Abstaining from the 1998 Local Government Elections in Mozambique: Some Hypotheses', *L'Afrique Politique* (Paris), 1999, pp. 125–45.

West, Sunguta, 'Ansar al-Sunna: A New Militant Islamist Group Emerges in Mozambique', *Terrorism Monitor* (Jamestown Foundation), 6(12), June 2018, 5–7.

Wilson, Ken B., 'Cults of Violence and Counter-violence in Mozambique', *Journal of Southern African Studies*, 18(3), 1992, pp. 527–82.

BIBLIOGRAPHY

Worsfold, W. Basil, *Portuguese Nyassaland: An Account of the Discovery, Native Population, Agricultural and Mineral Resources, and Present Administration of the Territory of the Nyassa Company, with a Review of the Portuguese Rule on the East Coast of Africa*, New York: Negro Universities Press, 1969.

Zamparoni, Valdemir, 'Monhés, Baneanes, Chinas e Afro-Maometanos: Colonialismo e racismo em Lourenço Marques, Moçambique, 1890–1940', *Lusotopie* (Paris), 7, 2000, pp. 191–222.

Zeghal, Malika, 'État et marché des biens religieux: Les voies égyptienne et tunisienne', *Critique Internationale*, 5, 1999, pp. 75–95.

Zenn, Jacob, 'Boko Haram's Conquest for the Caliphate: How Al Qaeda Helped Islamic State Acquire Territory', *Studies in Conflict and Terrorism*, 43(2), 2020, pp. 89–122.

INDEX

Note: Page numbers followed by " *t* " refer to tables, " *f* " refer to figures,
Bold indicates maps.

Abdala, Camissa Adamo, 78, 79
Abudo, José Ibraimo, 38, 40,
   73–4, 82, 86, 112
Afghanistan, 42
Africa Muslims Agency (AMA),
   20, 33, 39, 42, 59, 101, 132
African Muslims, jobs, 21–2
African nationalism, 10, 23–4,
   30
Africanization, 58
Afro-Asian sheiks, 28–30
Afro-Mahometan Association, 22
Afro-Shirazi polities, 8
Aga Khan Development Network,
   39
Aga Khan, 24
Aguebas movement, 83
Ahmadiyya brotherhood, 22
Al Calam (magazine), 108, 114
Al-Azhar University, 111
Algeria, 59
Alim Commission, 103–4
al-Qaeda, 42, 138

al-Shabaab, 6, 119–20, 123–4,
   129, 135, 138
Aly Dauto, Ussumane, 73–4
AMA. *See* Africa Muslims Agency
   (AMA)
Amin Dada, Idi, 41
Aminuddin, Sheik, 40
Amuji, Suleimane, 79
Ancuabe, 128
Angoche, 42, 77, 78–9
Ansar al-Sunna, 41, 44, 111
Ansaru Sunna, 111
anti-Asian campaign, 76
anti-religious policy, 3, 24–8, 30,
   34, 43, 57
anti-Sufis, 86
Anuaril Association, 22
Anuaril Isslamo, 28, 29, 30, 31, 40
Arabs, 8
Armed Conflict Location and
   Event Data Project, 1
Asian Muslims, 24–5, 55
Assane, Alberto, 79

233

INDEX

Assembly of the Republic, 47, 49–90
Associação Comoriana, 22
Associação Muçulmana de Angoche (Muslim Association of Angoche), 40
atheist propaganda, 25–6
Azize, Abdul, 133

Babu Salam, 76
Balama, 124, 125, 127, 130
Beira, 60, 73, 87, 112
Benadir Coast, 8
Berlin Conference (1884–5), 9
Bezme Tabligh Isslamo Cadrya Sunni, 22
Bible, 107
Bilal (newspaper), 114
bin Jimba, Abdurrahman Amuri, 41, 82
bin Sultan al-Busaidi, Sayyid Saïd, 8
Boko Haram, 138
British government, 28
Brotherhood (see also Tariqa/Turuq), 10, 21–23, 25, 28–32, 41, 44, 51, 55, 61, 82, 151
Burqa, 93, 102-5, 110, 122, 144, 146

Cabo Delgado, 8, 12, 23, 93, 96, 105, 111–12, 117–18
  anti-religious policy and revolts, 27
  armed conflict, 1–2
  introduction of Wahhabi institutions, 132
  LNG project, 2
  nature of insurgency in, 119–24
  sheiks and *mwalimu* attack, 10
Camal, Amade Chemane Júnior, 75
Cameroon, 106

Carimo, Abdul, 127–8
Catholicism, 23, 60, 61, 71, 98
CCM (Conselho Cristão de Moçambique), 51
census (1997), 52, 53, 53*t*
Centre of Islamic Training. *See* CFI (Centro de Formação Islâmica)
CFI (Centro de Formação Islâmica), 40–1, 44, 73
Chande, Ame, 111
Chissano, Joaquim, 50, 63, 64, 76
Chiure, 130–1
Christian Council of Mozambique. *See* CCM (Conselho Cristão de Moçambique)
Christian extremism, 108
Christian Mozambicans, 106–7
Christian principles, 77
Christianity, 56, 66, 96
Christians, 26, 36, 39, 54, 107–8
Christmas holiday, 50
church–state relations, 49, 50, 51, 57–61
CIMO. *See* Comunidade Islâmica de Moçambique (CIMO)
CISLAMO (Conselho Islâmico de Moçambique), 31, 32, 33, 36, 38, 40, 41, 43, 44, 72–3, 110–11, 126, 132
Clash of Civilizations (Huntington), 48
Commission for Demobilization, 37
Community of Sant'Egidio, 51
Comoros, 27
Comunidade Islâmica de Moçambique (CIMO), 112
Comunidade Mahometana (Indian Muslim Community), 22, 32, 36
co-optation policy, 25, 30, 55

234

INDEX

Council of Brotherhoods, 44
Council of Ministers, 142–3
Council of Muslim Theologians, 87
Council of Ulama of Mozambique, 87
Crescente (newspaper), 114
Cuamba, 78

David, Sheik Cassimo, 78, 79
Democratic Republic of the Congo (DRC), 106, 133–4
Deobandism, 22, 44
Department for Religious Affairs (DAR), 27, 31, 33, 34, 37, 44, 63, 64, 72, 145
Department of Foreign Affairs, 51
Dhlakama, Afonso, 55
Djá-Al Hak (magazine), 114
Djibouti, 106
DNAR. *See* National Directorate for Religious Affairs
Domingo (newspaper), 40
DRC. *See* Democratic Republic of the Congo (DRC)
Dulá, Nuro Amade, 28

East African coast: arrival of Islam, 7–10
Egypt, 110
'Eid affair'. *See* Muslim holidays affair (1996)
Eid Ul Adha, 26, 38, 45, 47, 76
Eid Ul Fitr, 38, 45, 47, 76
elections (1994), 38, 43, 45
elections (1999), 41–2
ENI company, 2
Episcopal Conference, 51
Ethiopia, 106
evangelization strategy, 59
ExxonMobil, 2

Facebook, 114
Faisal, Abdul Rahim, 134–5
family law, green paper on, 39, 45
Faquir Bay, Faquir Bay Nalagi, 78
Freedom of Religion and Worship Law (2020), 143
Frelimo (Frente de Libertação de Moçambique), 3, 4, 5, 24, 32, 52, 57
alliance conclusion between Muslims and, 70–1
anti-religious policy, 3, 24–8, 30, 34, 43, 57
banned proselytization, 30
banned use of all religious symbols, 105
Eid affair and, 54–5, 56, 65
elections (1994), 38, 64
elections (1999), 41–2
faith organizations property, nationalization of, 24
Fifth Congress (1989), 34, 63
free religious market, 34–7, 63–5, 66
'policy shift', 62–3
policy towards Islam, 79–84
removed Muslim candidates, 76–7
secularism policy, 61–2
Third Congress (1977), 25, 62
'fundamentalism', 36–7, 38, 39, 49, 60, 61, 67
funerary rituals, 28

Gaza, 98
Guebuza, Armando, 83
Guinea Bissau, 108
Gulf monarchies, 72–3

Hadhrami Arabs, 8–9
Haj, 156

INDEX

Hamza Mosque, 111
HIV, 88
Holy Friday, 50

Ilha de Moçambique, 73, 77–8
Independent Party of Mozambique.
    See PIMO [Partido
    Independente de Moçambique]
Indonesia, 35
Indo-Pakistani community, 37, 41,
    74, 81
Inhambane, 21, 26, 98
International Crisis Group, 118
International Monetary Fund, 34
Inusso, Ismail, 75
Iran, 55, 72–3
Iraq, 72–3
ISCAP. *See* ISIS Central Africa
    Province (ISCAP)
ISIS Central Africa Province
    (ISCAP), 135–6
ISIS. *See* Islamic State of Iraq and
    the Levant
Islam
    colonial, 21–4
    Frelimo's policy towards,
        79–84
    growth of, 95–101, 97t, 99t
    history of Islam in South East
        Africa, 7–10
    politicization of, 34–9, 48,
        55–6, 66
    position shift, 19, 43–5
    postcolonial, 10–16
    religious policy, 24–8
    term, 14–15
    twentieth century, 39–42
    See also Muslim holidays affair
        (1996)
Islamic Appeal, 20
Islamic Congress of Mozambique

(Sunni), 31–2, 33, 36, 38, 41,
    43, 44, 72–3, 87, 146
    relationship with CISLAMO, 40
Islamic Community. *See* CIMO, 75,
    111-112, 114, 146, 152
Islamic Council of Mozambique.
    See CISLAMO (Conselho
    Islâmico de Moçambique)
Islamic Development Bank, 35
Islamic extremism, 108
Islamic Forum, 40
Islamic fundamentalism, 108–9
Islamic Maghreb, 138
Islamic State of Iraq and the
    Levant, 117, 134, 135–9, 136t
Islamism, 7, 44–5
Islamist sectarianism, 131
Islamists
    and secularism, 4
    term, 15
Islamization, 47, 50
Ismaili Aga Khan Development
    Network, 114
Ismaili community, 40, 113–14
Ismaili Muslims, 24, 74
ivory and slaves trade, 8, 9

Jamaat Daawa al Islamiya (World
    Islamic Call Society), 32
Jamú, Sheik Abdurazzaque, 82
jihadi insurgency, emergence of, 1,
    7, 12, 119–24
jihadism, 5, 7, 131
jihadists, term, 15

Kenya, 118, 133
Khan, Aga, 114
Khan, Sharfuddine, 73
Kilwa Chronicle, 8

Latif, Abdul, 78, 79

INDEX

Leck, Abdul Kha, 75
Lichinga, 111
Likongo, Abdala, 133
liquefied natural gas (LNG), 2
Lunat, Nazir, 85
Luso-German treaty, 9
Libya, 59, 63

Machel, Samora, 145
Macomia, 130–1
madrasas, closure of, 26
Maharishi Mahesh Yogi, 64, 65
Mahomed, Abdul Amide, 75
Makda, Hassan Ismail, 75
Makua people, 21
Malawi, 28
Mamudo, Gulamo, 79
Manica province, 98
Maputo Muslim Community, 38,
    41, 42, 78, 113
Maputo, 31, 42, 76, 81–2
Marxism–Leninism, 11, 25, 62, 75
Matola, 110–11
mawlana Mágira. *See* Mussá Ismael,
    Sheik Abubacar Hagy (mawlana
    Mágira)
Mawlid, 29, 40, 101
Meagy, Assubugy, 78
Mecca, 10, 23, 26, 33, 81–2,
    87–8
militantism, 44–5
Ministry of Interior, 27
Ministry of Justice, 31
Miya family, 29
Moamed, Issufo, 27
Mocímboa da Praia, 1, 27, 79, 117,
    119, 124, 132
Mogne, Mohamed, 73
Mombasa, 8
Moon (sighting), 87-88, 162-3
Moses (prophet), 125

mosques
    Anuaril Isslamo, 28, 29, 30, 31,
        40
    closure of, 26
    construction and renovation,
        10, 19
    destruction of, 27
Movimento Islâmico de
    Moçambique (Islamic
    Movement of Mozambique),
    76
Mozambican National Institute of
    Statistics, 96
Mozambique Liberation Front. *See*
    Frelimo (Frente de Libertação
    de Moçambique)
Mucuthaya, Amisse, 133
Muhamad (prophet), 108
Mawlid, 29, 40, 101
Muhammad, Sheik Aminuddin, 87,
    109
Munazzamat al-Da'wa al-Islamiyya,
    39
Muslim Association of Sofala, 87,
    113
Muslim community, 15, 20
    divisions within, 20, 21–3
    dynamics, 5, 7, 14
    on Frelimo's power, 24–5
    in Lisbon, 27
Muslim Hands (organization), 39
Muslim holidays affair (1996),
    38–9, 43, 45, 47–67
    controversy and its actors,
        47–8, 49–52
    Frelimo strategy, 54–5, 56
    interpretations of the
        controversy and its origins,
        52–6, 53*t*
    religious competition, 49,
        56–61, 58*t*

237

INDEX

state mediation (since independence), 61–5, 66
Muslim League of Zambezia, 38
Muslim population, 21, 43, **46,** 58*t*
Muslim Union of Mozambique 87
Muslim World League (Rabitat), 32, 33, 35
Muslim–Christian conflict, 39–40
Mussa Bin Bique University, 86, 112
Mussá Ismael, Sheik Abubacar Hagy (mawlana Mágira), 29, 31, 40, 86–7, 89
Mustafa, Rachid, 75

Nacala, 77, 78, 83
Naimo, Abacar Abdul Satar, 77
Nampula, 1, 8, 30, 38, 60–1, 70, 74, 78, 111
Nampuio, Paulo Mautamurro, 75
Nampula, Jorge Adriano, 75
Nangade, 125
Nankalava, Faraji, 133
National Directorate for Religious Affairs, 80, 141
National Islamic Conference (2016), 128
National Islamic Conference I (2003), 108
natural gas fields, 1–2
Netherlands, 82
Nhacole, 125–6
Niassa, 1, 26, 38, 98
Nigeria, 138
9/11 attacks, 42
Nkomati agreement, 34
non-governmental organizations (NGOs), 4, 56, 59
Nordine, Ibrahimo, 35
northern Mozambique, 93–4, 98, 117, 125

Nova Sofala (Sufi sanctuary), 21, 29, 40
Nyassa Chartered Company, 9–10

'O Minarete', 115
O País (newspaper), 120, 142
OIC, 73, 115
Oman, 27, 35
Omani rule, 8–9
Organisation of the Islamic Conference (OIC), 35, 64
Organizações da Juventude Islâmica de Angoche, 40

Pakistan, 113
Palma, 120–1
Pangane, 130
Paquitiquete mosque, 112
Peace Day, 127
Pemba, 27, 77, 78–9, 93
burqa affair, 102–4, 104*f*
Pentecostal churches, 60
Pentecostals, 60, 61
PIMO [Partido Independente de Moçambique], 37–8, 45, 64, 78, 108
'pluralist' system, 34
population, 21, 43, **46,** 58*t*
Portugal colonial rule, 9–10, 28, 57
colonial policy (1960), 83
co-optation policy, 25, 30
religious policy, 21, 23
Portuguese, 8, 9, 19, 71, 81
attitude to Islam, 10
proselytization, 30, 34, 61, 64, 101
pro-Sufi Islamic Congress of Mozambique, 112
Protestant churches, 59, 60
Protestantism, 36, 57, 61, 98
Protestants, 51, 61

238

INDEX

Qadiriyya brotherhood, 21, 22, 55, 113
Qatar, 115
Quran, 15, 25, 27, 76

Rabitat. *See* World Muslim League, 32-33, 35
Radio Haq, 114
Rafayel, Sualehe, 125–7
Ramadan, 87–8
reformism, 28–30, 44
regionalism, 42
religious affiliation, 52–3
religious competition, 5–6, 49, 56–61, 58*t*
Resistência Nacional de Moçambique (Renamo), 27, 30, 34, 37, 38, 52, 54, 58, 63, 72, 75, 132
elections (1999), 41, 42
Revolt, 27
Revolutionary Committee of Anuaril, 30
Rhodesia, 27, 58
Rifa'iyya brotherhood, 21, 22
Roman Catholic Church, 9–10, 23, 30, 36, 37, 59–60, 61
Eid affair and, 50, 51, 57
Rome General Peace Accords (1992), 34

Salazar, António de Oliveira, 57, 71
Saudi Arabia, 27, 31, 55, 60, 81, 85, 110
Aly Dauto visit, 73
Sautul Isslam (magazine), 114
Savana (newspaper), 40
'sect', term, 13
secularism, 4, 50, 52, 62–3
Senegal, 106

Service of Associative and Religious Affairs (SAAR), 26–7, 31
Shadhiliyya brotherhood, 21, 22
Shafi'i school of law, 21
sharia law, 105, 106, 145
Shia community, 113–14
Shia Muslims, 124
Shia Ithna, 114
Sofala, 98
Somalia, 120, 133, 134
South Africa, 34, 113
southern Tanzania, 1
statistics, 116
sub-Saharan Africa, 106
Sudan, 55, 85, 110
Sufi brotherhoods conflict, 22–3
Sufi evangelists, 10
Sufi Islamic Congress, 115
Sufi leaders, 82
Sufis, 86, 111–12
Sufism and anti-Sufism conflict, 28–30
Sufism, 10, 11, 21, 31, 40, 88, 111
Sulemane, Momade Bashir, 113
Sultanate of Zanzibar, 9
Supreme Court (Mozambique), 47
'supreme disorder' (*fitna*), 15
Swahili culture, 8, 21
Switzerland, 82

Tanzania, 106, 117, 132
tariqa, 10, 21, 25, 41, 55, 57, 82
Tayob, Cassamo, 28–9
'teleology', 6–7
terrorism, 42, 105, 109,
Tete province, 98
TotalEnergies, 2
turuq (sing. *tariqa*), 21–3, 25

Uganda, 41, 133, 134–5

INDEX

ulama (community of the learned), 28–9, 31, 86
UN Monitoring Group, 118
União Democrática (Democratic Union), 52
União Muçulmana de Moçambique, 87
United Arab Emirates (UAE), 35, 115
United States, 60, 82
9/11 attacks, 42
Universal Church of the Kingdom of God, 37, 61, 64, 65
Universidade Mussa Bin Bique in Nampula, 40–1
University of Dar-es-Salaam, 27
Usafi mosque (Kampala), 134

Vazirma, Carimo, 73
Veil. *See* Burqa, 11, 93, 104, 106
Vilankulos, 79

Voz do Islam (radio station), 114

Wahhabis, 88, 111–12
Wahhabism, 4–5, 11, 22, 44, 101
rise of, 28–34
World Bank, 34
World Federation of Islamic Missions, 32
World Islamic Call Society. *See* Jamaat Daawa al Islamiya, 32
World Muslim Congress, 32
World Muslim League, 20, 31
World Vision, 59

Xai-Xai, 78–9
Xavier, Marcelino, 54

Yao people, 9, 21

Zambezia, 98, 114, 124
Zero Brigades, 83

240